The New Academic: A Strategic Handbook

The New Academic: A Strategic Handbook

Shelda Debowski

 Open University Press

Open University Press
McGraw-Hill Education
McGraw-Hill House
Shoppenhangers Road
Maidenhead
Berkshire
England
SL6 2QL

email: enquiries@openup.co.uk
world wide web: www.openup.co.uk

and Two Penn Plaza, New York, NY 10121-2289, USA

First published 2012

A catalogue record of this book is available from the British Library

ISBN-10: 0-33-524535-8
ISBN-13: 978-0-33-524535-2
e-ISBN: 978-0-33-524536-9

Library of Congress Cataloging-in-Publication Data
CIP data has been applied for

Typeset by Aptara Inc., India
Printed in the UK by Bell and Bain Ltd, Glasgow.

Fictitious names of companies, products, people, characters and/or data that may be used herein (in case studies or in examples) are not intended to represent any real individual, company, product or event.

MIX
Paper from
responsible sources
FSC
www.fsc.org FSC® C007785

The *McGraw·Hill* Companies

Praise for this book

This book is dedicated to my loving and much loved family:

To Alysia: mentee, critical friend and courageous explorer: may your entry into academe continue its smooth and strategic progression.

To James: just starting on your postgraduate journey, but already seeing the world as a series of research questions needing to be answered.

To John: for always being there through the tumultuous, neglected or triumphant years, and affirming that academe is where I should be.

And also to Robert E Wood: an extraordinary supervisor, mentor and sponsor who changed my academic path.

Contents

List of tables

List of figures

Preface

Talk to any experienced academic and they will acknowledge that they have made a number of wrong judgements in navigating through their career options. Most eventually worked out how higher education operated through trial and error, and fortunately managed to come out the other end, slightly more dented, but certainly much wiser. However, for every individual who succeeds, there are many others who surrender, drown, or are gently (or not so gently) persuaded that academe is not for them.

I have been an academic since I was invited to fill a one-year contract at 24 years of age. Although I returned briefly to my profession, I knew that my vocation was in higher education. Within a year I had made my move to the sector, initially as a contracted employee and later with tenured status. It hasn't necessarily been an easy career. I have worked across a spectrum of universities and encountered diverse leaders, cultures and political challenges, while completing a doctorate part time, raising two children, and maintaining a marriage. Not easy, but very satisfying! No other career would have offered me the opportunities to meet such a rich array of colleagues and friends, to constantly set new challenges and to pursue them, or to continue learning, with each day offering something new.

In reviewing my career, I can articulate three phases that I still see played out by many academics today. The first could be called *good citizen*. For 18 years I performed the roles that were expected of me, obtained additional qualifications, and continued to make myself indispensable. As a docile and obedient academic I accepted high workloads and waited to be rewarded. I applied for promotion and was unsuccessful. I worked harder and waited... and kept waiting, hoping someone would realize how essential I was to the fabric of the place. Thanks to my PhD mentor, the first person who ever offered strategic guidance, I finally realized that I had outgrown my employer and needed to find a more conducive work environment. I moved on to a new discipline and a more senior role with much relief.

In Phase 2 of my career, as a *strategic academic,* I made conscious career choices – not always correctly, but at least with careful consideration of the evolving environment and potential consequences. I developed a more critical understanding of the higher education environment, became an agent of change, and moved into key leadership roles to increase my university's effectiveness. While focusing on my own emerging research career, I also sought to assist others, discovering that my slow progress in consolidating my academic skills and understanding was a common malaise across the institution. We were all trying to put the puzzle together in a way that worked, but often did so in isolation, which greatly reduced our effectiveness. And few of us drew on the support of mentors, much to our detriment.

In Phase 3 I became an *engaged scholar*, moving to a more influential senior role where I could mobilize a team and resources to make a more significant difference to my academic colleagues. This has been my most fulfilling experience as it has supported hundreds of people and enabled them to flourish. I now work as *a translator*, offering a lexicon as to how universities and the sector operate; *a tour guide*, showing the best and most interesting ways to navigate new terrain; *an interpreter*, explaining how the actions of the university, sector or individual leaders can impact on the lived experience of academics and whole communities; *a change agent* – encouraging more self-aware leadership and conscious enactment of roles to improve academic environments, *a mentor* to many, and *a scholar* who is trying to make sense and build better frameworks to share these insights with others. Above all, I continue to be a *learner and explorer*, constantly discovering new insights about myself and this complex, evolving world.

The New Academic draws on these experiences, aiming to reduce the learning curve for new generations coming into higher education, and facilitating their transition from *novice* to *knowing*. I have seen first hand the challenges many face in getting established and finding a personal niche and identity. Discussions with hundreds of individuals illustrate limited understanding of the sector, career management or academic expectations. Many have not found mentors, partly because they feel afraid to ask. Participants in my workshops regularly note confusion, isolation and concern that their immense hard work is not achieving the desired outcomes. This book will illustrate why they have difficulty in getting traction. Effort is not the critical ingredient: strategic career management and a more conscious personal agency are the keys, as I will show.

The key elements of academic work

The higher education context is changing rapidly and will need agile and adaptive academics to be ready for the new world that is now opening up. Traditional academic practices are challenged by shifting employment patterns and growing pressure from external stakeholders. Academics need to read the environment and adapt their roles to maximize their impact and effectiveness. Over their career they will reflect variant priorities, particularly as they move into leadership. This book has therefore been designed to offer a detailed and insightful view of the different activities an academic might support. It encourages the reader to be actively engaged in judging which academic mix is most suitable for their particular context, and to then optimize their activities in their chosen portfolio.

The New Academic therefore explores four key roles: teaching, research, engagement and leadership. It also examines the process of entering academe and managing a strategic career. With these insights in hand, any academic (both new and currently employed) will be better equipped to capitalize their role and opportunities.

Missing pieces of the puzzle

In reviewing the current literature and theory base, it is clear that there is much we still do not know about higher education academic work. Some areas, such as writing for publication, supervising research students, lecturing, or tutoring abound with useful manuals and guides. Other areas, such as career management, research grant writing, engagement and leadership are much less visible in our body of knowledge. Drawing on allied disciplines and feedback from experienced and new academics, I have integrated practical but scholarly guidance on these missing elements. They are becoming critical components of academic work, although our scholarship relating to these role elements continues to lag. Perhaps this book may stimulate others to think more closely about these under-discussed areas.

There are many questions that each academic needs to resolve: Where does service fit in? At what stage should leadership roles be assumed? What's the best model for an academic career? How can teaching and research be balanced? These are but a few of the challenges my colleagues have shared with me over the last years. I have aimed to address them by exploring the holistic role of the academic, and suggesting that the role that is played may be determined by three key influences: the individual's own capabilities and talents; the environmental setting and support that is available; and the degree to which the individual commits to progressing their career: their personal agency.

Academic identity

While there are other books on the market that explore how to *operate* as a new academic, they rarely discuss the broader positioning of academic work and issues of academic identity. Too often, new academics are thrown into the hurly burley of university work without being encouraged to think about their role and how it contributes to the university, discipline and sector. With only extrinsic rewards in mind (such as getting tenure or promotion), the rough and tumble world can seem antagonistic, given its competitiveness and limited channels for advancement. In contrast, a strong understanding of why we work in academe, and the long-term value we hope to offer, encourages a more anchored sense of identity that can sustain the individual through any rough patches. And, of course, it then encourages a stronger strategic focus. Throughout this work the reader is encouraged to think about both the *why* and the *how*. It is not enough to simply enact practices. It is critical to understand why these activities are important contributions to society and knowledge production, and to the long-term needs of the individual.

Values-based roles

This book reflects a consistent theme: that academics are the heartbeat of the institution. Their interactions with students and the community are the interface between learning and its translation into the real lives of millions of people. This is an essential message that sometimes gets lost if academic work simply becomes a job. My goal has been to bring the reader back to the question of what academics contribute. To some extent, I have encouraged new academics to think about their vocation and the

influence they can have on the hearts and minds of their students, community collaborators and colleagues. Each of us has the potential to be a force for good. But first,
we need to build a robust sense of our own values and beliefs as to what we might
contribute. The reader will be encouraged to explore these in relation to their core
roles and participation as a member of academic communities. They are challenged
to think about the difference they might make as an educator, researcher, leader, and
engaged scholar.

Finally, *The New Academic* offers guidance on how to be strategic in career decisions and roles that might be assumed. The message is clear: academics can enact their
roles in many different ways. The decisions need to be guided by self-awareness, an
understanding of the sector and its evolution, our career ambitions, and many other
considerations.

It is time to start questioning and reshaping our sector to encourage more constructive academic contexts. In my interactions with many international colleagues
it is clear that higher education settings will need to be more flexible and more considered in how they nurture their academic workforce. As our baby boomers move to
retirement, the small pool of graduates is unlikely to meet the demand that universities will experience for qualified workers. While this opens up many opportunities for
talented new academics, it also poses a challenge for universities: how will they ensure
their academic workforce stays with them? Positive cultures and effective leadership
are going to be ever more critical in promoting workplaces that nurture, encourage and
stimulate academics. This work will also challenge new academics to look critically at
their work cultures and the leadership styles that they experience. They have a role in
influencing and encouraging better workplace practice.

The structure of the book

The book is therefore divided into five sections:

Section 1 explores the broader context of higher education to help new academics
successfully prepare for entry into university work. It will assist in choosing a suitable
employer, establishing the role, and securing good mentors and sponsors.

Section 2 examines the process of building excellence in teaching. It explores the
broad educational principles that encourage student learning and engagement, practical strategies to manage typical challenges, and the associated activities of scholarship
and research in teaching and learning.

Section 3 highlights successful practices academics employ to build highly successful
and influential research careers. This section illustrates the need to be strategic and
far-sighted in planning a research career. It also highlights the importance of acquiring
more sophisticated research management skills to ensure time is productively spent.

In *Section 4*, engagement is examined, illustrating the importance of building a stronger focus on scholarly engagement to establish a presence across the university, discipline and the broader community.

Section 5 offers a more holistic view of building a sustainable approach to working as an academic. Career management, leadership and working in academic settings are explored, completing the exploration of the new academic context.

Acknowledgments

My gratitude is extended to the many academics who have generously shared their expertise, lessons and failures. I hope this work might be of value to them in their ongoing support for new generations of academic protégés.

The group that has most assisted this book's development are my mentees and programme or workshop participants. I have been fortunate in interacting with so many talented and committed people. They have engaged enthusiastically in creating a more strategic approach to being an academic. Their feedback and insights have assisted in refining the models that are shared throughout this work. Our joint sense-making and exploration of complex questions have enriched my initial ideas and challenged me to think more deeply about the concepts being developed.

Section 1

Getting started as an academic

1   Academic work

Academic work is one of the most rewarding yet frustrating and challenging roles any-one could undertake. It is complex, dynamic and rapidly evolving to accommodate the expectations of its many stakeholders. Long-established traditions are being challenged in a changing landscape where academics are public property and constantly asked to do more, in a better way, and with increasing efficiency. So why do we stay, and why are you reading this book? There are many reasons we choose to be academics. The most critical is a fundamental love of learning and a desire to share that with others. This is a key driver that attracts us to this rapidly evolving sector.

As a new academic you face a very different world to that experienced several decades ago. Universities now fill an expanded brief relating to teaching, research, community engagement and advocacy, supporting stronger economic gains for their nation. The traditional view of academics as remote intellectuals who ruminate, cogitate and pontificate to their heart's content is a thing of the past. The vastly widened participation of students and the growing diversity of expectations from stakehold-ers have changed the roles we play. The preparation of an intelligent and educated workforce has become an increasingly important part of our educational focus, justi-fying government funding and contributing to the perceived relevance of our work to society. Our research plays an important role in identifying and transmitting new knowledge to encourage higher standards of living, increased longevity, and improved solutions to many of the issues facing mankind and the world at large. Our broader en-gagement with society encourages lifelong learning across the community and enriches the interchange between universities and the general population. While these different roles are highly fulfilling, they do require careful balancing with other elements of our academic activities.

This first chapter offers you a broad overview of the context of academic work and why we choose to work in universities. It also highlights the changing nature of academic identity and the need to be very strategic as to where you focus. Coming into universities now is an exciting but challenging time. This book will offer you important guidance on how to survive and thrive, despite the many shifts in higher education that are occurring.

The changing higher education setting

The evolution of higher education (which will be explored more fully in Chapter 2) has changed the nature of academic work in terms of span of roles, performance expectations and conditions of employment. The complexity and variant messages as to which elements of academic work matter has generated considerable challenge for many of us as we grapple with demonstrating research, teaching and engagement excellence.

As the primary intellectual asset of a university, the academic workforce acts as the vehicle through which education, research and knowledge are enacted and translated more broadly across the community. With this growing recognition of our importance has come a stronger focus by university leaders as to how we can best be 'guided' to perform to our utmost. The emerging organizational architecture of universities reflects a keen desire to increase the effective deployment of academic staff. Universities have played with a range of faculty structures, grouping different disciplines together, flattening or increasing hierarchies, and introducing new management layers and systems. Similarly, research concentrations are being increasingly formalized through the development of centres and institutes and university prioritizing of research strengths. Structural change is one of the givens in our academic setting. Most of us will be located in an array of schools or faculties as universities try to group their academics into cognate areas that 'make sense', to achieve economies of scale and encourage collaboration.

Academic identity

For many years, we have focused on our disciplines or cognate knowledge areas as our primary academic identity. Think about how you identify yourself when you are asked to describe your role. For the most part, you probably focus on your disciplinary base: your tribe (Becher and Trowler, 2001). After studying and working in your field for so many years, your beliefs and values will be highly influenced by that grounding, determining how you teach, research and interact with your colleagues and the wider community. However, strong adherence to that heritage can also be a limiting factor in reaching your full potential as the context of higher education continues to shift. This is one of the many ambivalences we need to consider when working in academe.

Although the discipline has been a strong anchor for academic identity it is losing some traction as people move across, or into new, disciplinary specialisms or fields of knowledge, undertake interdisciplinary research, or experience structural reconfigurations of academic groups. The strong affiliation to a particular subject area no longer offers the same assurance. Instead, each academic needs to search more deeply for an identity that can operate across disciplines and, possibly, role shifts. There is an evident move towards seeing academic work as a profession that requires a repertoire of skills and capabilities that might be deployed across a number of different contexts. This alternative depiction of our role offers exciting new possibilities and reduces the anxiety of detaching from a particular disciplinary allegiance. It emphasizes the need to consciously assess our capacity to operate in variant settings and to seek continuing enhancement of our core capabilities.

In tandem, we need to explore the underlying purpose and function of being an educator, researcher, scholar and leader. While each academic may reflect these respective aspects of academic work, the interpretation and enactment of these roles can differ markedly. The relative mix of emphases will be partly determined by opportunity, the organizational context, and our personal capabilities, talents and preferences. The changing higher education context encourages a more creative engagement with variant role depictions and numerous alliances. Moving away from the discipline as the primary marker of academic identity widens the choices that we might explore. This professionalization of the domain of core academic capabilities will be explored throughout this book, encouraging a deeper consideration of what it means to be an academic.

On a more practical level, the conventional scoping of academic work has markedly shifted. We have seen a growing rise in explicit performance expectations and changing role requirements, partly stemming from a formalization of university management and corporate governance. Academics are regarded as a critical source of intellectual capital for the institution, contributing to the reputation and standing of the university and generating considerable income to sustain the broader university enterprise. New innovations in educational practice, interdisciplinary initiatives and university–community relationships are but some of the contributions being made. Academic involvement in university governance has expanded, particularly to ensure good educational practice and the maintenance of high-quality academic outcomes. The traditional picture of the remote and disengaged academic is long gone. Instead, we see an increasing emphasis on performativity (Becher and Trowler, 2001: 270), where we must demonstrate our achievement of specified outcomes to gain access to resources and status (Gappa et al., 2007). In effect, we have been wired into the mainstream of university life. Our challenge is to optimize this opportunity and see it as an avenue to achieve our potential.

Working as an academic

Within these changing conditions, we can see some large challenges emerging for those wishing to work, survive and thrive as academics. Foremost is the need to achieve high-quality outcomes in the core activities of teaching and research. The quantity, quality and impact of our efforts are widely monitored and critiqued. The breadth of our activities can be substantial, ranging from teaching and developing courses of study, coordinating groups of teachers and tutors, supervising research students, seeking grants, publishing, and building a strong academic track record. For most academics, this is our work core – where we aim to focus the majority of our time and energy. With the growth and influence of international benchmarks and metrics to judge excellence, academics are being placed under increasing scrutiny as to their effectiveness and efficiency in performing these roles.

Despite the pressure to demonstrate high-level performance in teaching and research, we are also expected to contribute to the collective good of our institutions and to enact our expertise across local, national and international communities. Involvement in department activities, committees, working parties, advisory groups, and the building of collaborative partnerships are important ways of influencing the development of the higher education sector and society as a whole. These activities are sometimes dismissed as time-consuming or disruptive, but they are important facets of our academic contribution and impact. As this work will show, there is increasing recognition of the need to more widely translate our research and teaching: to be engaged scholars. This opens up a richer dynamic to share our learning and contribute to a more robust future. It increases the valuing and recognition of our interactions with colleagues, industry and the community.

Building a sustainable career

The academic role rarely ceases, potentially operating 24/7. The separation between work and personal settings has been largely removed, making it more challenging to maintain some space for family and personal pastimes. There is increasing recognition that academics need to work in a way that is more conducive to long-term emotional and physical well-being. While high performance is a clear message that is being conveyed consistently across the sector, there are other expectations that you will expect to achieve: to be a balanced individual who maintains a personal life. As members of a wider society, we need to accommodate the numerous demands of academe, loved ones, friendships, self-care, hobbies and other life interests. A key thread through this work is the need to build viable practices that enable these other interests to also thrive. You will be offered guidance on how to flourish: to achieve a high level of performance with a strong sense of direction and purpose. We will explore the conflicting challenges of 'satisficing' and perfectionism: achieving a good outcome to support your career objectives, while avoiding burnout and destructive personal behaviours. You will be encouraged to think about how you might make a difference through your personal actions and support of others who model good practices.

This brief overview highlights five things about our academic context: the conception of academic work is rapidly changing; academics are more firmly integrated into the university mainstream; we must demonstrate escalating performance that reflects both quality and quantity; we must operate effectively across a number of platforms to be significant contributors – and finally, we also wish to live in a balanced and sustainable way while still positioning ourselves as high-achieving academics. It sounds like a tall order, but it is possible!

Why be an academic?

Given this complex work context and the limited remuneration and security, many people might ask: *Why in the world would you be an academic?* Fortunately, there are many benefits that can be found in working in higher education. Some of the more common answers are listed below:

- ***The love of learning***: There are few other professions where you are paid to follow an intellectual interest and satisfy your curiosity.

- ***To share your passion:*** To share that love of learning with students, colleagues and protégés is a particularly fulfilling aspect of working in universities.
- ***To continually seek new challenges:*** If you are someone who seeks variety and new challenges, academic work can be rich in unpredictability and new opportunities. (Although, it does have its fair share of routine and 'churn' where tasks must simply be done.)
- ***To work with colleagues who are intellectually challenging and inspirational:*** As knowledge incubators, our universities recruit and cultivate talented and innovative thought leaders that you can meet, work with and learn from.
- ***To make a difference:*** Few professions offer the same chances to influence the future in the way that academic work can: through educating students, working with community groups and conducting and promoting research.
- ***To work flexibly:*** The capacity to work from home, adapt around personal commitments, and work in a way that best suits each individual's preferred style, is a strong lure for many.
- ***To travel:*** The opportunity to visit new places and meet colleagues from across the world is also a significant benefit.

In essence, working as a faculty member offers excitement, satisfaction and an ongoing sense of self-determination. Academic work offers one of the better contexts to find meaningful work and self-fulfilment (Fairlie, 2011; Seligman, 2011). It also offers one of the most powerful settings to operate as a creative individual – if time and priorities are managed effectively. The development of streamlined systems and practices can ensure these benefits are realized.

While the advantages are significant, the higher education sector has seen some erosion of conditions that were once evident. Some of the more critical challenges are briefly listed here.

- ***Security has decreased:*** The casualization of the academic workforce has led to an increasing use of contracts to enable flexible employment practices (Feldman and Turnley, 2004; Coates and Goedegebuure, 2010). In particular, many researchers are employed on grant funding, sometimes for decades, thereby experiencing high levels of uncertainty (McAlpine, 2010; Department of Innovation, Industry, Science and Research, 2010).
- ***Workloads have increased:*** With tightening resources, technological developments and escalating student demand, higher education institutions have increased expected teaching loads and reduced administrative support to assist academics.
- ***Available 24/7:*** The growth in information and communication technologies has hampered the capacity to separate personal and professional lives. There is no real downtime as academics operate well outside the established 'working hours' to manage their academic roles. It is not unusual to email a colleague during the weekend and receive an answer almost immediately.

- *It isn't for the money*... Most academics could earn much more by working in industry or as consultants. Money is not a key driver, although we do require sufficient funds to resource our work roles, research and related travel.
- *Stakeholder expectations have grown markedly*: The increasing cost of a tertiary education has encouraged students to look closely at the quality of the education they receive, and to give strong feedback if they are not pleased. There are more diverse groups making their expectations known.
- *The goal posts are always receding*: Academe is an unusual work context, in that the better you get, the better you need to be! The use of peer review for many activities creates a strong judgemental context in which every effort is weighed, evaluated, and often found to be insufficient. This constant quest for perfection or an approximation of excellence can be a significant pressure, and can lead to high levels of personal insecurity and stress.

Despite these factors, we stay. And love it. It isn't for the money and it is rarely for the fame or notoriety. Many of us will never be widely recognized for what we do, but we know that we make a difference and that our work and passions also enrich and excite us (Hermanowicz, 2003). These challenges do need to be managed, however. Ensuring you have a strong appreciation of the context in which you work, and taking personal ownership of your career and role enactment, are two key strategies that will ensure the benefits far outweigh these challenges.

Defining a successful academic

Interestingly, there has been little debate about what makes a successful academic. Most universities define their expectations through the promotion criteria that determine recognition and advancement. Four key indicators of academic success are commonly emphasized.

- *A strong research track record* comprising numerous, esteemed publications, citations by others of published works, successful grants and funding to undertake research, successful supervision of research students to a timely and good quality completion, and possibly, patents and other notable forms of intellectual property and commercialization from research activities.
- *Educational excellence*, as measured by student and peer evaluations, innovative teaching practices and advancement of the discipline, scholarship and research relating to educational practices, and awards and recognition for teaching excellence.
- *International and national collaborations* with colleagues, industry partners, other disciplines and community groups to promote the translation of your knowledge and expertise into practice or policy.
- *Leadership* of groups; initiatives to achieve optimal outcomes for all involved.

There is no one single approach to being successful. Each of us builds a profile that is a particular mix of activities and roles. To achieve the optimal disposition of your time and talents, you will need to make a careful assessment of your capabilities and to then work towards maximizing their potential outcomes. However, determination of priorities can be strongly assisted by a clear understanding of the work context, clarity as to university performance expectations, clear self-knowledge of capabilities, and effective identification of potential opportunities. Career decisions need to be based on good judgement and a sound understanding of both consequences and implications.

The strategic academic

Escalating expectations and a widening range of responsibilities, combined with de-creasing security of tenure and employment, create a complex environment for new academics (Cantwell, 2010). There is little room for trial and error. Wasted effort can make the difference between continuing employment and looking for a new career outside academe. There are many PhD and postdoctoral candidates who aspire to be full-time academics, but find it difficult to break in.

For some, being in the right context, with good support and the opportunity to achieve quality outcomes is part of their success. However, an equally useful approach is to plan and manage your academic career in a strategic and informed manner. There are many examples of people who work incredibly hard, but achieve only moderate success as academics. In some cases, the work environment may be unsupportive. In many others, despite good working conditions, the individual simply finds it difficult to develop the right approach to get ahead and make the most of their talents. This book will show you how to operate as a *strategic academic*: drawing on a well developed sense of personal agency predicated on strong self-belief and awareness of your capabilities. You will have a better sense of the environment in which you operate and understand the rules and requirements of your employer, discipline and other significant influences. Choices can be assessed to determine both long- and short-term implications. You will be encouraged to harness a ready pool of mentors and sponsors who can advise and help to weigh options.

The role of the academic also evolves as people become more expert, leading to additional opportunities for leadership and influence. Many academics find it hard to segue into these more senior roles, holding tight to their initial identity and established approaches that assisted their initial survival. It is important to look towards the next role(s) and to plan well ahead, seeking new opportunities and collaborators who can support that growth and development. Above all, it is essential to see the larger picture in which academe operates, so that each decision is taken with conscious deliberation and recognition of the likely impact on your long-term career strategy. These issues will all be explored through this work.

The New Academic recognizes that higher education has become more political and much more stringently governed. It explores the various issues that could derail you if they are not recognized and carefully negotiated. In essence, this is the handbook that many academics wish they had received when they first started their careers. This work is the culmination of many years working with new academics and accumulating the shared wisdom of many successful academics. It offers you a guide to success so that you can clarify what is important and how you can flourish as a new academic.

The following chapters are therefore designed to offer:

- A realistic preview of academic work and the way it operates in our changing, globalized world.
- A clear road map of emerging trends that need to be recognized and addressed in order to perform to a high standard of academic excellence.
- A practical guide to the holistic nature of academic work that recognizes the complementary nature of research, teaching, engagement and leadership in strategically positioning your career.
- Practical tips on managing different elements of your role.
- Guidance on how to develop sound career management strategies, so that every decision contributes to your long-term goal of being a leader in your field.

The world of academe can seem strange and bound by inexplicable rules. This book will offer a practical guide on setting yourself up for success and will help to explain the reasons for some of those strictures. We will explore the four key foundational areas that underpin successful academic work: teaching, research, engagement and leadership. In the process, you are encouraged to explore your role and identity as an academic. What are the key goals you seek to attain? How would you describe yourself in terms of your role and purpose? What do you seek from your university to enable you to flourish and achieve your ambitions? Who is there to support you along the way? This book will offer you a number of frameworks and views to help you examine these complex questions. Each section offers a practical but scholarly perspective on one particular area. The concluding chapters explore a more holistic view of academic work, providing guidance on how to establish a more informed approach to achieving your goals and operating as a strategic academic.

The goal is to help you move towards a highly successful career – as a leading academic and an academic leader.

2 Academic work in a competitive and globalized sector

As one of the longest-serving institutions in Western society (Taylor and Machado, 2006), universities have influenced the development of nations, key leaders, and our diverse knowledge base. Conversely, they have been greatly influenced by escalating societal expectations.

First established as guilds of scholars that operated in a collegial manner, universities later evolved towards teaching and research as the key platforms on which they operated. In the twenty-first century, the higher education sector entered a new phase, as more students entered higher education and an undergraduate degree became a necessary rite of passage for most school leavers. There has been a growing focus on the role of universities in assisting economic prosperity and national goals (Deem et al., 2008; McArthur, 2011). A more critical emphasis is now placed on vocational education, which has resulted in a number of universities reshaping their missions to better support students entering the workforce.

At the same time, universities have aimed to retain their strong focus on research and scholarship, employing different modes of activity. Research may, for example, emphasize *discovery* (research to advance knowledge), *integration* (linking knowledge across disciplines and knowledge systems), *application* (to translate knowledge into practice), or *teaching* (taking the learner to a higher level of understanding) (Boyer, 1990). With the growth of the knowledge economy, these emphases have also emerged in other related sectors, providing opportunities for collaboration while also increasing potential competition. These growing influences have affected each university, particularly in how it positions curricular, research and external engagement activities.

This chapter therefore offers a brief review of the emergent higher education context and implications of these changes – for universities and the staff who work within them. As a new academic you will benefit from a good understanding of these trends and their relationship with your likely roles and work contexts. Your functions, employment conditions and performance indicators will be strongly determined by various policies, funding practices and ideologies that influence particular educational systems. As a strategic academic you will need to understand how and why your university operates in a particular way, and to consider how those conditions may impact on your roles and priorities. An ability to pinpoint the particular characteristics of a specific university can also determine which university you seek to secure as an employer.

The purposes of higher education

The increasing diversity of students entering university has stimulated strong debate around the perceived purposes of universities (Stevens, Armstrong and Arum, 2008). In recent years, one of those debates has centred on what functions universities should fulfil, with the following primarily being identified:

- education of the masses to ensure they can obtain viable employment
- avenues of intellectual inquiry, scholarship and research
- repositories and generators of knowledge
- innovation incubators, and
- catalysts for community development.

While these generic purposes may be evident across most universities, the relative prioritization and focus can vary greatly, depending on the origin and funding base of each institution. Many universities continue to offer a comprehensive curriculum that will support most learner needs, whether for a vocationally oriented outcome or a broad-ranging liberal education (Markwell, 2007). However, the goal of educating the masses to prepare them for a productive and employable future has grown in priority, particularly in nations where universities rely on some funding from government (Paivitynjala and Sarja, 2003; St George, 2006; McArthur, 2011).

The nature of higher education institutions

Higher education institutions range from research-intensive universities where research is the most critical outcome, to others, where teaching or community engagement takes precedence. Religious groups or philanthropic benefactors privately fund some institutions, while others rely heavily on government subsidy or student fees. Many institutions are specialized, focusing on particular disciplines, fields of study, student types, or specific programmes of study. Others support a large, comprehensive suite of programmes and offerings. In some nations, the term 'university' is only awarded to institutions that are recognized for their scholastic endeavour and capacity to graduate doctoral students. Other countries employ different models and structures. In developing nations, universities may be strongly supported by their government. In return, their role and functions may be tightly focused on supporting national priorities. The functions and identity of each institution can be influenced by many factors, including the institutional tradition, funding sources and their requirements, stakeholder and community expectations, leadership vision for the university, demand for the institution's offerings, and the position and affiliations of the university within the sector.

The range of higher education institutions varies across different nations. The United States Carnegie Foundation for the Advancement of Teaching, for example, highlights 33 different types of institutions in the United States, including 96 research universities with very high research activity, and community colleges that focus on a very different mission (see: http://classifications.carnegiefoundation.org/). This diversity partly reflects the ways in which the United States has built its sector, with states and regions playing a strong role in determining many institutional identities. At the other end of the spectrum, Australia has a largely homogenous sector, mainly funded by the Federal Government. Even then, the universities have created a range of categorizations to seek some differentiation (Marginson and Considine, 2000).

Funding of higher education as a driver

The recent Global Financial Crisis has stimulated an urgent focus on higher education funding. An Organisation for Economic Co-operation and Development (OECD) review of international higher education highlighted two opposing trends: increasing investment in higher education by governments in developing nations, and diminishing national sponsorship of higher education in many established countries (OECD, 2010; Quiddington, 2010). Funding by government has dwindled in some countries from 80 to 30 per cent of university income (Clarke, 2004; Levy, 2006). In some nations this has been offset by an increasing reliance on student loans and fees to compensate for the reduced government sponsorship. Although the real value of their investment may have diminished, governments still seek to influence the directions and priorities that are pursued in universities. Allocated funding is often contingent on demonstrated compliance or support for practices that are seen as compatible with the political ideology of the time. The traditional view of universities as independent authorities and voices in society has been strongly impacted by reliance on government sponsorship.

University activity has also shifted from focusing on education and research to ensuring there is sufficient funding to support core activities (Marginson and van der Wende, 2007). Thus, the rise of the manager in universities has been a very necessary, but notable, development in the last few decades (Marginson and Considine, 2000; Shattock, 2003). This has generated considerable discussion about the rise of managerialism, corporatization and privatization as various business practices have been introduced.

Massive funding cuts and commensurate staffing rationalizations illustrate the challenges that have been evident across many developed economies, as shifts in funding have occurred. Philanthropy, attracting foreign students, packaging learning to attract different types of students, and increasing engagement with business and community have all become important strategies to ensure universities remain financially viable. Many of these initiatives draw on academic expertise as the main commodity that is being marketed to attract these funding sources.

Universities have also demonstrated high levels of adaptability in responding to funding sources' expectations. In Australia, for example, funding allocated for teaching excellence resulted in large investments by universities to promote high-quality teaching and improve student satisfaction. With the more recent shift to measure research performance through the Excellence Research Australia (ERA), many institutions have refocused their attention on evaluating staff research productivity. This is but one small example of how funding sources and government can influence the ways in which universities operate, including the (re)design of academic reward, recognition, performance and recruitment practices (Ransome, 2011).

Globalization and its impact

A major influence on the sector has been the globalization of higher education. Universities now compete with institutions situated anywhere in the world. The increasing ease with which we can access information on any university, and different national strategies, has generated a global platform where policies, ideas and innovations are sourced and duplicated with remarkable alacrity. This has opened up a much stronger invigilation of how each university compares with others (Marginson and van der Wende, 2007; Bradmore and Smyrnios, 2009) and, in turn, has influenced student choices about university desirability (M. Clarke, 2007).

The most common source of comparison relates to research performance, which is more readily assessed and benchmarked using common metrics. The initial rankings developed by the Shanghai Jiao Tong University (http://www.arwu.org/) have now been joined by a number of other benchmarking schemes – although most only partially capture the real story about each institution. While some, such as the Times Higher Education Rankings (see: http://www.timeshighereducation.co.uk/world-university-rankings/) seek to evaluate the full range of educative practices, many ranking schemes primarily emphasize broad-based research performance. The universal benchmarking of research has served to even out many national differences as universities seek to establish their ascendance in the international research stakes. China, for example, is notable in its rapid rise in the research league tables (Marginson, 2010). The push to be research excellent is also being stimulated by government performance assessments in a number of countries, including the United Kingdom, Australia and New Zealand (Bradmore and Smyrnios, 2009; Sampson and Comer, 2010).

The public access to information about universities has stimulated concern for showing high-quality performance against international and national comparators. Universities spend considerable time reviewing their growth and student profiles, refining curricula, developing partnerships and collaborations, and building a strong presence in their community (Bradmore and Smyrnios, 2009). This concern for performance and reputational enhancement has promoted ongoing formalization of leadership in the sector. We have seen an expansion of senior executive roles, growing expectations of senior academic leaders, and stronger risk management to protect the university's interests. New portfolios, such as external relations and marketing, have become well established, reflecting the need to build an outward focus and branding.

These influences have also increased the concern for reputational management. In tandem, the rise of management practices and an increased focus on building long-term strategies has driven many changes in each university as they try to differentiate themselves from competitors.

Globalization has stimulated many other changes to the sector. Students and staff are being recruited from anywhere in the world, resulting in increased competition to attract the best talent. Universities are no longer located in a single place, with many now operating across multiple campuses, regions and/or nations. This has had a huge impact on many academics. Most travel regularly and rely on technology to communicate with their far-flung students or colleagues (Smith, 2009; Bourn, 2011; Trahar and Hyland, 2011). Academics are global workers, straddling time zones, countries and cultures.

Universities are also building many alliances with like institutions across the world (Fielden, 2011). The building of university networks has been particularly active as common interests and profiles act as a unifying mechanism to share knowledge, resources and strategies. At the same time, globalization has seen an increasing opening of the sector as more diverse forms of educational providers emerge. There is particularly active competition from international, private or non-university educational providers. Thus, the global nature of education has created a very dynamic and rapidly changing sector.

Technology

Universities are experiencing a further shift in their focus through the increasing influence of technological advancement. Information infrastructure, systems, student learning, record keeping and knowledge sharing are all changing markedly as universities embrace new ways of managing their data, knowledge and interactions. The escalating speed of transactions and sophisticated integration of complex systems have opened up increasing possibilities for thinking more creatively about how universities operate, and the processes that will best support their large ambitions.

With the increasing integration of corporate systems there is also greater capacity to monitor outcomes, evaluate effectiveness, and assess the performance of individuals and the organization as a whole. This has had a major impact on university strategies and assessment of institutional outcomes. It is now easier to assess some elements of academic performance with publicly available data, although this has skewed the ways in which academics are evaluated.

Technology is having a major impact on how teaching and research operates. Most students now expect support from an effective learning platform, and to be able to access their learning resources from their computer. They interact with their fellow students through learning management systems and anticipate rapid responses from administrators and their teachers.

Research strategies have also changed as the capacity to meet, exchange ideas and work collaboratively have become more readily managed through virtual means. Super computers and enhanced technologies have increased the sophistication of research and the capacity to answer ever more complex questions. However, these rapid transitions in technological capability also put major pressure on both institutions and individuals to remain current and competitive. The financial costs of maintaining large-scale infrastructure in universities is significant and escalating. Similarly, the need to re-educate staff to keep pace with new advancements has become a critical priority.

Teaching and learning

The competitive environment has generated a stronger focus on whether quality educational outcomes are being achieved (Hénard, 2010). With increasingly easy access to publicly accessible data, the calibre of the learning environment and student outcomes have been more prominently emphasized by many institutions.

In recent years there has been an escalating concern for monitoring the quality of the student experience.

- How well supported are students when they enter university?
- Are university teachers effective?
- Is the calibre of teaching sufficient to encourage high-quality graduates?
- Are graduates able to find suitable employment relating to their studies?
- Do graduates contribute to the university's reputation?

Students do not always get what they want from their university experience. When they come to university they join a community where every person or thing they encounter contributes to their overall impressions. The learning environment, student advisers, tutors, lecturers, online support, library and student unions are all part of the complex matrix that determines a student's perception of educational quality. As a teacher, you will be a critical influence, impacting on every student who comes in contact with you. Your passion, credibility and commitment will be important elements that ensure a positive student experience.

Unfortunately, the majority of higher education institutions have moved away from a more personalized approach to education, generating many challenges for their students and teachers (Tennant et al., 2009). Small classes generally occur only at final year undergraduate or postgraduate levels, increasing the risk of students being lost in the system. Students who work part time may participate online rather than face to face. This diminution of the relationship between teacher and students has some unfortunate consequences. It is not uncommon, for example, for a student to leave the university after several years of study without having one person able to provide a character reference (Light, 2004). Despite the increasing isolation of the student, they note a strong desire to feel part of a learning community. This places additional pressure on you as the teacher to create a supportive learning environment (both online and face to face) to encourage student engagement.

Research

Research has been the primary differentiator between universities and other post-secondary institutions for decades. The degree of research-intensive activity varies greatly, however, with some universities operating from a primary focus on research, through to those that have particular pockets of research excellence. The research focus is partially determined by the university mission, origin, community and funding base. University leaders and managers play a significant role in guiding quality research outcomes and promoting an intensive focus on these priorities.

The competitive environment for research has become a significant influence on institutional activities and priorities, with increased external scrutiny of institutional research performance. In the United Kingdom, Australia and New Zealand, national measures of institutional research performance also drive funding to institutions, thereby creating further incentives to lift productivity and quality outcomes.

There have been significant shifts in the research context over the last decade, pushing universities to review their research priorities and strengths. Some of these shifts include:

- The globalization of research, opportunities for virtual collaboration, and increased recruitment of researchers and students from anywhere in the world.
- Greater competition for talented research staff and students, leading to a stronger emphasis on the quality of the research environment, the reputation of institutional scholars, and the growing reputation of the institution.
- A strong emphasis on scientific-orientated (STEM) research that generate highly cited, peer-reviewed journal articles.
- Increased recognition of research ethics and integrity issues.
- Escalating emphasis on measuring research productivity, effectiveness and impact.
- Increased collaboration with allied research areas across the world.
- A growing recognition of the value of research collaboration with industry and other community partners.

The professionalization of university research activities has seen the development of a large university infrastructure and associated support services. Over time, the breadth of these agencies has expanded from an initial concern for research management and governance, to a growing emphasis on capacity building and collaborative enhancement. Universities are also formalizing the development of centres, institutes and research groups, building stronger expectations as to the leadership and management that should be evident.

Engagement

Universities are increasingly connected to their local, national and international communities. They need to engage with their local stakeholders, encouraging the translation of their knowledge and research into larger applied contexts. National and international engagement plays an important role in strengthening each university's contribution to economic and social outcomes, while also enabling greater interchange with other bodies that might enrich the institution's own activities. Many universities are spending considerable sums to re-engage and connect with their alumni. Similarly, engagement with industry and other potential partners in research is seen as a very important part of building strong connections between the academic and broader communities (Bolden and Petrov, 2008).

Role diversification

Multiple academic roles are emerging as universities respond to the broader political and economic landscape. While the traditional roles of a research-intensive academic, or a teaching/research academic, still predominate, many universities now offer alternative career paths for experienced academics. Research, or teaching development, support roles focus on helping colleagues to build their academic skills. In some institutions people can be seconded into these roles, then move back into their substantive positions. These experiences are very powerful learning opportunities.

With the increased competition over research performance we have seen a new role called the teaching-intensive academic. Universities have introduced these roles for different reasons. In some cases, they encourage good teachers who are less active in research to focus on their specialism as good teachers. National systems that judge university research performance against the number of staff employed to research can deploy less active researchers into these teaching-only roles. In other instances, academics may be employed specifically as specialist teachers to meet an identified need. A possible impact from being appointed to a teaching-intensive role is the likely reduction in research productivity. On the other hand, it can be a good avenue to build a teaching track record and demonstrate excellence, before seeking a broader role. A consequence of this diverging range of career options is a growing uncertainty as to academic identity (Billot, 2010; Gale, 2011; Waitere et al., 2011). This is likely to remain a point of debate for some time as the higher education context continues to evolve.

This brief overview of a very complex topic serves to illustrate the challenge you may face in determining which university will be the best fit for your talents and capabilities. As you evaluate employers, consider their scope of activity, level of research intensity, and support offered to employees. The funding base of the institution will be an important factor to assess: will they be able to offer you the support you need to build your research career? What are the workloads that you will be asked to fulfil if you take employment with a particular university? Are the facilities appropriate to the sort of work you hope to do? Due diligence about the university and its reputation is one of the first important steps in being a strategic academic.

3   Entering academe

There is no single way to become an academic. For some people, the process is a smooth transition from graduate, to tutor, to full-time academic. For others, the path may be convoluted and disjointed, integrating various roles that gradually evidence suitability. Some lucky people find themselves in the right place at the right time and with the right credentials to be considered a desirable candidate for a suitable position. Even without a fortuitous alignment, you can maximize potential opportunities by understanding how academic careers operate in higher education.

There are some academic principles that operate fairly consistently across the world. First, academic work is generally built on an apprenticeship model, where new people must prove their competence and show evidence of effectiveness before they are allowed to move to accredited status as a tenured or long-term academic. Second, the hurdles to move from entry-level appointments to more senior roles are zealously guarded and protected by promotion committees, unions and tradition. To become a professor, you must work through various rites of passage to demonstrate your suitability and capacity to meet the established expectations that your university has constructed over many years. You will need to understand these requirements and 'tests'. Third, it is important to recognize that finances are strong determinants of university strategy and related employment practices. Your career opportunities may largely be determined by your potential employer's capacity to fund new staff, more than your capacity to perform. The use of casual staff to support academic activities is a growing phenomenon, driven by uncertain funding and student demand. Unfortunately, the main group that has experienced the consequences of these strategies are entry-level academics. It is important, then, to be well informed about the options and sufficiently prepared to act on opportunities.

Types of academic work

There are several employment paths that may be available to you. The most common is the traditional path: following the completion of a research doctorate or equivalent (Akerlind, 2009). In this apprenticeship model, graduates have demonstrated that they can perform a substantive and original piece of research and write effectively. These are important prerequisites to an academic career. With doctorate in hand, would be academics may then seek full-time employment as either a teaching/research academic, full-time researcher, or possibly, full-time teacher. For many, the most desirable role is as a teaching/research academic that may result in a tenured position. This role is generally seen as more secure in that it draws on the resources of the school or faculty to fund the position. The academic is expected to teach, undertake research, and fulfil various service roles.

Workloads and roles differ greatly between disciplines, universities and nations. Science-based disciplines may structure workloads around large-class teaching and an intensive research focus, while professional specialisms may require considerable hours supporting student work-based learning, smaller classes, more face-to-face interaction, and greater engagement with the profession. Academic roles may include teaching offshore at international campuses, or any number of other expectations.

For a new academic, the challenge of establishing a credible teaching track record can become all-consuming. Certainly, there will be considerable pressure to demonstrate satisfactory teaching within a short space of time. At the same time, it is imperative that a solid research track record is also established. In many university systems academics must spend considerable time working as probationers before being judged worthy of a tenure track appointment. The opportunity to become a tenured staff member has decreased, as universities rely more heavily on rolling contracts to maintain their flexible employment options. This puts more pressure on contracted/non-tenured academics to maintain their competitive edge (Shaker et al., 2011).

Research-based appointments are often linked to research projects or programmes of work that have been funded. The length of appointment will therefore be dependent on the funds that have been gained for the project. In some instances, researchers may receive shorter contracts to cover potential shortfalls in the project budget. Postdoctorates are another channel for employment, with a range of approaches employed: university-funded, grant-based, or competitive fellowships are common. Research roles offer the benefit of a dedicated focus on undertaking productive research. However, it is critical that at the end of the contracted period the researcher is well positioned to move to a new role. Those years must not be wasted. The goal is to build an even stronger track record over that time. Sabbatical, long-service and maternity leave entitlements may operate differently when people are employed in positions of this nature.

There are many other avenues of employment that an early career candidate might consider. Academics sometimes commence in casual (or adjunct), research or teaching roles and then move to administrative positions where they can continue to support their university's work. This can be a demanding existence with only minimal support from the university, although efforts are being made to more fully include these staff in university life (Percy et al., 2008; Ginsberg, 2011). In the last decade, a growth area for academics has related to research, student and faculty development service roles. In the United States and Canada, academics may hold dual roles, holding a faculty-based appointment and working in a service role that operates across the university. Clinical academics also fill a dual role: continuing to service patients in their professional clinical capacity, while teaching and/or researching in their university. This is a very challenging and demanding role. Teaching-intensive appointments are also a possibility, offering a good way to get established in a discipline group.

In some situations, universities may appoint well-credentialed individuals as adjunct staff. These appointments are commonly seen as important ways to bring expert staff into the institution, but without the full commitments of a salary, office, and other employment conditions. These individuals may be involved in teaching or research, operating as active advocates of the university in seeking sponsorship and alliances with industry and other partners. In some situations, academic staff also seek more extensive experience in industry or their broader discipline. They might take a placement in a particular work setting, or exchange roles with another colleague, working in their position for a stipulated time (Nicoll, 2009).

Your personal context may also determine the span of opportunities you access. More options are available if you are willing to move between regions or countries. If your preference is one location, be more open to exploring diverse channels to gain a foothold into local universities.

A key message from this brief overview is that there will be different avenues for entering academe. Each offers particular benefits. While waiting for the desired role, look for other ways in which service to the discipline or university might be enacted. The key issue is to start to build some clear evidence of experience in the sector – in whatever way possible. Casual teaching can be an important first step, and can reduce the challenges of learning to teach while also working to establish your research track record. A benefit of casual work is that it can be relatively easy to secure, although it may not be as emotionally or fiscally satisfying.

Securing an academic position

As large employers, universities are required to operate within strict guidelines as to how they employ new full-time staff. This can work to your benefit, as it means that each candidate should have the opportunity to showcase their credentials and experience for consideration by the selection panel.

The following process is a typical sequence for a position to be filled.

1   The academic position is identified as requiring recruitment (either through new funding, a resignation, growth in student numbers, or some form of organizational restructure).
2   The supervisor reviews the job description and prepares an advertisement to seek applications. The selection panel may review this before it is publicized, and it may need to be approved by the dean or other senior figures. In some situations, the university may have a generic duty statement for academic roles. However, it is common practice to identify a set of selection criteria on which candidates will be assessed.
3   Once advertised, candidates will be invited to submit their dossier for consideration. Academic dossiers often comprise four parts: a letter outlining the key strengths and background of the candidate; a curriculum vitae (CV); a response to the selection criteria and an academic portfolio (discussed later in this chapter); and the names of three referees may also be required.
4   A selection panel is convened, normally with a mixture of genders and a representative who is not within that particular work area.

5   Panel members review the applications, based on the identified criteria, and then determine who will be interviewed. They may also develop the interview questions.

6   Short-listed candidates will then attend an interview to explore their suitability, and may be asked to present on a topic to their potential colleagues. If candidates are located overseas, they may be interviewed by videoconference or phone.

7   The chair of the panel may open and conclude the interviews, and other members will normally ask one or two questions. While a good panel size is three people (Fernandez-Araoz et al., 2011), academic selection panels may be much larger. This may make it hard to view the panellists, let alone monitor their respective responses.

8   Following interviews, possibly, presentations, and referee checks, the successful candidate will be invited to accept an offer.

9   Hopefully, unsuccessful candidates are quickly advised that they will not be of interest in this instance. However, not all universities extend this courtesy.

The interview

There are four things a good panel will wish to verify during the interview.

1   Does the candidate demonstrate the capacity to perform the role?
2   Do they demonstrate the necessary professional skills to work in an academic/research role (e.g. communication, literacy, people skills).
3   Will they fit the existing culture?
4   What skills and talents do they offer to enrich the current staff mix?

In properly structured interviews each candidate will be asked the same series of questions to create a reliable assessment context. The questions are normally open-ended, designed to test the depth of each person's knowledge and their appreciation of the key elements of the role. Behavioural questions ask the candidate to describe an experience similar to something that might be encountered in the role. For example, in an academic interview, you might be asked:

- 'Please outline an incident when you experienced conflict with a colleague and explain how you dealt with it.' Or...
- 'Explain how you would build a research partnership with an industry partner.'

These questions encourage an explanation of the context, drawing out background experience and how you deal with complex situations.

As the questions are explored, the panel will assess each answer and make notes to discuss their observations later. On this assessment, they will then determine who might be the best candidate, or, in some cases, who might need a second interview if two candidates are very hard to separate.

Of course, the other function the panel must fulfil is to lure the desired candidate into the position. They need to sell the benefits of working with this group and helping to make it even more successful. A realistic job preview is very important. If you are assured that you are moving into a cutting edge research facility that will offer you the best context, for example, and then discover the reality is vastly inferior, you will soon be looking for another position. An honest and fair review of the work context is an important part of a good selection process.

Candidates are normally offered an opportunity to ask questions or make any further statements. This is an important chance to showcase elements that may not have been profiled through the questions. It is also a critical time to ask questions about the role, the work context, or possible career development opportunities.

In addition to the interview, academic appointees may be asked to give a presentation. The presentation is designed to test for communication skills and depth of expertise, and provide the academic community with a preview of each candidate. While the selection panel remains the main arbiter as to who is chosen, feedback from the audience about the presentation can be very influential in making a final judgement.

Finally, referees are normally contacted. While the referee may be asked for a general commendation, the panel may also seek some more specific advice on issues that have arisen during the interview.

Tips for successful interviews

To maximize your chance of being selected from the interview, consider the following.

- *Research your potential employer:* Examine the strategic plan and where the university is heading. Explore the website, student information and media releases. Become familiar with the key terms that the university is badging as its point of difference. Think about what they mean and how you might support them if you are employed. If you are after a research role, look into the background of the key players. Think about how you might connect with their interests.
- *Be very well prepared in terms of your own background and knowledge:* Review the selection criteria and consider the types of questions that might be asked. Think about examples you can offer to illustrate your suitability. If there are areas you are a little less confident about, do more research to ensure you have a good general knowledge.
- *Dress the part:* Look professional and neat. Don't bring a large amount of material with you – a simple folder with some notes and some paper to jot down questions can be helpful. But only use this if you have a complete mental blank.
- *The handshake…* Western countries place a lot of importance on the type of handshake a person offers when they meet someone new. The interview

handshake needs to be confident, firm but not hard, and efficient. This is something worth practising before the interview. Ask for feedback and practice. This is a useful professional skill when networking too.

- *Read your audience:* As you answer questions, monitor the body language and interest of the panel. If they are fidgeting or restless, you are not answering as you should. Don't be put off by someone who is frowning. They may just be trying to concentrate on what you say. If more than one person is frowning, be worried. You may be sending the wrong message.
- *Don't be afraid to ask for questions to be repeated:* Not all panellists are good at asking questions. Ask for it to be repeated if it is complicated or hard to answer. Alternatively, rephrase the question and check that you have understood it correctly. It will give you a few more seconds to frame your response.
- *Don't talk too little or too much:* Each question will hopefully generate about three to five minutes of talk by you. Give some examples, and aim for clear, concise, informative answers. They wish to hear how you think and articulate an answer.
- *Appear confident, even if you don't feel it!* The goal is to assure the panel that you are ready to take ownership of the role. If you can, outline some of the ideas you have for the position. Smile and demonstrate your enthusiasm, passion and confidence.
- *Maximize your impact in remote interviews:* There will be some interviews where you will need to present via telephone or videoconference. If possible, avoid telephone interviews. The interviewing university may be happy to pay for you to visit a local videoconferencing facility. Alternatively, Skype and other forms of online conferencing can enable a visual and verbal interaction with an interviewer. Prepare as carefully for this interaction as you would for a face-to-face meeting. Dress the part and present in an area that is organized, neat and tidy. Ensure you look confident and face the panel or interviewer with a confident look and well prepared answers. Make sure you won't be disturbed during the interview.

Negotiating your position and conditions

If you are the successful appointee, don't lose the opportunity to make sure this really is the right place for you and to push for some benefits to assist you in your settling in period. There are three key issues you will need to explore.

First, how well will this new organization support you? If this is your first appointment, you will require some substantial on-the-job learning. Will you be given time to attend foundational skills courses in teaching and/or research? Is there a mentoring scheme to assist you? Will you be required to carry a normal workload straight away, or is there capacity to reduce your load slightly while you learn the ropes? Is there a good balance between teaching and research expectations, or will you be more focused on one (Gale, 2011)?

While discussing these issues with your potential supervisor, consider that individual and how he or she is approaching the discussion. Can you work with them? Your manager is the most likely reason you might leave this role (Fernandez-Araoz et al., 2011). In visiting your potential workplace, monitor the staff and the culture that is evident. Do they look positive, upbeat, engaged? Or are you facing a corridor of closed doors with little sense of a community? All of these issues are very important. Leadership and culture will strongly influence your performance and effectiveness (Bland et al., 2005; Gratton, 2007; Fernandez-Araoz et al., 2011). (See Chapters 18 and 19 for further guidance.)

Second, how will your career be assisted? Will there be opportunities to present at conferences, to participate on committees, to work with more senior leaders? What are the expectations of your role? Will you be judged on your research performance, but have little time or resources to build your achievements? It is very important to be very clear about the level of workload you will be expected to carry.

Third, what are the conditions that you can negotiate? While your salary may be relatively non-negotiable, it is not unreasonable to request a start-up grant to kickstart your research. This can assist you with purchasing some specialized resources or assistance, or help you attend some initial meetings that will build your potential collaborations. This is especially critical if you are establishing your presence in a new city or country.

The evidence trail

A critical element in obtaining a position as an academic is the preparation of a dossier of evidence that proves you are well credentialed, sufficiently experienced, and able to deliver a high-quality outcome. There are four sources of evidence that you may need to provide to interview panels. These are briefly described below.

The curriculum vitae (CV) documents your history and achievements to date. Typically it is structured into a series of sections.

1   Personal and contact details.
2   Qualifications and skills.
3   Achievements, awards and recognition.
4   Work history (including your core duties and major accomplishments in those roles).
5   Publications and other academic outputs, grouped into categories for ease of reference.

The CV should guide the reader through these sections with minimal effort. Use clear headings, provide brief explanations about roles you have filled, and ensure there are no spelling or typographical errors. This is a personal record that you need to keep up to date.

The academic portfolio provides the linkage between your CV and your evidence base (Seldin and Miller, 2009). Most portfolios are grouped into three sections:

Teaching, Research and Engagement (or Service), providing guidance on how your career strategy is being developed and the evidence you have accrued to demonstrate your success or development. Table 3.1 documents the typical components that are found in academic portfolios.

There are two types of portfolios commonly developed by academics. The summative portfolio is designed to showcase your best accomplishments, illustrating your progressive growth and escalating profile in the academic community. Intended for consideration by selection or assessment panels, it is less likely to explore development issues. Developmental portfolios, on the other hand, are designed to provide a reflective view of your goals and your progress towards achieving them. They map your progressive development of new skills, drawing on evidence to guide that evaluative process. These portfolios are often used for annual performance reviews, and components of them can be very useful when meeting a new mentor to discuss your ongoing developmental needs. Portfolios are generally developed as short (five pages or so) summary sections for each element of the role, followed by supportive appendices where the detailed evidence may be presented.

A challenge associated with portfolios is the necessity of building an evidence base. Look out for unsolicited feedback, media commentaries, or anything else that shows you are a high performer. The more you can illustrate wider appreciation of your talents, the easier it is to build a credible dossier. It is useful to build summaries of each type of evidence so that they are easier to review and evaluate. For example, if you have student evaluations of your teaching, prepare a table to summarize how your ratings have changed over the time you have been teaching. A single page summary is more useful than numerous single class reports. Qualitative responses are also helpful in highlighting particular strengths and qualities that you feel are major assets. When documenting these, list the class and year from which the quote was drawn, and keep these on file in case you need them. Remember that the reviewer does not wish to wade through large files of documentation to verify your potential. Make it easy for them.

Response to selection criteria

Use the selection criteria as headings, and make sure you show how you meet those expectations, offering a few examples to illustrate your background and suitability. Show you understand the context in which the institution is operating, and offer clear guidance on how you would fit into their context. Highlight your strengths and potential clearly. If you have particular capabilities that you feel might also assist them, outline how these are relevant. You will find the process of documenting your credentials also becomes a useful reflection process.

Many institutions are moving to online submissions, and may ask for an expression of interest or a covering letter with your CV. This is designed to attract the largest pool possible, but it can also make the selection process very difficult for the panel, as it needs to investigate each application to see if candidates meet the requirements. If you simply send a generic response to the panel, you have diminished your likelihood of being chosen. The panel is likely to receive a large number of applications from around

Table 3.1 Academic portfolio components

1	*Teaching*	
1.1	Teaching and learning context	Describe your teaching context and roles: the university mission and its particular educational strategy; the particular learner cohorts; the courses you teach, and any other elements that influence how and what you teach.
1.2	Teaching philosophy	Your teaching philosophy statement outlines your goals, how you interpret your role as a teacher, the methods you employ to reach those goals, and your support for learner needs. This statement is a very dynamic reflective process that evolves each time you review it. You will find that your first version will be quite superficial. Feedback from others can assist in clarifying your thoughts.
1.3	Teaching and learning achievements	As you progress you will be expected to build a portfolio of evidence that demonstrates progressive growth in your teaching skills, including student and peer feedback. Summarize the evidence: tables offer a useful summation of student feedback over progressive years. Whilst it is very gratifying to receive notes and emails from students, when you seek promotion or employment the hard evidence of rigorous evaluation and other forms of clear recognition will be the most critical sources of evidence that you offer.
1.4	Leadership of teaching	From the early years as an educator you will have opportunities to demonstrate leadership. This can be as simple as leading a team of tutors, overseeing the redesign of a course, assisting with student orientation days, or sitting on various committees to help reshape curricula. Keep note of these contributions – they are very important. They serve as an indication of engagement and demonstrate your growth as a teaching leader.
2.0	**Research**	
	The research portfolio operates in a similar way to a teaching portfolio. It profiles your context, philosophy, outcomes and role as a research leader.	
2.1	Research context	The specific role you play in a research community, other demands on your time, particular obligations you must meet, or commitments that you already have in place, will influence what you can achieve in your research role. Clearly document your context to explain these parameters.
2.2	Research philosophy	It is very important to have a clear sense of your research strategy. In your portfolio, make sure this is clearly outlined to your reader. You need to be clear about the particular path you are hoping to follow and the strategies that you are hoping to explore to get there. Think about your goals for the next five years and this will help you build a clear picture of your ultimate destination. (Chapter 11 will offer more guidance on this aspect of research strategy.)

(continued)

Table 3.1 (*Continued*)

2.3	Research achievements	This is probably the easiest section of your portfolio. Map your various outcomes relating to research publications, grants, collaborations, student supervision, patents, citations and any other form of metric evidence relating to your research effectiveness. You may find your university has an internal form of research assessment that benchmarks each researcher. Review this data carefully and, if it is useful, include that evidence.
2.4	Research leadership	As with teaching, it is important to look for opportunities to start to take a leadership role in research. Build a progressive documentation of these and consider what difference you made as a result of enacting that role. Look for evidence of impact and start to build this into your dossier.
3.0	**Engagement (or Service)**	
		As noted in Chapter 2, engagement is becoming an increasingly important part of academic work, connecting your teaching and research with the wider community.
3.1	Engagement philosophy	Again, your philosophy outlines what you are seeking to accomplish. It is better to be a strategically engaged academic than one who simply responds to whatever requests emerge. Think carefully about the profile you wish to build and how engagement contributes to your academic role.
3.2	Engagement outcomes	Similarly to Sections 1 and 2, aim to provide a comprehensive list of the ways you have demonstrated engagement. Again, it can be useful to collect evidence for your dossier to ensure that others can see the contribution you have made. Driscoll and Lynton (1999) offer some useful pointers on documenting your impact.

the globe. They will be keen to whittle the field down to a small number as rapidly as possible. Provide clear guidance to the reviewers as to why you are an exceptional candidate, outlining how you meet the criteria – even if it is not required.

Referees

Your choice of referees is also critical, but can be difficult at the start of a career. This is something to work on as a strategic goal: building a pool of sponsors who admire your work and are happy to affirm your potential and value. Make sure you secure their permission to list them as referees, and send a copy of your application in good time. If they only have knowledge of a specific area of your activities, this can be mentioned when you list them as referees. You might also like to send your referee a list of the things you hope they might mention. Many will find this helpful in talking about your qualities if called on. Be aware though that some referees are less than helpful when their input is sought, and may even be detractors. Try to select your referees carefully, and if you are unsuccessful following an interview, seek feedback on the outcome from the panel chair.

Unsolicited approaches

Many universities employ a pool of casual staff to assist with teaching and research needs that are more short term. Positions to be filled are often not advertised, but instead, offered to known candidates who are available. Getting yourself on that list of candidates is a potential option to get the first break into academic work. Part-time or casual work can be a good way to market your skills and build some connections with the discipline area. It helps you to establish your identity and to demonstrate your academic expertise in the role. Being known will be helpful when more substantive roles emerge later.

If you plan to use this method of seeking employment, prepare your dossier then make an appointment to see the head of the area and any other key leaders who you feel might be suitable. (This could require some investigative background work.) They may not be overly interested at that time, but you never know when something might arise. The information will be retrieved, and it may offer you that first move into academic work.

Entering academe is a little like a treasure hunt: you never know what may be waiting for you as you scan the horizon. Being prepared with a good CV and academic portfolio ready to submit will set you up for success. Be open to slightly different, unconsidered career channels – they may give you the first entry point to enter academe.

4 Getting started in a new academic role

'Here's your office. Toilets and coffee are that way. Good luck!'

Entering academe as a new employee is both exciting and somewhat daunting. The pace of work and the expectations of newcomers have both increased as the demands on higher education have grown. In some cases, new academics will be well looked after and strongly supported. They will be carefully inducted and meet with their academic head. They may have a reduced workload for the first semester. They will be clear about the support they can access, and they may enjoy the guidance of a buddy or mentor over that early period. This is a great way to begin setting the new academic up for a successful, smooth entry.

Unfortunately, not all commencements are as smooth. The reasons for less effective beginnings are many. In some cases, the academic head may be less interested in fulfilling the important role of inducting new staff. The culture may be less supportive, or people may simply be very busy, spread out across different areas or tied up with research or teaching. Whatever the reason, it can be alienating and lonely to arrive, ready to engage with faculty colleagues, only to discover that there is nothing in place to make this happen. So this chapter has been designed around that context. It outlines the processes and issues that you will need to address to be sure that you are fulfilling the right role and meeting the implicit expectations that you will be judged against when you come up for assessment. It offers you some pointers about surviving and thriving in less optimal surroundings.

Getting settled

Your first week in your new role is likely to comprise three key activities: clarifying your role and responsibilities, reading and reviewing policies, induction materials and background on the university and your work group, and commencing your network building. At the end of Week 1, you need to know what the broad rules of the game are, how you fit into the bigger picture in which you are operating, and what performance targets you must meet. You will continue to refine this understanding over many more weeks, but at this early point, you need to have some confidence that you are on the right track. The following tips can assist you in building this background knowledge.

Meet with your supervisor if possible, or another senior staff member

Ideally, you need time with a senior person to discuss your role, the broader context, how things work, and what you can expect in the way of support. This should be the start of a series of discussions. If you do not receive an invitation to meet with your head within a few days, set up the appointment with the head's secretary yourself. Don't wait. This is a critical discussion that you need to have. In meeting with your supervisor, you are establishing an important relationship. You are showing that you are proactive, goal-oriented, and keen to maximize your time with the group. You are also more likely to be sponsored if opportunities arise.

There are many areas that you will need to clarify in that first discussion. Table 4.1 offers some ideas about areas you may wish to explore in getting established. Later meetings can explore longer-term directions, your ongoing development, and career strategies.

Walk around and get to know your colleagues

Ideally, a welcome morning tea and a tour by a colleague sets you up to meet the group you will be working with. This is a warm and inviting start that helps establish you as the new person. It won't always happen, particularly if you start during teaching or high-pressure periods. Don't languish in your office waiting for someone to remember. Take the bull by the horns. Look up the website and identify staff in your community. Learning a bit about them can be a useful preparatory process to help you in later conversations. Prepare a short one-minute spiel about who you are, and wander down the corridors, knocking on doors, to introduce yourself. Visit the tearoom, if there is one, and again, introduce yourself to those who are present. You will find people are generally welcoming, although they may have been thoughtless initially in not making the first move. (If you experience some rebuffs, don't be put off. That simply helps you to identify people you won't be seeking to pursue as collaborators.)

Get to know the administrative and professional staff in your area

A failing of many academics is to see administrative and professional staff as 'irrelevant'. They can be incredibly important to you as you establish your role, offering you guidance and support. Find out about their roles, how you can best work with them, and what the limits are in terms of seeking assistance. Treat them with professional courtesy and they will watch out for you too.

Find out how things work

Some of your first week will be tied up with getting your computer set up, filling in forms, obtaining basic stationery, working out how the photocopier operates, and

Table 4.1 Clarifying your work context with your supervisor

Area of discussion	Possible questions to ask
The work context	• What are the main challenges facing the work group? • What are the key priorities I need to emphasize? • Who are the people I should get to know and seek help from? • Can you recommend a mentor to assist me during this settling in period?
The teaching context	• What is a typical teaching load for this group? • Will I receive a reduced workload while I get established? • Are there particular policies and strategies that I should know? • How is teaching performance measured? What standard do you expect of me? • Who would you see as excellent teachers in this work group? • Who should I contact if I have questions about teaching?
The research context	• What are the policies and issues I need to be aware of? • How is research performance measured? • What is expected of me in terms of my research performance? • Who are the star researchers in our work area? • Are there research groups that I should aim to join? • In terms of our discipline, are there external groups I should be seeking to enter (e.g. networks, professional societies...)? • Who should I contact for advice on research?
Engagement/Service	• Who are the main stakeholder groups that connect with this work group? • What are your expectations of me with respect to service/engagement? • During my first year, am I expected to undertake a formal service role (as opposed to being a generally supportive and engaged contributor)? • If so, are there roles that are less demanding so that I can build my confidence and skills in teaching and/or research more fully before getting too committed?
Development strategy	• Are there courses or workshops that could assist me? • Are there particular support schemes that are available for a new academic like me that I should be aware of? • Is there someone who can assist me with setting up my web profile and university information processes?

learning the names of key colleagues. At the same time, you need to move towards a wider understanding of the political setting in your work area and across the broader university. Talk with your colleagues about any advice they would offer you. A useful question might be *What advice would you offer to someone just starting out here?* An open question of this nature can be very informative. People may share observations about the culture and how it operates, key people who carry high influence, the effectiveness of the senior leaders, the tricks of the trade to survive, and who to avoid. . . You may hear life stories, grievances, and different views of university trends and directions. Don't commit to a particular view: just listen. You are hearing how the culture operates, and will start to make sense of things over the next few weeks. The conversations will help you to identify people who are positive, active contributors to the school, and those who are mired in history and grudges. Focus on building relationships with those who are constructive and helpful. You need to harness your energy and enthusiasm by linking to others who create a dynamic workplace.

Clarify your performance targets

With all of these many conversations and discussions, make sure you build a clear picture of what is expected of you. Hopefully this will be clearly outlined by your supervisor, but it is worth triangulating this guidance with other people and sources. Review the promotion guidelines, recognizing that you need to start planning for your next career transition from the very first days in your new role (Buller, 2010). As discussed in Chapter 2, it is also very helpful to review the larger sectoral trends and issues that are likely to impact on your discipline and role.

Identify and address your knowledge and skill gaps

You will require further development, even if you are well prepared and expert in your field. If your role includes teaching, contact your support services to discuss their courses, online support, and any other assistance they can offer you. Similarly, identify how research is supported in your university, and make contact with those who can give you some background and advice. Without guidance of this nature, you may find you have lost a good six months in trying to work out how things operate. Investment in your development is a sound strategy. Despite feeling busy and pressured to get a lot of things done, enrol in introductory courses if they are available. The benefits you reap will outweigh the time you lost.

Find a mentor

At this very early stage, try to connect with a person who is willing to help you get established and offer advice. In some institutions, this will be set up for you. In others, it will be up to you. Look for a person who is respected, knowledgeable, and willing to assist. You will soon identify someone of this nature in your familiarization activities, but if not, ask your head for guidance. This liaison may be of short duration, but it can be very helpful to have someone who is happy to answer 'silly' questions.

The first six months

The key goals you will be focused on in the first six months are:

- Establishing your credibility.
- Clarifying your role, responsibilities and performance requirements.
- Setting up your role and systems.
- Building your network of colleagues.
- Surviving, particularly in balancing the various work activities and roles.
- Clarifying how the culture works.
- Meeting your performance expectations.

You are likely to feel like you are in a whirlwind, rushing from one thing to the next and working out what works, who to trust, and how to thrive in a complex setting. This book will offer you many tips on how to achieve those goals. Some key principles to bear in mind are that you are just at the start of the process. You are not expected to be perfect, just required to demonstrate a capacity to satisfactorily meet the basic standards of performance. This first six months is your baseline – you will progress from there.

Keep your sense of humour and balance. Don't get caught up in the politics or take sides in debates. These are not your problems and you are better keeping some distance while you get to know key players more fully. However, do not remove yourself from your community. It is very important that you attend all staff meetings and other forums to gain a strong understanding of the environment in which you work.

Extend your network of colleagues, particularly aiming to meet other early career academics in a similar situation to you. It can be very helpful to explore the broader institutional context, comparing notes, and building a larger understanding of how policies and practices operate across the larger setting.

Look out for good systems and techniques that other colleagues employ. Academics are often poorly skilled in using their email and technological tools. Take the time to learn from trainers and other experts so that the most efficient practices are being used. This can save considerable effort and preserve precious discretionary time.

Recognize that this is the tough time. The many different areas that a new academic must learn and navigate can be time-consuming and very demanding. Lectures may take two days to prepare in the early days, and you will need to allow time for learning to teach effectively, understanding the student record systems, designing on-line resources for students, and marking assignments. At the same time, you may be working feverishly to produce the papers that are expected within the first year of appointment and straddling administrative duties that have been assigned to you.

An important issue to monitor is whether your workload is fair. There has been considerable debate for many years about the particular roles that new academics are assigned. In some cases, a reduced load is given, recognizing the learning curve that must be navigated in the first six months. In others, newcomers may be asked to accept large, complex roles (such as teaching a large first-year class or managing a group of casual teachers). Check the loads of other staff to make sure the allocations are equitable, and speak out if it is clearly not so.

Above all, keep the goal in sight. It can be easy to start to lose the sense of why academic work is worth the effort. Hold on to the passion, enthusiasm and vision that you came with. The world of academe is worth the effort, and things will get easier.

5 Successful approaches to mentorship and sponsorship

The academic game has many hidden rules and may require some agile responses to opportunities. It can be hard to work out which directions will achieve the best outcomes and to identify the pros and cons of different options. Two of the most critical, but under-recognized, factors that contribute to a successful academic career are mentorship and sponsorship. Mentoring is linked to the retention of early career academics (Dunham-Taylor et al., 2008) and more rapid career progression (Hegstad and Wentling, 2004). Mentors and sponsors offer an expert view of your capabilities and potential and the different paths that are emerging. They can help you fast track through the hurdles that are likely to come your way and keep the right balance in building your profile. Successful academics note the value of mentorship in expediting their careers. In some cases, initial associations that commence as strong support for an emerging academic can span many years of long-term collaborations.

While some academics are fortunate in having generous benefactors who are there from the start, many have to find, and then cultivate, suitable people. This chapter therefore explores the process of identifying and then engaging suitable mentors and sponsors.

What is a mentor?

A mentor is someone who can assist you in reflecting, planning, and managing your career strategy (Nakamura and Shernoff, 2009). Their primary focus is to assist your development by offering career and psychosocial support (Young and Perrewe, 2000; Scandura and Williams, 2004; Brown et al., 2009; Sawatzky and Enns, 2009). Mentors are often more experienced senior colleagues who share their knowledge and expertise with you to assist with decision-making. Their knowledge of you and your background, combined with an informed assessment of the environment in which you are operating, ensures you are receiving appropriate guidance to make good decisions and judgements. In essence, they act as a microscope, horoscope and telescope to provide different views of the present context and future possibilities. They enable a close and personal interaction that is intensive and sustained, unlike other forms of support that may be more 'interventionist' in intent (Gibson, 2005). A particular contribution is their focus on social learning– that is, how the real world operates, and how you can best fit into that setting (McDowall-Long, 2004).

While mentors are generally sought from more experienced colleagues, peer mentors also offer many benefits through sharing their own insights and learning. Reviewing common experiences, and cross comparisons with peers, offer an important mirror into the lived experience that is occurring and the broader institutional setting that is in place. Peers are particularly valuable in offering emotional support during times of change and growth, as their own journey is similarly unfolding.

The benefits of mentorship

Mentorship brings many benefits to both parties. As the mentee or protégé you will be assisted in:

- developing and refining professional skills and knowledge
- building professional and collaborative networks
- developing deeper insights about academic and professional communities
- exploring potential career options and strategies
- reviewing your personal and professional capabilities
- identifying areas of growth and learning that will be beneficial.

Mentors also benefit from offering their support. Through their interaction with protégés, they can:

- review their own career path and reflect on accumulated knowledge and insights
- leave a legacy through guiding and supporting talented new academics
- develop new skills and insights through mutual discussion and enquiry
- learn of new fields of knowledge and issues that could inform their own work and reflections
- identify potential talent that might be recruited into their own research group or projects
- develop potential research partnerships and collaborations, and possibly
- develop joint publishing/projects as time progresses.

Of particular note is the recognition that academic mentorship can be a lifelong partnership – with the role of the mentor and the nature of the relationship changing over time (Duda, 2004a).

Clarifying the mentoring focus

The process of entering academe is a very big transition for many people. It requires considerable agility in straddling the complex, complementary, but competitive fields of research and teaching. It is rare to find a mentor who can provide guidance on all areas of need. Different people have different areas of knowledge and expertise. A very high achieving academic with an outstanding track record, for example, might have little to offer in terms of advice about balancing family and work. Then again, they might!

The first step in the mentorship process is to be clear about the support that you seek. The choice of mentor is partly driven by a careful assessment of your current and future needs. As the following options illustrate, there may be quite an array of areas that could benefit from some guidance. The mentor may be able to address some of these, but is more likely to have particular skills and talents that relate to one or two areas. In fact, there is increasing recognition of the need to build a 'portfolio of mentors' (Higgins, 2000; de Janasz and Sullivan, 2004).

During the first few months of commencing in a new university, an **orientation mentor** can be invaluable (Sullivan-Brown, 2002). These mentors would normally be someone who has a good knowledge of the institution, the personalities that are likely to be encountered, and the way in which academics work and the broader institutional context function. Their internal networks and practical know-how can provide the necessary entry into a number of beneficial communities and ensure you are forewarned about some of the likely pitfalls. Cultural, teaching, research and policy contexts can be outlined, along with some indication of performance requirements and, possibly, some cautionary tales. In some universities new staff are appointed an orientation mentor for the first few weeks. This does not preclude finding others who can also help to interpret this world. In fact, it is useful to have several sources to ensure the messages that are being conveyed to you are correct. You need the right information to ensure you establish yourself as a great new asset to your school and university. Orientation mentors need to be familiar with the broad functions of your university, faculty and/or research community, but may not be senior members. However, it can be beneficial to have someone who has a more senior role as their broader perspective can identify any risks that need to be avoided and the opportunities that can be maximized.

Entering a new work setting can sometimes be a hazardous occupation, particularly if the academic community is divisive or highly competitive. In these situations it is critical to get a clear sense of the political and social context in which your work will operate, particularly if resources are tight and workloads are high. Even in good work settings it is useful to learn how you are expected to operate, and how the annual cycle works. **Contextual mentors** can offer practical insight into the academic context, protocols for academic work, and guidance on those who have knowledge, influence or power in a particular work setting. They can also offer advice on how you might best manage your relationships with important members of your academic community. These mentors often become apparent quite quickly on your arrival. They are likely to introduce themselves and share some tips for survival. Your discipline head or peers may also operate in this capacity. Contextual mentoring often operates on an 'as need' basis, and may be sought when required, rather than set up as a formal arrangement.

Career mentors play a very important role in guiding effective career management. A successful academic career requires considerable planning and consideration of long-term strategies to identify and maximize opportunities that arise. Normally a career mentor will be more senior, with an academic record that parallels the type of career you are seeking to build. The mentor's considerable experience will assist in guiding your steps and strategies. Their review of your academic track record to identify gaps and vulnerabilities can be particularly valuable. While career mentors may be found in your local community, they may also be located elsewhere. Your supervisor may fill this role (Richard et al., 2009), but it needs to be recognized that sometimes guidance on careers and academic progress is better discussed with someone who does not have a stake in your everyday outcomes. (For example, your supervisor may ask you to take on considerably more service roles than they could reasonably request. Their first priority may relate to getting the work done, rather than helping you balance teaching, research and engagement, or considering your future needs.) Supervisors can offer considerable support and resourcing to help you progress your career goals, and should see this as part of their role (Scandura and Williams, 2004). Career mentors may also be sourced outside academe, particularly if you feel that you wish to explore more diverse career opportunities (Higgins, 2000; de Janasz and Sullivan, 2004).

A key priority when moving into academe is to build a comprehensive understanding of your particular discipline and to establish a strong presence as an up and coming figure. While the PhD offers a preliminary insight into the field, it is only a small part of a wider macrocosm. As a new academic you will need to build a much bigger picture of the emerging issues and opportunities that you will encounter. A **discipline mentor** is someone who has a wide breadth of knowledge of the discipline and intricate understanding of the lines of research that are emerging internationally. They may also have a strong reputation for teaching and research supervision excellence. In essence, they know the game and understand the international, national and university landscape. These mentors are expert in their field. Their networks will be extensive, linking to other international scholars who are also contributing to the growth of the discipline. They may sit on national committees, be widely published and cited, and fill many different roles in representing disciplinary interests. Discipline mentors are particularly valuable in guiding a new research interest, exploring how the intertwined roles operate or in identifying potential areas of collaboration. They are often looking for new individuals to refresh their expert pool, and will be pleased to explore possible areas of development with you. Generous discipline mentors can offer entry into the networks, assist your integration into reviewing roles, and identify important opportunities for you to access. While you may find great discipline mentors close to your office door, look more widely across your field too.

As a new researcher you face a time of immense learning, frustration and challenges as you step into new fields of endeavour and forge your reputation for being an independent researcher. It is therefore very helpful to identify someone who is willing to act as a research mentor. **Research mentors** can fill a number of roles that will guide you through this learning period. First, they can offer guidance in critically reviewing emergent research ideas, proposals and publications. In this capacity they offer five benefits.

- *Supportive* – recognizing and acknowledging your strengths.
- *Constructive* – identifying areas requiring work, and how they might be improved.

- *Insightful* – exploring potential areas of related interest which might be included or strengthened.
- *Informative* – providing insights into the competitive process and how it operates.
- *Realistic* – advising if the grant or publication is ready.

Second, research mentors can provide guidance on the strategic deployment of your effort. Is this the right journal to target? Which publication channel will generate the greatest benefit? Which conference will be best for this research paper? Is my time better spent on two more papers or a grant submission? Third, they can also provide support during the academic acceptance/rejection process and its associated emotional upheavals. Finally, research mentors offer another avenue to access relevant networks and associated opportunities.

In a similar vein, you might seek a **teaching mentor** to assist you in planning and reviewing your educational practice and impact. Experienced teachers can offer many types of support – from modelling good practice, sharing resources, critiquing your methods or designs, to guiding your research about your teaching. Look for teachers who have been recognized for their excellence and who demonstrate passion and dedication. Inspirational people are infectious and will buoy you up, while supporting you in taking some risks to be innovative.

If you are leading a project team or a group of research students, you will need to build some basic leadership skills as rapidly as possible (see Chapter 18). As you move into leadership roles, look for a **leadership mentor** (Duda, 2004b) who is well regarded and respected for their generosity, effective guidance of groups, and capacity to achieve the utmost from the team's efforts. A leadership mentor can encourage your reflection and skill development in guiding and supporting others. They can be particularly helpful in exploring the complex issues that arise when managing tight resources, talented people, and demanding deadlines. You might also seek support in this area from professionals in your university, or coaches who can work with you in your development.

Peers who are keen to share their experiences and reflect on their progress with colleagues in a similar position can also provide mentorship. **Peer mentor** support can include the exchange of information, learning, insights, academic practice, networks, peer review of teaching, sharing of resources, support, energy, enthusiasm, social interaction and reflections. These mentors fill a very different role – uncertainties, vulnerabilities and future aspirations are but some of the areas that can be explored in a non-threatening forum of this nature. It is particularly important to build a friendship network in your academic community, and to identify people who would be pleased to act as peer mentors. You will gain strong affirmation and encouragement from each other. These relationships will be less formally managed and may operate through an occasional lunch or coffee break. It is important, though, to make time for these discussions.

There are, of course, other aspects that you might wish to seek help to explore. If your life has moved into straddling a young family and a career, it can be very useful to seek advice from someone who has successfully managed both (or at least, that might be how it seems to outsiders!). The types of mentors you seek are really endless, and will reflect your evolving needs and challenges.

Successful mentors

Successful mentors generally demonstrate generosity, positive advocacy and realistic consideration of the academic environment (Lee et al., 2007), effective communication, listening and questioning skills, and the capacity to see the mentee's context (Bozionelos, 2004; Waters, 2004; Brown et al., 2009). While successful mentors have a wealth of experience on which to draw, it is important that they recognize that the path of the mentee will not replicate their own history. Instead, the mentor offers a means of weighing options and judging the most desirable course of action. This capacity to move beyond thinking about self and into the skin and context of the mentee is a very important precondition for success.

Successful mentorship is predicated on some basic understandings as to how the interactions will operate. Some of these principles include:

- The primary purpose of the mentor is to help the mentee identify, review and weigh options, make informed judgements, assess risk-taking, and make strategic decisions. The setting of challenging, aspirational goals is the mark of a good relationship.
- The mentor can greatly assist this process by questioning and probing to provide opportunities for the mentee to reflect, explore and question their own perspectives. The mentor is not there to simply give advice and instructions on how things might/should be done.
- Ideas and observations should be communicated and explored in an open, non-judgemental fashion.
- Any feedback should be at the request of the mentee and reflect the individual's context and background.
- The discussions should primarily relate to the mentee's agreed development goals and priorities.
- Discussions about intellectual property and ideas should be treated as confidential.
- The discussions can be quite wide-ranging, as new ideas, expertise, models of good practice and lessons learned are exchanged, but each session should result in productive outcomes. This is not an opportunity to have a talkfest or listen to the mentor's memoirs.

Successful mentees

As the mentee you play a critical role in this relationship. The time a mentor spends in discussions and furthering your interests needs to be repaid through commensurate effort on your part, and evident follow-through on agreed goals. To get the most from a mentoring relationship, aim to demonstrate:

- Courtesy and respect for the mentor's knowledge, skills and reputation.
- An openness in communicating needs and expectations (Waters, 2004).
- A keen desire to learn, explore ideas, and seek guidance or feedback.
- Responsibility for identifying, reviewing, and weighing options.
- Willingness to receive honest feedback and to act on that advice, or at least, reflect on it (Young and Perrewe, 2000).
- Commitment to pursue agreed goals and plans (Young and Perrewe, 2000).
- Willingness to experiment, trial new processes and procedures, and move beyond the comfort zone.
- Responsibility in managing the meetings and interactions.

Identifying suitable mentors

The process of identifying suitable mentors will differ for each individual, depending on the type of mentor being sought and the level of support being offered by the university or school.

Formal mentorship opportunities are often offered as part of development programmes (e.g. Debowski, 2007) or as discrete programmes (e.g. Allen, 2003; Szumacher et al., 2006). New approaches, such as mentoring circles (Darwin and Palmer, 2009) can be a valuable way of building skills and confidence with colleagues. The training of mentors also increases the likelihood of successful mentoring partnerships (Kochan, 2002; Omary, 2008). In some cases, the university may offer support in sourcing and matching mentors and mentees. However, the ultimate success of a formal mentoring programme depends on the commitment of the mentee. Passive, distracted, or disinterested mentees will not keep their mentors engaged: they have much better ways to spend their time.

If you are not able to access formal programmes, it is still very easy to build a robust approach to finding and initiating good relationships. Once you have clarified the priorities you wish to explore with your mentor, you can then identify suitable 'candidates'. You might, for example:

- Ask your supervisor, head of school, or head of research centre to suggest some names.
- Conduct a literature search on your discipline area to identify some leading academics publishing in your area of interest. Review their profiles and contact them to explore your needs.
- Review conference paper abstracts to identify potential people of interest attending a conference. Attend their presentation and make yourself known to them. Be prepared to ask intelligent questions! If you would like more time to prepare, send an email following your return to the university.

- Canvass the opinions of your colleagues as to who might be a good mentor.
- Investigate leading academics in your local university and consider whether any might be suitable mentors.
- Seek the assistance of your research or teaching services, or other agencies that can recommend successful academics. You will find that certain people are regularly noted by many sources.
- Monitor your university publications to identify people of interest.
- Attend networking and other university functions to identify potential mentors.
- Visit a potential mentor's own university if you are travelling to a related event.

Once you have identified a potential mentor, conduct some due diligence on them, particularly with respect to their track record, reputation, current activities, projects, and suitability with your desired focus.

Make contact with them to see if they would consider being a potential mentor. This is best conducted as a personal contact – either in person or by phone. Following this initial contact, email your current CV and a short review of your academic interests, achievements and goals. Your mentor may also share their profile for your background information.

Building an effective relationship

Once a mentor has agreed to participate, it will be necessary to initiate the relationship. The first meeting is normally an opportunity to clarify expectations and agree on how the relationship might operate. Some useful questions to assist in the discussion include:

- What do we want to achieve from this relationship?
- What are the main areas that our discussion might emphasize?
- What time frame are we considering?
- How will the mentoring process work?
- Who is responsible for maintaining the connection? How should this be managed?
- Where shall we meet?
- How often?
- What are the expectations in relation to preparation?
- What are our understandings with respect to confidentiality, respect, honesty and trust?

Following this first meeting, you will need to maintain the relationship. Ensure the role to be played by each partner is clearly understood. Promptly act on any agreed goals that have been discussed: each meeting should show a progressive development of the identified strategy. As the mentee, take the initiative in arranging regular meetings and other opportunities to interact (Foote and Solem, 2009). Be at the meetings on time, or a little before, and prepare for the discussion to maximize the outcomes. It is useful to share materials and revisions well ahead of time. Critical questions that need to be explored are usefully shared prior to the meeting so that the mentor can think about them. There may be opportunities where the tables can be reversed: mutual sharing of contacts, insights and new ideas can support the mentor's growth. Frequency of interaction increases the benefits from the mentoring, particularly in guiding career strategies (Bozionelos, 2004).

When is it over?

Not all mentoring relationships succeed or last. There are many factors that can impact on the durability. In some cases, the personalities may be ill suited. In others, the need is short-term rather than a long-term focus. Some academics find that they may outgrow their mentor or their context changes. Others will move to new employers, new disciplines, or out of the sector entirely. In many cases, the meetings will span longer gaps or shift into a more collaborative focus. The most critical issue is to be open about the status of the relationship and to discuss any interactive challenges that are emerging. Recognize that the relationship will change over time as the goals are achieved.

Sponsors

Mentors offer particularly close support so that their mentees can test ideas and gradually build viable strategies for implementation. In effect, they offer developmental guidance on career strategies and processes and help you clarify your goals. Establishing the identified skills, capabilities and evidence can take some time, requiring a sustained relationship.

Sponsors are primarily focused on helping you achieve those identified goals by providing avenues for you to fast track your strategy. They are generally people who have significant power, influence, capacity and willingness to create new opportunities for you. Some typical actions a sponsor might take include facilitating networking opportunities, sponsoring entry into key networks, recommending their protégés for roles that will offer good profile or experience, and acting as a referee as needed. To perform these functions, the sponsor needs to be aware that you exist! Many early career academics patiently wait to be noticed, to little avail. Be proactive in seeking support. Make contact with potential sponsors and proffer your CV and a brief career profile. Outline your goals and the support you are seeking. You are then on the radar and the sponsor will keep you in mind. And, of course, if you do get offered opportunities – take them up and make the utmost use of them. This may mean looking at all other commitments to see what needs to be dropped. You will need to make sufficient space to shine in these higher profile settings. Keep your sponsor informed of your progress and make sure you convey your appreciation.

Coaching

It is important to both build on your strengths and assets and identify areas that require development. If your writing or communication skills are poor, for example, you are likely to have some major challenges in forging an academic career. Rather than struggling alone to address the issues, consider hiring a coach to assist you. Coaches are skilled in working with one individual to correct long-standing habits and errors. They can analyse the issue, identify small learning goals, and work step-by-step through the incremental changes that are needed. Because they are focusing on one particular learning outcome and will need to meet with you regularly, progress will be sustained and evident. Coaching can be an important investment in your future. Your mentor can assist in identifying possible areas for this intensive support. Your supervisor might also offer feedback on areas that are holding you back. Don't see these as criticisms – regard them as learning opportunities and act on them.

Mentors and sponsors are an essential part of your career strategy. Aim to have at least one mentor at any time and ensure they are rewarded with your development in the agreed areas of need.

Section 2

Making a difference as an effective teacher

6 The changing context of higher education learning and teaching

In the last few decades, higher education learning and teaching has been a significant focus for theory building, research and debate. The growth in student diversity, and variety of educational institutions, has forced the sector to more closely explore the evolving learning environment and the consequences of educational policy and practice. In this chapter you will be offered a brief overview of some of the emerging issues evident in the sector.

The focus on teaching quality

The growing influence of globalization has stimulated a heightened emphasis on educational quality (Tennant et al., 2009; Hénard, 2010). Universities have established large quality assurance agencies to measure, evaluate and act on data about teaching quality and student outcomes. Entire national strategies revolve around measuring teaching quality (Martin, 1999; Barnett and Coate, 2005; Siddons, 2008; Matthews et al., 2011). There is also increasing activity internationally through the AHELO project, intended to create international disciplinary-based educational standards (OECD, 2011). The growth of metrics to explore student retention, satisfaction and achievement, graduate outcomes, and the destinations of graduates (Yorke and Longden, 2004; Edwards and Coates, 2011), has generated a significant concern for the number of students who fail to thrive in higher education (Peelo and Wareham, 2002; Crosling and Heagney, 2009; Arum and Roksa, 2011).

Research has illustrated the significant link between teaching quality, student motivation, and outcomes (Ning and Downing, 2011). Equally, there is vigorous discussion around the need for education to fulfil its designated purposes, although, as we saw earlier, these purposes may not be clearly articulated or, indeed, adequately debated. The current emphasis on benchmarking student outcomes, for example, may have unintended consequences by reducing the concern for student learning in favour of delivering content to meet predetermined and prescriptive graduate outcomes (Barnett and Coate, 2005; Hattie, 2008).

Risks to teaching quality

This is a time where support for university teaching is under considerable threat. The escalating student demand for education, with concurrent diminishing funding, has seen a push for teachers to oversee larger classes and increasingly *manage* the educational process, rather than *engage* with it. This instrumental approach sees education as a *product* rather than a *process,* posing considerable risk to the long-term valuing of higher education. If we see teachers as merely devices to ensure students have jumped through the necessary hoops to graduate, we have hugely diminished the value and importance of higher education and underestimated the power of a quality learning experience.

The pressures of working across multiple platforms and locational settings with a diversity of students, while simultaneously attempting to build a strong research track, have certainly created an environment where academics may see teaching as a less critical role. Institutional cross-subsidizing of research, from student fees and teaching funds, affirms the perceived relative weighting placed on research versus learning. The ongoing demarcation of academic roles to categorize people as teaching and research, *research-intensive*, or *teaching-intensive,* further serves to differentiate people according to some crude measures of purpose and worth. As Tennant et al. (2009: 35, 47) note, teacher identity must be fluid and will increasingly need to accommodate multiple foci to effectively operate in our complex sector. The growth of knowledge economies, and the socio-cultural role education plays, requires flexible and adaptive teachers. Insufficient recognition of teaching and its critical role in higher education is an ongoing challenge for the many academics who take their educational responsibilities seriously.

The student experience

We are seeing a vigorous international debate around the different ways in which we can enhance the quality of higher education learning and teaching. Government concern for increasing participation rates of low socio-economic students, and a greater diversity of learners, has encouraged consideration as to how we can create a more inclusive curriculum that supports diverse student cohorts (Crozier and Reay, 2011). This has certainly sparked considerable debate about how we can achieve better success rates for student retention. There is much greater recognition that new students benefit from structure, socialization opportunities, and skills development to successfully transition into the more sophisticated demands of a university existence.

Many universities have identified the student experience as their signature strategy, guaranteeing a high-quality experience for students who enrol. In recent years we have gained a much better understanding of the multiple factors that contribute to that quality experience and learning engagement (Light, 2004; Yorke and Longden, 2004; Leach and Zepke, 2011). Central to a quality student experience is the commitment, passion, and expertise of the teacher, something that excellent teachers regularly demonstrate (Hay, 2011). The socialization and interaction activities that students encounter outside the classroom are important, complementing the provision of a rich and meaningful learning experience within the class setting (Matthews et al., 2011).

Students who move away from home to undertake their studies are a group that may be particularly at risk. The complexity of building a new friendship base, acclimatizing to university existence, increased freedom, and possibly, a very different set of cultural practices, creates significant challenges. The recognition that students are not homogenous has stimulated increasing concern for making curricula internationally and globally relevant. However, the concept of internationalization remains a somewhat confused, and in fact, largely misunderstood, concept for many academics and administrators. Audit reports of Australian university strategies to encourage internationalization, for example, show a strong tendency to see this principle as related to sending students abroad. As with many other learning and teaching concepts, there is considerable work to be done in unpacking and better understanding both principles and practices to ensure a quality student experience.

Increasing participation in higher education has also generated a push to use technology more effectively to enable students to learn asynchronously: at any time, any place. Universities see the provision of e-learning as a marketing strength, although there is decreasing separation between institutions as technological gains continue to move forward. Considerable money is being spent on building digital platforms, learning management systems, web-based access for students, online library systems, student portals, and a range of interactive technologies that signal the university is at the forefront of learning innovation. Flexible learning offers enormous potential for enriched learning experiences, but also places considerable pressures on academics to straddle face-to-face interaction with students and the development of integrative and effective interchange through technological means. While there has been considerable research around e-learning and the way it can be enacted, we have not necessarily engaged with how we ensure students remain connected with their teachers and fellow students, particularly with respect to their affective development (Tennant et al., 2009). The broader questions around building blended learning approaches, creating a social community between teacher and students, and maintaining 'the heart' of the educational experience (Palmer et al., 2010) still requires further exploration.

The focus on the economic benefits of higher education, and the preparation of students for a productive future, has perhaps tilted the balance a little too heavily towards graduate outcomes that are work related. There is growing concern for counteracting those pressures, and recognizing the importance of educating students who have the moral and ethical principles to live healthy, productive and balanced lives. This debate, while still emerging, highlights the need for academics to remain attuned to the role they might play in helping to create a healthier society. The capacity to offer and stimulate compassion and social contact is a powerful opportunity for educators at a formative stage in a student's life (Light, 2004; Palmer et al., 2010).

The academic focus

The desire to link higher education more closely to societal imperatives has opened up many opportunities for academics to align their educational practice more closely with the professions, industry, and society at large. The design of curricula that have contextual relevance and prepare students more fully for the world of work and service offer rich and meaningful experiences for both teacher and student. In many cases, the academic's engagement with these broader communities also encourages deeper consideration of the ways in which higher education can better support the evolving world in which it is situated. These exchanges can further benefit the academic by integrating applied research into their teaching, particularly through real examples and stories.

For some years there has been a strong suggestion that academics should be able to meld their research practice and knowledge with their teaching activities: demonstrating a strong teaching–research nexus (Brew, 2010a). This philosophical stance argues that it is important to integrate research into teaching, and certainly to ensure that students receive a research-informed experience. An introduction to research is particularly important for undergraduates who have moved from a generalized learning context in secondary school, to a theoretical learning platform in university (Cantwell et al., 2010). The broader assumption that academics will be able to effectively link their own personal research and scholarship interests to their teaching assumes that these two domains of activity are complementary. However, the growth in large-scale teaching, and reduction of 'boutique' subjects featuring an academic's research interests, has generated more challenges in achieving this synergy. More critically, there has been considerable debate around the assumptions that excellent teachers are excellent researchers. Research shows there is little correlation between good research and good teaching (Marsh and Hattie, 2002; Hughes, 2005). Thus, while the principles are worthy, they have proven more challenging in creating a viable framework for the sector to apply (Visser-Wijnveen et al., 2010).

Academics with teaching roles are expected to develop professional teaching skills. The process of developing effective skills in teaching is complex. It requires a comprehensive understanding of educational practice, pedagogy, student needs and university systems and policy. Many universities now provide educational programmes for new teachers, and in some cases, insist that teachers must be qualified in order to teach their students. In addition to formalized instruction, positive leadership and modelling within schools and departments plays a significant part in encouraging quality teaching (Debowski, 2012). An academic community committed to quality learning offers powerful support during these formative processes. Peers, mentors, and professional support services can also assist the development of integrative frameworks. Practice, perseverance, feedback, and an ongoing commitment to learning and development, are further elements that lead to success in university teaching.

Evaluating teaching quality

The professionalization of teaching requires regular, informed assessments of teaching effectiveness. It is critically important that teachers are self-aware, reflective, and able to identify incremental learning goals through regular self-review. Considerable energy has been expended on designing assessment systems to evaluate teaching effectiveness, and more recently, to establish some international benchmarks. The complexity of assessing the impact of teaching on students has made this a particularly challenging area to consolidate (Hénard, 2010), and continues to attract strong debate, particularly concerning the reliability and validity of evaluative tools. While international measures of *student engagement* (such as the Course Experience Questionnaire (CEQ) (Wilson et al., 1997) and National Survey of Student Engagement (NSSE) (see: http://nsse.iub.edu/) have been widely adopted, there is much less consistency as to the evaluation of *teacher effectiveness*. Most universities have developed institutional tools to provide feedback and guidance to individual teachers. Measures include formal surveys of students, the development of teaching portfolios, and peer review of teaching. In many settings, the decision to use these evaluative measures is left to the teacher. However, those seeking promotion or tenure will be expected to demonstrate a history of data-related evidence to corroborate their claims.

Recognition of excellent teaching has been in place for some years, particularly through national schemes. For example, in Canada, the 3M Fellows have been very successfully sponsored (http://www.mcmaster.ca/3Mteachingfellowships/) and Australia's national teaching awards have seen the recognition of hundreds of teachers, teams, programmes and administrators (http://www.olt.gov.au/awards). Universities have established schemes to acknowledge university teachers who show excellence, commitment, and strong impact on their students. For the most part, these award schemes operate through peer and student nomination processes. The teaching portfolio and a teaching philosophy are key elements of the evidence base that must be tendered for recognition as excellent teachers. This highlights the growing concern for creating a more scholarly approach to educational practice.

Implications for new academics

The first few years of teaching can be quite complex, potentially including large classes, multi-campuses, different class groups, different content areas, and the need to design curricula from scratch. It is probable that your teaching will not marry closely with your research interests. Despite this diverse portfolio, you will be expected to demonstrate competence in your teaching while also building your capabilities in research.

For many new academics, uncertainty as to what matters poses considerable risk. In their efforts to be very good teachers they may tip the balance too heavily towards the goal of being a perfect teacher. This can compromise their efforts to also build a good foundational track record in research. Growing from novice to experienced teacher takes time and perseverance. While new teachers might feel that they lack the credibility of more experienced colleagues, what they do offer is a close connection with students, and often, a willingness to take the time to engage and learn. However, this will only take a new teacher so far. The development of professional knowledge and expertise is fundamental to long-term effectiveness as a university teacher. If your university offers a programme to guide you towards good teaching, make this a priority in your development schedule. It will save many years of trial and error that could be detrimental to your long-term career prospects. Most universities now require evidence of competent teaching before academics can progress towards tenure track. The acquisition of a professional knowledge base, and insight into pedagogy, are important steps in becoming a fully fledged, bona fide academic.

From this broad overview it can be seen that there are many different pressure points and initiatives being taken to cultivate higher education environments where learning is both valued and effective. As a new academic, you will need to build a clear understanding of what is valued in your university and the key strategies that have been established around learning and teaching. Your university will have some clear messages about the initiatives it has identified as critical priorities. You will be expected to reflect those policies and principles in your own professional practice. Take the time to understand this broader institutional context as it will help you identify your key performance foci and incremental development goals.

This section on teaching and learning offers a practical guide on how to operate as an effective, confident and creative educator. In the next chapter you will be offered an overview of some of the core theoretical principles and knowledge areas that are now internationally recognized as critical foundational principles for excellent teaching. While this broad snapshot will merely offer a scaffold for your consideration, it will help you to determine which areas are best pursued in your development strategy. The design of a curriculum is then explored in Chapter 8. Following that, Chapter 9 will offer tips as to how you might manage the administrative and educational requirements of your teaching in a sustainable manner. Chapter 9 also takes a closer look at typical challenges that new academics might face in their teaching. Chapter 10 then explores our current understanding of learning and teaching scholarship and research so that you can develop a well researched and knowledgeable professional framework.

After reading this section, then, you should feel a little more comfortable in navigating the learning and teaching landscape. To some extent, this will partly derive from your greater confidence in using some of the language that is associated with higher education learning and teaching. It can be a strange new world in the first few years of working in a university. Hopefully, this section will ensure that you feel much more confident about embarking on your new career as a university teacher.

7 Key principles for achieving quality learning

In the last 40 years we have gained more understanding about university students: how they best learn, and the techniques and principles that provide the most effective support and guidance. This chapter will first explore the characteristics of quality teaching, followed by a review of some of the key concepts and principles that are now being promoted as desirable practices. By the time you have finished this chapter you should have a clear understanding of strategies that enhance the students' experience, and the key foundational processes that need to be considered.

Defining quality teaching

How do you know you are a good teacher? Most of us hope we are, but it can be hard to judge our impact on students. Fortunately, there has been considerable research as to the teaching qualities that make a difference to students and their level of learning engagement (Blaxter et al., 1998; Light, 2004; Yorke and Longden, 2004; Kuh, 2008; Ruohoniemi and Lindblom-Ylänne, 2009; Denson et al., 2010; Devlin and Samarawickrema, 2010; Ning and Downing, 2011). Although these debates are still continuing, there are some core practices that have been identified. To be a quality teacher:

- Ensure you have a comprehensive knowledge of the subject area.
- Link your field of knowledge to the students' own context, personal lives, values, and experiences.
- Ensure your course has a reasonable workload so that students can engage with their learning.
- Design classes that offer a range of experiences and learning challenges.
- Ensure your classes are well planned and organized.
- Provide students with clear goals and direction as to what they will be learning.
- Provide clear guidance on academic expectations and standards.
- Build opportunities for students to interact, engage with their learning, and each other.
- Offer clear structure, explanations and guidance to your students so that they can build their own conceptual understanding.

- Encourage students to question, seek clarification, and explore their understanding in a safe and supportive environment.
- Regard errors and misunderstandings as an excellent opportunity to learn and grow.
- Ensure assessments are appropriate, challenging, and engaging.
- Provide opportunities for students to receive formative feedback so that they can learn and improve their understanding.
- Integrate feedback that is constructive, informative, and timely.
- Empathize with student needs, and offer some flexibility in addressing their issues.
- Be available (to a degree) outside class time.
- Share your enthusiasm and passion when teaching.
- Seek feedback on your teaching effectiveness.
- Learn your students' names (where possible).

These characteristics reflect a serious focus on thinking about the students and their educational needs. Quality teaching largely relates to building a constructive learning context, ensuring your courses are well designed, meaningful and effectively managed, and engaging with your students as their teacher. To accomplish this, it is useful to think a little more about the theoretical underpinnings that guide educational practice.

The student experience

At the heart of higher education is a concern for providing the right setting for students to succeed. **Learner-centred teaching** emphasizes that students must take responsibility for their own learning (Weimer, 2002), encouraging us to think about the role teachers and learners play in the educational process. As educators, we need to understand what students bring to their learning experience and how we might best encourage them to take responsibility for their own development. The focus in your teaching, using this philosophy, is to recognize that the teacher's role is to provide the right conditions for learning, facilitating the student's engagement with developing skills, understanding, and a deeper knowledge of themselves. In this framing, students attend class because they regard the learning context as an important contribution towards their learning.

This shift in focus away from didactic, teacher-centred approaches promotes a stronger consideration of the partnership between teacher and learner, and more consideration of the particular student needs. Effective learning experiences are likely to include many different learning activities that encourage student engagement and challenge them. Active learning of this nature can be confronting for new teachers, who may feel more comfortable and secure if they have a scripted approach to follow. However, tightly structured teaching will not engage students effectively, and may result in high absenteeism as they experience little 'added value' from being physically present.

Considerable focus has been placed on the undergraduate experience and the conditions under which students flourish. Some groups stand out as having more complex needs: first generation, first year, and international students all experience particular challenges in settling into university life and meeting academic expectations.

It is important that students encounter quality teaching throughout their studies, but particularly in their first year as they build their first impressions of the subject field, university learning, and their perceived fit with higher education. The **first year experience** is a particularly critical point for undergraduates (Yorke and Longden, 2004; Johnston, 2010; Willcoxson, 2010). While most would agree that new students need close support and strong associations with their teachers, the first year is a time when many will, in all probability, experience extremely large classes, anonymity, and potentially, inexperienced tutors. This places a student at considerable risk. The transition from high school to university can be quite a shock, particularly through moving from a structured school setting to a freer, more self-determining structure (Morosanu et al., 2010). Those who are coming from low socio-economic contexts can experience particular challenges in the transition to higher education (Crozier and Reay, 2011), as they may also be the first family member to attend university. Many first year students also find they have selected the wrong course of study (Yorke and Longden, 2004), and may be feeling demotivated and anxious.

Despite the large sizes of many first year classes, teaching should offer dynamic opportunities to learn, engage, and acquire the necessary skills that will help students survive in a university setting. A high impact practice for first year students is to integrate small group experiences so they can build some of the necessary skills and engage with fellow students and teachers (Kuh, 2008). Other strategies include creating opportunities for collaborative learning, critical enquiry, regular writing, and engagement with your research (Kuh, 2008). Integrating collaborative learning opportunities to work with other students on assignments and projects also helps. These might include team-based assessments, joint assignments, research, or in-class exercises. Students also enjoy pursuing and exploring issues, applying their experience, using new technologies, and engaging with challenging questions (Kuh, 2008).

Inclusivity also supports a quality learning experience (Tennant et al., 2009: 85). When designing your programme of teaching, including assessments, it is critical to think about student diversity. Your learners will come from different nations and cultures. Some will be learning in a second language, and many will have personal, social, emotional or learning challenges that can complicate their learning experience. Others may feel disconnected, finding it hard to build friendships at university. Some students will be undertaking paid work to fund their study, thereby straddling two opposing worlds. Your students will also bring a range of experiences and background knowledge to your programme, and will have different learning styles.

As the teacher, you will play a key role in building a respectful and inclusive setting where diversity is valued and built into the learning setting (Tennant et al., 2009; Biggs and Tang, 2011; Dunne, 2011; Sanderson, 2011). A goal of effective learning is to build a global learning context for students – where they locate their learning in an internationalized context. Useful strategies include participating in small groups and participative exchanges, including large-class interactions and dialogues, rather than merely observing (Tennant et al., 2009: 91). As an effective teacher this requires a careful consideration of the ways in which your interactions and student participation are orchestrated. Simple ways of internationalizing the learning context include promoting international students as 'assets' from which much can be learned (Ryan, 2011), drawing in the student's own personal experiences, integrating examples from different countries, building an international perspective around your theory base, and opening opportunities for students to undertake assessments that allow them to relate the exercise to their own personal context. These may appear simple practices, but they reflect respect for the diversity of backgrounds students bring to their learning (Biggs and Tang, 2011). Recognizing the rich possibilities stemming from a transcultural learning setting can open very different realizations for all members of your learning community (Johnson and Kumar, 2010; Ryan 2011). The involvement of students as co-creators of the curriculum offers another way to ensure learning is inclusive (Bovill et al., 2011). A range of learning approaches will assist all students, as they will be offered different perspectives to look at the same problem, gaining richer insights as a consequence.

Language can be a challenging area for both international students and their teachers. While students are required to demonstrate their basic capabilities before entering university, the capacity to speak and write for an academic context can be particularly complex (Benzie, 2010), and can marginalize students from their peers and the learning experience. The more opportunities you offer to encourage student participation and practising of their language skills, the better. Ensure too, that students do not huddle in their own cultural group. Establishing learning groups that encourage students to work within diverse, transcultural communities is all part of the rich tapestry of our global existence.

Although these principles have been highlighted as particularly benefiting students at risk, they equally apply to all students.

Clarifying the reason for teaching

Why do we teach? What do we hope to achieve through our engagement with students?

Consider the following question: *What are the outcomes that you hope your students will gain from their educational experience?* Your response helps clarify your beliefs as to the overall role that teaching plays in the student's university experience. As university educators, we are the main vehicles that ensure the university's goals relating to student outcomes are achieved. And yet, many of us find it hard to explain what we are seeking to accomplish through our interaction with students. If we believe that the purpose is merely to get students through their degree, or deliver content, then we are less likely to focus on designing and delivering authentic and meaningful learning experiences.

Barnett and Coate (2005: 59) suggest our role should emphasize educating well rounded students who:

- are critical and articulate knowledge consumers and creators (*knowing*)
- engage in both the practice of learning, and the application of that learning to their broader world (*acting*)
- develop self-realization, positive self-efficacy, and strong identities that draw on robust values and beliefs (*being*).

This reconceptualization of curriculum highlights the significant role that teachers can play in the development of the student – as academic, citizen and engaged individual. As teachers, we have the potential to design learning that offers rich layers of experience and engagement for our students. Being clear about our reason for teaching, and the general and specific outcomes that we aim to stimulate, provides a stronger foundation for thinking about curriculum design. While the general outcomes may operate similarly across all of your teaching roles, the specific emphases you seek to support may differ markedly, depending on the student cohort and its context. A first year group, for example, has vastly different learning needs to a final year group.

Encouraging effective student learning

Marton and Säljö (1976) identified two modes of learning that are encouraged through different forms of educational practice: **deep** and **surface learning**. Surface learning occurs when students focus on information that can be efficiently memorized and reproduced. This form of learning is primarily employed when teachers require students to demonstrate the acquisition of facts and information. Deep learning, on the other hand, encourages students to build a comprehensive understanding of how the concepts fit together and the connectivity of ideas and concepts. It promotes learning as a means of understanding, and encourages students to see things in a more integrated way. The long-term goal of deep learning is to construct a more informed view of the world and how it relates.

The way we teach has a big influence on the learning approach students adopt. They resort to surface learning when they are overwhelmed with the amount of content that has to be acquired or navigated, where limited feedback on their progress is offered, if they feel ill-prepared for the course of study or, if this is the mode of learning they have commonly been exposed to in their past educational experiences (Martin, 1999). Courses that are heavy on content, loaded with superficial exercises, or offer little opportunity to build more intensive understanding of concepts, are most likely to encourage surface learning. This is a major challenge for many academics, as they may see transmission of content as the most critical function of their teaching. Deep learning opportunities require time for students to reflect, engage, and take ownership of their learning: the teacher's role becomes more closely allied to mentor, guide and catalyst, than conductor. This concept also reflects the recognition that students need to take responsibility for their own learning (Hattie, 2008).

Deep learning strategies also encourage the development of **critical thinking** (Golding, 2011; Hammer and Green, 2011; Moore, 2011). Evidence of critical thinking can be found in the ability to construct an argument, sieve fact from opinion, judge the worth of an argument, and develop a logical and persuasive argument (Stassen et al., 2011). Davies (2011) notes that critical thinking is a hard concept for university students. Their learning experiences play a major part in building these competencies. If students are only exposed to learning and assessment activities that are facile and shallow, they will have few opportunities to build these capabilities. Given the increasing emphasis on preparing students to operate in a complex knowledge society (Debowski, 2006), we need to provide many chances for students to acquire these skills.

A particular application of critical thinking is **problem-based learning** (Pepper, 2010; Ruiz-Gallardo et al., 2011). Designed to contextualize learning, it has been employed extensively in medical programmes, with the goal of encouraging students to see the complexities and challenges associated with working in real situations. To determine an optimal outcome, students must draw on many sources of information, wide-ranging knowledge and, to some extent, their intuition. The process is made more powerful when students work collaboratively in learning communities on the problems (Kuh, 2008). Problem-based learning has assisted new generations of medical practitioners to be more creative in their analysis of complex issues. This process is also extensively employed in business courses and other professional programmes. It is an engaging way to help students integrate their learning into their conceptual schema. Activities of this sort also encourage those broader outcomes associated with curricula that emphasize knowing, acting and being (Barnett and Coates, 2005).

In our role we need to identify **threshold concepts:** the learning that students find challenging (Kiley and Wisker, 2009; Land, 2011). In some cases, they will clash with existing beliefs or well established concepts. Or there may be a large gap between what is known and what now needs to be understood. Watch for instances where students stall and find new concepts hard to integrate or apply. Allow time for them to work through the mental barricades, offer additional ideas or explanations, and possibly consider other ways to consolidate their learning. Focusing an assessment item on the concept can offer opportunities to build deeper understanding. Most of us encounter these roadblocks in our teaching. The key issue is recognizing that these are critical learning opportunities that need to be supported.

As university teachers, we are expected to integrate a **research focus** in our teaching. There are different ways we can achieve this (Healey and Jenkins, 2009; Schapper and Mayson, 2010). Firstly, we reflect a scholarly approach to our teaching, providing students with an insight into research and the different views that are held around the subject. Secondly, we may encourage students to develop effective research skills and capabilities through assignments, activities and other forms of engagement with research practice. Thirdly, we may engage students in research and enquiry through project work or other forms of investigative processes.

Contextualized learning

There has been a growth in real-world learning experiences – especially for undergraduate students. Two key approaches have been work-integrated learning (WIL) and service learning (France, 2004; VanWynsberghe and Andruske, 2007; Cipolle, 2010; Harris et al., 2010).

Work-integrated learning has been around for many years, particularly for professional disciplines (e.g. Litchfield et al., 2010). Designed to provide students with exposure to real-world settings, these processes bridge the divide between theoretical learning and real contexts of working with people, on authentic tasks, and in complex social settings. The increasing engagement of universities with their communities has opened up a desire to encourage work-ready students. Students may undertake an internship, complete a research project, or fulfil a practicum experience linked to their major field of study. In each case, the goal is to create an effective interface between university learning and the real setting of work (Jackson, 2010). If you are involved in WIL, you will find that these activities require considerable preparation (Freudenberg et al., 2010). You will need to think through all of the likely contingencies and work with the hosting workplaces to ensure both host and student experience a rich and rewarding interaction. In some cases, you may need to put considerable effort into preparing the students for their placement and the role they must play in the real world. You may also be required to visit each workplace and assess the student's performance.

Service learning operates similarly, but with the intention of providing the student with an opportunity to offer service back to the community (e.g. France, 2004; VanWynsberghe and Andruske, 2007; Cipolle, 2010; Harris et al., 2010). Universities that encourage this form of engagement often see the growth of individuals as global citizens to be a critical learning outcome. The students will normally apply their university knowledge in the community, and later reflect and review their experience to make sense of the new learning (Kuh, 2008). Aim to integrate that learning into class discussions, reflective exercises, and other subsequent activities.

Capstone projects are another variation – providing students with the opportunity to engage deeply with their entire educational process towards the end of their degrees. By completing in-depth projects, exhibitions or papers, students are offered the opportunity to demonstrate the skills they have acquired (Kuh, 2008). If your students have this opportunity, consider how you can create linkages between your teaching and that culminating experience.

These forms of interaction between student and community offer great richness and personal benefit to all concerned. As their teacher, there is rich potential to integrate these experiences back into the curriculum. Classroom discussions can consolidate the students' growth and encourage rich sharing with their peers.

The learning platform

e-learning is now viewed as part of the essential fabric of university teaching (Crisp, 2009; Ellis et al., 2009; Tennant et al., 2009; Boettcher and Conrad, 2010; Gikandi et al., 2011). Most universities host a learning management system (LMS) and require their teachers to mount critical information for each of their courses online. Unfortunately, many offerings are static and poorly designed, offering very little interactivity or engagement with the student. Many lectures that are placed on the web are uninspiring and poor indications of the type of learning students are exposed to. The challenge then, is how to use the available technology in a constructive and creative manner. Fortunately there has been much research and experimentation to better understand effective online learning (Yorke and Longden, 2004; Willcoxson, 2010).

Online learning platforms offer immediate support to each student at point of need. This means that the student has control as to when they access this support, and the degree to which they will engage with the experiences that have been integrated. Student learning can be considerably enhanced through ready access to self-guided reflections, testing of conceptual knowledge, increased interaction with peers, identification and sharing of insights with fellow students and the teacher, and opportunities to review and deepen cognitive understanding of the core content. The development of effective online learning requires time and careful planning to ensure students are offered sufficient guidance on the learning they need to explore. Effective online learning is well structured, links effectively to the student's knowledge and prior understanding, and ties closely to the course of study and the required learning outcomes (Ellis et al., 2009). Assessment practices have also been greatly enhanced by the use of e-learning, offering students capacity to undertake self-quizzes, engage in discussion groups, and test their learning through a range of interactive strategies (Crisp, 2009; Gikandi et al., 2011).

The multifaceted role of the teacher in an e-learning environment comprises developer, moderator, feedback provider, problem solver, and catalyst for student engagement. While some interactions between teacher and students might be formal and strongly structured, there will be many opportunities for students to interact with each other without the intervention of the teacher. However, an online community with an absentee teacher will lead to very limited engagement from the students. If you are using online strategies, respond rapidly to student problems, encourage active participation in group discussions, and focus student discussions to keep them engaged. The design of the website, and the degree to which you have built high levels of support, also play a role in increasing student engagement. However, it needs to be recognized that students do have limited discretionary time. Where students are asked to expend inordinate amounts of time online, they will start to look carefully at whether the investment is worth the expenditure of time and energy.

Clearly, your investment in building an effective e-learning platform can offer major benefits to your students, particularly if they find it difficult or impossible to attend your teaching sessions. Developing online learning strategies will require significant dedication in order to produce quality learning resources and experiences. Beware though: it is very easy to be hijacked by the lure of creating glitzy presentations and online features. Ensure any activities you spend time developing are clearly aligned to your ultimate learning outcomes and reflect your understanding of the student learning needs. The investment in developing a quality online presence needs to be justified in terms of student impact. If you are teaching a diverse, translocated group, where language skills are a problem, or students have difficulty in coming to class because of work and personal commitments, the building of effective learning resources and support online will be a very critical part of the support that you offer. If your class is a small one, and students attend each week, you may be better advised to put your time into interacting with them more intensively. The choices we make as teachers in terms of where to put our effort must constantly be based on our best judgement as to how the student will benefit the most.

Many teachers will employ a dual approach of offering a face-to-face instructional programme and online support. Called **blended learning**, this educational practice provides the student with additional assistance so that they can work asynchronously at point of need while still gaining direct access to their teacher (Garrison and Vaughan, 2008; George-Walker and Keeffe, 2010). The relative mix of online and face-to-face support varies greatly, depending on the subject, students, and teacher. Successful blended learning requires careful consideration of the learning outcomes and how they can best be achieved. The reasons for each learning element, and the integrative process that has been designed, will need to be clearly conveyed to your students so that they understand the criticality of engaging with the provided resources/activities or learner groups. With the advent of mobile technologies (such as iPads, phones, and other devices), the accessibility of online interactivity has greatly escalated. These innovations are creating some exciting possibilities. Be careful though, that you don't become seduced by the technology! Every learning activity should have a purpose and complement the other experiences you offer.

This short overview explored some of the key principles that have been developed around learning and teaching. It highlighted the need for us to be considered and informed about why we teach. While we have some clear understanding on how to design and create meaningful learning experiences for students, there are also many challenges in achieving this in the limited time available. In some instances universities are seeing online instruction as the answer. However, as can be seen from this overview, the connection between student and teacher lies at the heart of an engaging and productive learning experience. Whether online or face to face, the design of an engaging learning experience must be the critical focus of effective teaching.

8 Applying the principles in practice

The translation of learning principles into practice can be quite complex, depending on the particular teaching environment in which you are operating. This chapter explores the design of an engaging, good quality, and educationally sound teaching programme.

Creating an effective learning design

Consistency underpins good learning design (Toohey, 1999): strong **alignment** between learning goals, desired learning outcomes, the teaching strategies, and the assessment processes to be employed ensures students have clear signposts as to the important learning goals they should emphasize (Biggs, 2012). Constructive alignment ensures that the students receive a clear and consistent message about what will be covered, the teaching strategies that will be employed, and the required assessment and outcomes to be evaluated. Most critically, this process ensures that any assessment activities are clearly and logically linked to all other design elements. Students quickly assess course expectations to determine the level of effort they will need to expend. The learning design strongly predicts the level of student engagement.

Figure 8.1 illustrates the key conceptual stages that contribute to a well planned learning experience. Each will be explored in turn.

Who are my students?

An understanding of your students and their likely needs will greatly assist in designing a suitable course of study. There are many questions you might ask: What have they studied previously? What is their likely graduate destination? Do they require particular outcomes to prepare them for their future careers? Will they need to learn particular methods and techniques? How diverse are they in background and knowledge? How motivated will they be? Is there any common background that can be assumed? Are there potential threshold concepts that they may find challenging? Will they be experienced in working in groups? Are there fundamental academic practices that I will need to encourage?

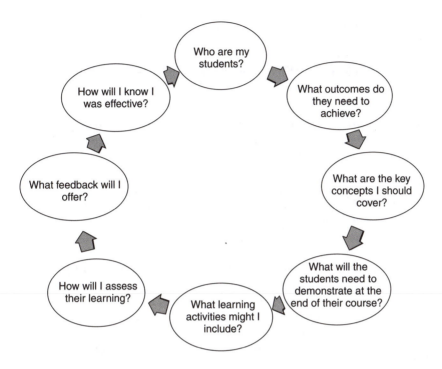

Figure 8.1 Designing effective learning

These are but some of the questions you might ask before you start to plan your programme. Students may find it helpful to have these considerations outlined in your unit information, particularly if you are assuming they bring background knowledge with them.

What outcomes do they need to achieve?

The next step in the process is to consider the outcomes you hope your students will demonstrate. Learning outcomes describe the ultimate end point of the course of study that you will guide every student towards. These are important signals to the student as to the learning goals they should target.

There are many outcomes you might regard as priorities in your teaching, including: acquiring knowledge, memorizing or retaining information, applying skills and understanding, building critical thinking skills, or developing as an individual learner. These are, of course, not mutually exclusive, but you may need to be somewhat selective, depending on your particular disciplinary context. If your primary function is to prepare work-ready students you will need to think about authentic learning that facilitates their entry into the complex world of work. If, on the other hand, your programme seeks to develop critical learners who demonstrate research skills and a greater sense of understanding around particular disciplinary contexts, you might design a programme of a very different nature. Multiple goals and outcomes can be supported through your educational strategy.

Sources of guidance that might assist you in thinking about learning outcomes include:

- *Graduate attributes that your university has identified as being critical outcomes for its students.* Many of these are very similar across most universities (Barrie, 2007). For example, they commonly reflect a focus on three key areas: effective citizenship, generic skills, and professional/job-related capabilities.
- *Professional standards and requirements of your discipline if you are in a field that is accredited by an external body.* These standards and guidelines can be quite prescriptive in some fields and should be well understood before you start developing your plan.
- *Information on prior learning students will have completed.* For example, if you are teaching a higher level course you will not wish to repeat the same material that was covered in earlier units. Instead, you might scaffold from the previous learning to encourage students to engage more deeply and critically with the earlier materials and concepts.
- *Expectations of the course as a preparatory programme for future courses.* You may be obligated to provide guidance to students on particular skills and understandings that will prepare them for their next courses of study, or perhaps a capstone project at the end of their study.

There are many other sources that you might access. These include conferring with industry experts or colleagues and benchmarking against similar courses in other universities. In addition, think carefully about where your field of knowledge is heading. An educator's responsibility includes anticipating the emergent trends and preparing students for an evolving world. Lecturing from textbooks can limit the opportunity that students have to think much more carefully about the future directions and how they might contribute to that evolution.

From this brief overview it can be seen that it is very important to investigate the context in which the teaching is located. We don't teach in isolation. For the most part, we are contributing to a meshed learning environment that enables students to develop a body of knowledge, the capacity to be critical thinkers, and to become effective contributors to the larger socio-cultural setting in which they live. You have an obligation to think deeply about your educational contribution and how you will add value through your engagement with students.

What are the key concepts I should cover?

With a strong understanding of the key outcomes you wish to encourage, you can then think about the critical concepts that students will need to explore and apply. A useful technique to employ at this stage is **concept mapping**. This is a simple graphic technique that maps key concepts or principles to be emphasized through the course. It helps to identify a structured hierarchy of ideas and to consider how much time each may require for students to cross the threshold. In some disciplines, a curriculum matrix may be collectively developed with other colleagues, limiting duplication and ensuring that there is good complementarity between year levels.

What will the students need to demonstrate at the end of their course?

Instructional objectives describe the particular skills and capabilities that you expect students to demonstrate by the time they have completed their course. Toohey (1999: 149–151) offers a very helpful overview of the evolving understanding of instructional objectives. She suggests that they fulfil three key functions: providing guidance on what needs to be learned and assessed; clarifying for students the purpose of the course and the outcomes they will need to demonstrate; and offering a framework for negotiation of student-orientated assessment that can meet the designated learning outcomes. She argues that effective instructional objectives need to be small in number, meaningful, contextualized, clear about the standards of performance to be achieved, and capable of accommodating the different levels of achievement that students will demonstrate. The construction of your instructional objectives will guide your design programme.

What learning activities might I include?

Once you have a clear sense of the learning outcomes and instructional objectives, you will then need to consider how you deploy your limited teaching time.

The mark of a good teacher is to provide varied, engaging, highly relevant learning experiences that support the development of the necessary competencies students should acquire through their university education. Your choice of learning experiences will partly depend on the students and their particular learning context. For example, if you are teaching first year students you will need to be conscious of their need to acquire rudimentary academic and professional skills, such as critical thinking, presentation skills, research skills, an understanding of academic integrity, group learning, and perhaps some specialist competencies. Some structured developmental learning, with students completing a small piece of work and receiving feedback on their efforts prior to submitting their formal assessment, can be a powerful way of encouraging this complex skill acquisition. Senior students will engage in more complex activities that require them to integrate their prior learning with their new knowledge and expertise. The use of problem-based learning encourages this deep integration and synthesis.

In designing your programme you might choose a number of different approaches. The traditional approach comprises a series of lectures, tutorials, seminars and/or laboratories. In this mode you will have strong control over the learning stage and content to be covered in each session. An alternative is to apply a problem- or project-based strategy, with students gradually building the skills to complete a complex piece of work in a carefully structured and supportive environment. You may find that there are different approaches that are commonly used within your discipline. Psychology, for example, has long-established traditions of introducing students to experimental settings. At a more practical level, consider how large your group is likely to be. One thousand students requires different approaches to 30. Will some students be studying remotely, or are they all likely to be attending face-to-face classes? These considerations will also guide your instructional design decisions.

To encourage deep learning (Biggs, 2012) you will need to allow time for the students to explore new concepts and consider how they relate to their broader understanding. Some of these concepts will be fundamental threshold concepts that require considerable focus throughout the curriculum. These issues all need to be thought through to ensure you have allowed sufficient time to build understanding and then consolidate those insights.

No matter what design you choose, students will need time to explore their learning as they progress from first acquaintance to deeper understanding. They may travel through several stages.

1   *Familiarization:* They will need time to become acquainted with the new concepts. In some instances, this requires intensive time to ensure students have gained a full understanding. It may be necessary to offer concrete examples, build some linkage back to their own existing knowledge and understanding, and perhaps, explore the concepts using a range of different perspectives and technologies.
2   *Test and apply:* The opportunity to then test and apply this knowledge can help build deeper understanding. You will need to allow time for this in your programme. Assessments can greatly assist with this stage.
3   *Feedback and review:* Ensure students receive timely and informative feedback on their successful application.
4   *Integration:* Further opportunities for the student to reflect, practice, and then evaluate the success of their efforts will help to consolidate and integrate their learning.

This simple model of learning underpins many good learning designs.

Some common teaching traps

There are many traps for new teachers when designing a course – particularly if the previous steps have not been followed. Three common pitfalls are outlined below.

Pitfall 1: The 'kitchen sink' model

You do not need to include every conceivable concept that was ever linked to your subject area. This approach will strongly encourage surface learning, limit long-term benefit to the students, and generate high stress. Teaching that encourages deep learning will have a much stronger impact on the student. This style of educational process also recognizes that the learning concepts and broad foundational principles are much more important than particular elements of content that may change as new research and developments grow. Helping students think critically, analyse, and interrogate future knowledge will be a much stronger contribution to their learning than insisting that they develop a memorized suite of facts and information. Consider too, that students who have become engaged will more likely read more broadly – particularly if the assessments are well designed.

Pitfall 2: The fast-food menu

If you are drawing on a textbook to guide students in their reading and reflection, you have a ready source of material to explore and review. The danger here is that you may go into 'automatic' drive and simply adopt the textbook and its recommended approach without careful consideration of the match with your student needs and broader learning outcomes. It is particularly risky to simply adopt the author's presentations, multiple-choice questions and other activities without careful consideration as to whether they really support your learners. This is especially critical if you are teaching in a transcultural setting where students come from much more diverse backgrounds and experiences. Treat your textbook as a useful resource, but don't shortcut on carefully planning the learning experience.

Pitfall 3: The movie marathon

Some academics rely heavily on visiting speakers, arguing that they offer an insight into the real world that students need to understand. While an occasional visitor can be very helpful and educative, there is a real risk that students will simply experience a kaleidoscope of different people without any real framing or continuity of understanding. Students want more than this from their educational experience. If you do use visiting speakers, orientate them carefully so that they contribute a unique perspective that complements other elements of the course. Solely relying on visiting speakers to teach your course may greatly reduce the quality of the student learning experience as visitors will not have a full understanding of the curriculum or the students.

Improving student engagement

Three areas where careful planning and innovation can make a substantial impact on student engagement relate to your lecturing strategy, tutorial design, and effective use of group learning techniques. These are briefly overviewed, highlighting some of the pedagogical principles that can assist your interaction with students.

Is the lecture dead?

Lectures remain a common element of most undergraduate courses, although there is considerable debate concerning their effectiveness and function (Scevak, 2010; Cannon and Knapper, 2011). Think back to your own experience of lectures: what stood out? The occasional good one? For the most part, lectures are not the highlight of a student's encounter with higher education. Rather, they are regarded as a necessary evil that must be tolerated to pass a unit. This could be one of the reasons that students elect to absent themselves, relying instead on lecture downloads from their university websites. How then, can you create engaging lectures?

Traditional lectures function as a dissemination tool, with a captive audience listening passively to an expert source. For the most part, the goal is to provide students with guidance on what should be understood. Unfortunately, the lecture is quite inefficient if used as an information dissemination process. Students will drift after 20 minutes unless you are a particularly powerful raconteur. Think carefully then about the purposes you hope to accomplish with this precious time.

One of the major weaknesses of lectures is that many teachers try to cover far too much – even if that content is already provided through other sources, such as textbooks. This pushes them to talk intensively at students for the allotted time. Think carefully about your concept map: what were the key ideas that you needed to explore through your teaching? Keep this in mind as you plan your presentations. Cannon and Knapper (2011) offer an invaluable guide as to how you might optimize your lecturing impact. They note the importance of carefully structuring your lecture to guide students as to the important points – interspersing other media to explore concepts, limiting the amount of information presented on PowerPoint slides, and integrating opportunities for students to explore their understanding. Various active learning strategies can be used to encourage students to consider their interpretation of the ideas. For example, they might be asked to write down a question that they are still unsure of, or something they have learned. This might be shared with their neighbour. The use of peer discussion, sharing of ideas, and testing of concepts works effectively in any size classroom if the activities are carefully thought through and students know they may be asked to share their ideas.

Resuscitating the tutorial

Similarly, the potential value of tutorials is vastly underestimated. Lublin and Sutherland (2009) offer an invaluable guide to maximize the potential of tutorials. They note the criticality of building an effective relationship with your students and ensuring all members have opportunities to fully participate. It is particularly important to encourage students to take ownership of their own learning (Parkes and Muldoon, 2010). The tutor initially acts as both guide and coach, scaffolding and structuring learning in the early part of the relationship, but with the goal of moving towards stronger student ownership of the learning process as they gain confidence. In some instances, students may require strong 'encouragement' to participate (Souza et al., 2010).

Tutorial activities should align with, complement, and support the broader course goals (Cantwell et al., 2010; Parkes and Muldoon, 2010). The tutorial programme provides the ideal platform to sculpt different activities that encourage students to challenge, test and apply their understanding. Student commitment will be greatly enhanced if you clearly establish your expectations as to their preparation and weekly contributions at each tutorial. If your students are required to present their research to their peers, it is helpful to guide them on (and assess) effective presentation techniques. Remember that learning outcomes are not merely content driven, but should also support the student's broader development in communication, intellectual and social capabilities.

Group work

Group work is a very important strategy to increase student engagement and learning. Students benefit through interacting with diverse individuals, negotiating outcomes, communicating, listening, and working collaboratively. Group work can be extremely frustrating to students – particularly if they are allocated to a group that they perceive as dissonant or ill-suited to their own personal values and ambitions. On the other hand, learning to work with diverse individuals is a necessary skill in our knowledge economy.

You can employ group work in different ways, ranging from informal, opportunistic learning points where students work informally in classes to apply or test a concept, to more structured, long-term associations that encourage group identity, focused purpose and deep learning (such as a tutorial or project group). Tennant et al. (2009) offer a useful overview of the principles and development of group strategies. They highlight the criticality of supporting the group's formation and growth of identity. It is particularly important to recognize that student groups do need structure and established parameters to ensure all understand the requirements and their responsibilities.

How will I assess their learning?

Assessment has received considerable attention in the last decade (Toohey, 1999; James et al., 2002; Adler-Kassner and O'Neill, 2010; Brown, 2010; Buller, 2010; Biggs and Tang, 2011). It has been recognized that many of the assessment activities students are given fail to test the appropriate learning, and, in fact, send strong cues that the material that was being covered in class really didn't matter in the first place. Teachers who wish to encourage a deep approach to learning take considerable time to craft their assessment requirements. They aim to promote an experience that encourages meaningful engagement with the content and its deeper concepts. Some of the principles that can contribute to effective assessment processes include:

- Aim for a variety of assessment practices that will test for different forms of knowledge and understanding.

- Ensure that anything you assess has high validity – that is, it is measuring something that is important.
- Provide students with the assessment information at the start of your programme: this will help them see the relevance of the material that they're covering and will encourage them to think more deeply about how those activities will relate to the final assessments.
- Include assessments that encourage writing (Light, 2004: 54).
- Provide clear criteria in advance to guide the students in their preparation of the assessment piece (Tennant et al., 2009: 25).
- Consider using formative assessment: providing feedback on small developmental tasks to check for early understanding. This is particularly helpful for first year students.
- If you include group work, assess the effectiveness of the group dynamic and interactions, as well as the product the group has produced (Light, 2004: 53). Consider providing time in class for students to meet and work on their activity. Many find it hard to manage out-of-class meetings.
- If you are teaching a programme where you can access publisher-provided cases and multiple choice questions, think very carefully before employing them. While they are convenient and little trouble to use, they will be far less influential than an exercise that you have constructed with your understanding of the students in mind.
- Don't be afraid to allow students to negotiate or deconstruct the assessment items. While you may spend considerable time designing assessments, they don't always come together. The opportunity for students to renegotiate criteria, suggest alternative framings, ask for a different time frame, or seek alternative assessments that they can match to their personal context, all signal that they are taking the assessment seriously and wish to use it to maximum effect. The key principle in this negotiation is to recognize that the assessment task is designed to demonstrate certain learning outcomes. As long as these expectations are clear and readily interpreted by all concerned, flexibility in redesigning the assessment is quite feasible.
- Ensure student assessments are marked insightfully and offer appropriate feedback to clarify things that are not sufficiently understood (Tennant et al., 2009: 25).

When designing your programme, it is critical to think about assessment and its relationship to your broader instructional objectives and learning outcomes. Students need to be clear about what is expected of them. The first thing they will look at when they are handed a new syllabus is the assessment section. They understand that this will determine the areas they need to emphasize through the course of study and the degree of effort they will need to apply. When you are writing assessment instructions it is very important to be absolutely clear about what is required and how the assessment will be evaluated. Develop your assessment checklist at the same time – it helps to check that the activity is feasible and suited to the overall course requirements. Students benefit from knowing the evaluation criteria at the start of the course, as they can then focus on the key learning you are seeking. Be aware though, that the assessment path you set will be the one they explore in their learning.

Think about what each assessment will add to the overall learning of the student. Ideally, each assessment will offer a different learning experience and consolidate the core concepts that underpin your course of study. Explaining to students how these all link together illustrates the relevance and interrelationships and will greatly increase their motivation. The potential use of e-assessments has grown exponentially as student access and technological capability have improved. Crisp (2009) offers a valuable overview of how you might integrate various assessment strategies using technology.

You may find that some assessments fall at a bad time for many of the students. For example, there are particular weeks in a semester where students may have three or four assessment items due. It is important to be flexible and open to renegotiation as to due dates.

Setting group assessments has become a popular assessment method (Willis and Millis, 2004). To maximize their impact, think about the goals of the assessment and how you will measure those intentions. A useful strategy is encouraging peer evaluations as both formative and summative processes to increase the cohesion of the group and its focus on the required outcomes (Williams et al., 2004).

A particular challenge for academics nowadays is to identify plagiarism or cheating. Academic integrity is a confusing concept for many students – particularly those who have just come from high school where group work and collaboration are strongly encouraged, or from a different university system overseas (DiPietro, 2010; Bista, 2011). It can take some time for students to understand how to reference effectively, work in groups without integrating each other's materials in their assignments, and acknowledge authorship. Despite careful exploration in classes, you will encounter plagiarism and cheating. Most times you will find that there is good guidance from your university as to what should then be done. You can help avoid this problem by carefully designing assessment tasks that reduce the possibility of copying earlier assignments.

What feedback will I offer?

Feedback is one of the strongest predictors of student learning (Hattie, 2008). We often forget that it closes the loop and offers the only individual support to the learner that they will receive. It needs to be targeted, informative and helpful in guiding the student's learning. And yet, it also needs to be managed sustainably to ensure you cope and can keep the feedback flowing back to your students.

The provision of feedback can take many forms and will depend to a large extent on the type of assignment that you have set students. It will also depend on the learning priorities that are being emphasized. For example, students submitting an essay could be provided feedback on their research skills, coherence, conceptual understanding, critical thinking, ability to write an argument, or any number of other outcomes. If you were to assess all of these areas, each assignment would be covered in red ink. This can be very demoralizing to the student and could take you an extremely long time to complete. Think carefully then about the learning you wish to prioritize, and share this with the students before they start the assignment. This enables them to focus on the learning outcomes that you have identified as critical to this particular course of study. Of course, you might decide that all of those areas were critical. If that is the case, students need to know about this before they commence the assessment. Consider offering formative feedback before their work is being appraised for marking purposes. Models, examples of good work, and encouragement to seek formative feedback from their peers can also assist in building their evaluative skills.

Students appreciate explanatory and diagnostic feedback when they are being assessed. If you are asking them to complete an assessment item they have a right to expect useful feedback that will further guide their learning. Debriefing students on the overall performance for a key assessment piece can be a helpful way of clarifying what is expected of them, while also increasing accountability for the overall assessment design.

Marking is not an exact science. It can generate many opportunities to be biased towards certain students. A clear delineation of the criteria and explanation of levels of achievement will greatly encourage equity and fairness. The development of a rubric (Lublin and Sutherland, 2009) can be a useful method to map the student's performance against established criteria, while also ensuring equity and transparency. The rubric offers additional benefits in providing more detailed explanations to students and decreasing the time required to mark each assessment. It is a critical tool when multiple markers assess the same course.

How will I know I was effective?

Teaching is about continually testing and modifying practices to improve your educational practice and impact. Feedback offers you guidance on particular strategies and their effectiveness so that you can respond to these cues promptly. To review your teaching effectiveness, you require evidence to show that you have had an impact on student learning and their engagement. This requires a systematic approach to seeking feedback from various sources.

Your own reflection and measures of improvement are one source of guidance. When assessing students, for example, it is important to consider how well the students demonstrated their learning in the assessment activities. This review of student outcomes closes the loop in the learning process and may require some remediation if the intended learning experience was unsuccessful.

Student feedback is a second source of guidance on your effectiveness. Your university is likely to have at least one and maybe more evaluation processes that you might access. Evaluations of teacher effectiveness will typically seek student feedback on the teacher's relationship with the students, specialist knowledge, whether the learning experiences were meaningful and engaging, and the effectiveness of assessment and feedback. Clearly, these are all very critical indicators that you will want to know about and keep monitoring. If you can access these services midway through a semester, students will value the opportunity to share their insights so that you can act on the feedback and identify potential issues. If you do not have access to a mid-semester option, you can create an opportunity to seek feedback from students by simply asking them to note what they have gained to date from the experience, and what they would suggest needs changing the next time the unit is conducted. This will simply take five to ten minutes at the end of the class, providing a rich array of qualitative information that can be considered and actioned. When students are asked for feedback, make sure you act on that information and respond in return about what you have gained from their advice. Failure to do this will increase their belief that this is not taken seriously by teachers (El Hassan, 2009).

Your reaction to adverse feedback can be influenced by many things, including your gender (Boye and Tapp, 2010). Reactions can vary widely, partly based on the degree of vulnerability you feel and the feedback emphasis. Those who have been unaware of particular challenges, may, for example, deflect responsibility for the problem to other sources, (the school, timetabling, the students. . .). Another response might be to question the validity of the instrument or the capacity of students to give authentic and informed feedback. The reality is: take ownership and think carefully about how you might address the underlying issue.

Another invaluable form of feedback can be through peer observation of your teaching (Barnard et al., 2011; Boye and Meixner, 2011; Bell, 2012). This is being particularly encouraged in many universities, as it stimulates ongoing discussion around pedagogy and fruitful interchange of ideas that can enrich people's instructional strategies. It is also regarded highly when you come to build your dossier for tenure or promotion. Your peer reviewer need not have a good knowledge of your discipline and the methodologies you employ. A fresh view of the learning dynamic, student engagement, and your capacity to share both knowledge and passion, can be very beneficial in highlighting and perhaps questioning some well established habits and practices. You might ask your colleague to focus on a particular aspect of your teaching, to monitor the level of student engagement, or to examine more generally the broad emphasis of your teaching. To gain the utmost from this experience it will be important to park your ego at the door. Listen carefully to the feedback, acknowledge and thank the feedback provider, and then spend time digesting and considering what you might change. A peer observer would normally seek a similar reciprocity from yourself, thereby opening up the opportunity for some robust discussion around what each does and why.

Effective teaching is guided by a clear understanding of the student, learning goals, and consistent, fair strategies that build student engagement. Understanding your role and the various approaches you might apply offers you considerable support in designing an interesting and helpful curriculum. Remember, though, that it won't be perfect. Each time we teach, we learn, and these new insights will re-inform our practice for the next time.

9 Managing your teaching role: practical tips and strategies

Your teaching role is just as critical in building your academic career as your research activities. However, the demands of teaching can be all-consuming if you are not well organized. This chapter offers some practical tips on managing the demands of your teaching role in a sustainable manner. Some typical challenges will be explored, illustrating how to balance being a quality educator with your other essential roles.

So much to do, so little time!

Your teaching roles are going to loom large in your mind, as they impact on every student with whom you interact. This can create real tension as you try to operate to a high standard while retaining time to maintain your research focus, engagement activities, and personal roles. Many new teachers get the balance wrong – partly because they have not learned how to organize their teaching activities, and partly because everything takes a little longer in the early stages of teaching. Like your students, you will be absorbing a vast array of cues as to what works and what doesn't. You may also over-prepare in order to protect yourself from not having 'the answers'.

The first survival strategy is to manage your role as strategically as possible. The following tips may assist.

1 ***Draw on available sources:*** Don't start from scratch when planning your course: conduct a thorough review of available resources and sources to build your understanding and conceptual map.
2 ***Prepare your courses carefully, well ahead of time***: Preparing for a course cannot be a last-minute exercise. Ensure that you have sourced any reading material, thought about your learning design, considered your assessment practices, developed your online course, prepared course readers, put items into the reserve collection in the library, had materials printed, and ordered textbooks well ahead of the deadlines. The lead up to a new semester can be very congested if you need specialist support. It is best to seek help earlier rather than later.
3 ***Set a time limit on your tasks***: It is all too easy to allow your preparation time to stretch from days to weeks. Set a time limit on how much

time you might reasonably expend on preparing each week's material. It is better to put more time into thinking about your learning design, and how selected activities will guide your students, than building an intensive, encyclopaedic coverage of each topic. Note that your students should be undertaking preparatory reading, and your role is to guide their integration of that understanding. Remember that your students are not experts: they do not require the detailed coverage that you might be seeking to develop. (Of course you do need to be confident and competent, and able to display a good foundational-level knowledge.)

4   ***Seek variety in your teaching approaches:*** Your programme may include a range of learning opportunities, including visits, guest speakers, YouTube clips, student-based activities, mobile phone technology interactions, etc. Plan these activities well ahead to ensure there are no hiccups closer to the time.

5   ***Identify potential risks and problems ahead of time:*** A good strategy is to anticipate likely problems before they occur. Think about the students and their background knowledge, consider the areas you'll be covering, and then identify any potential issues that might emerge. From this analysis you are likely to identify some key areas that could end up being learning bottlenecks. Consider how you will address these. For example, you might prepare more detailed notes for the students so that they don't need to come to you for assistance, but can rely on the pre-prepared material instead. You might consider integrating an optional session to better prepare students for the challenge they may potentially encounter. Another option might be to provide some optional practice sessions to be done online. The principle here is that you are trying to reduce the amount of time you will need to do one-on-one counselling. The more you can anticipate and pre-empt any problems, the better.

6   ***Respond quickly to emerging problems:*** Where something unexpected does emerge as an issue, act quickly to set up guidelines or information that will support other students in your course. Send a message out to all of your students as soon as possible to advise them of the new information or the problems that have been identified. This will help reduce the number of individual emails you will need to answer.

7   ***Take the time to learn about your necessary systems and processes:*** You will need a working knowledge of the student records management system, your online learning system, guidelines and protocols for teaching and learning, and any teaching templates. Time spent learning about these systems will be quickly recompensed.

8   ***Stagger your assessment dates:*** Monitor your workflow to ensure assessment items are manageable. Block out relevant dates in your calendar to ensure you have sufficient time to manage your imminent marking load.

9   ***Do not over-assess:*** This is a particular risk for new teachers: they feel that students need to demonstrate every feasible element of their learning. Instead, focus on two to three key assessments that capture the majority

of the critical concepts you wish to see demonstrated. Then consider how you might integrate other feedback and practice opportunities in your class design. This can include encouraging peer interaction, group feedback, and activities where you might offer guidance to the entire class. Again, this practical approach will ensure you are not weighed down with marking throughout the entire semester, while still offering students regular opportunities for feedback and review.

10 ***Set up marking keys, comments shortcuts, and other timesaving devices***: The goal of assessment is to offer informative, quality feedback without spending inordinate amounts of time marking each assignment. Rubrics, marking keys, and comments shortcuts are very useful devices to reduce the amount of time you spend assessing (Buller, 2010).

11 ***Pace yourself when marking:*** Review student work in small chunks of five to ten assignments, and take regular breaks. Fatigued markers make mistakes that will be challenged by students and require significant remediation and justification.

12 ***Use your technology to good effect:*** If you use voice-recognition software, develop a template to provide student feedback and record your verbal assessment of their work. Digital recordings might also be emailed back to students.

13 ***Keep good records of any issues or learning that occurs during your course implementation:*** The next time you run your course you will have useful notes that will guide your preparation and highlight the areas that require revision.

It can be seen that these tips are not overly complex. However, they will reduce the amount of wasted effort you might otherwise expend. Being prepared, organized and future focused will greatly help you in managing what can feel an overwhelming task.

Managing a large student cohort

A particular challenge for any teacher relates to managing a large class of students. While there is no single definition of what constitutes a large class, it is likely to comprise hundreds of students, complex teaching and learning processes, oversight of tutors, multiple lectures, and numerous repeat sessions to accommodate all students. As the coordinator you are likely to experience huge demands from students in terms of phone calls and emails.

Strategies to encourage student participation, and manage the administrative loads associated with coordinating this large community, are two particularly critical priorities. The following tips can assist.

- ***Establish your presence with the students so that they feel connected with you:*** Consider how you might encourage positive interactions between yourself, your students, and the community as a whole. This might be achieved through your formal teaching role, via email, and through the online learning system. There are a number of useful guides that can assist you in building more effective interaction with your students (e.g. Heppner, 2007; Buller, 2010; Hanover Research, 2010; Biggs and Tang, 2011; Svinicki et al., 2011).

- *Plan carefully:* Large classes need to be meticulously planned: they require careful project management to ensure all bases are covered well ahead of time. If you are coordinating a team of tutors, this will be particularly critical. Tutors are often less experienced in teaching and value the guidance you offer, particularly in the form of detailed outlines for each teaching session.
- *Set up your online support early:* It will be critical that you have a strong online presence to address common issues, provide models and examples for student review, encourage regular student interaction, and link to resources, video clips and anything else that may assist your students in an efficient manner. The learning management system will enable live and asynchronous interaction and the building of a student community. You will need to oversee and monitor the activities of the learning platform, so this will need to be scheduled into your regular activities.
- *Provide clear guidance to your students:* Be very clear about the structure of the course and its management. Provide detailed notes and guidelines in the course material to reduce possible queries. Remind students of the broad structure and design at regular intervals. At the start of each week outline what you expect of the students in the coming period and how these activities contribute to their overall learning. This will help to reconnect them with the course as a whole and ensure everybody receives a consistent message.
- *Develop your large-class repertoire:* There are some very useful resources that can help you encourage higher order thinking in your large class (Heppner, 2007; Buller, 2010; Hanover Research, 2010; Biggs and Tang, 2011; Cannon and Knapper, 2011). Questioning, management of student activities, and guidance of student reflection are important strategies to enrich large classes.
- *Offer support classes to assist students having difficulty:* In addition to making yourself available before and after the scheduled class time, plan for special sessions as assignments become due. These may operate as drop-in sessions. The investment of an occasional hour is well worth your time. You will be able to discuss particular problems with students and then convey this to their peers before more encounter the same issues. This proactive commitment will entail much less time than you would otherwise spend with a line of students waiting at your door.
- *Seek feedback and models:* Seek peer or professional feedback on your effectiveness. Invite a colleague to monitor student engagement, the effectiveness of your interactions with them, and your presentation skills. You will also find it helpful to view large-class expert teachers in action.

Managing tutors

Hopefully you will not face a large class in your first years of teaching. It is preferable to have an opportunity to develop your teaching skills in a less fraught setting. However, not everyone is offered this gentle start to their academic teaching career. You may need to coordinate a team of tutors and/or markers, many of whom will be adjunct or casual appointments with variant teaching experience (Ginsberg, 2011).

The following steps offer you some practical ways of building a consistent and high-quality approach to ensure students are well supported by the teaching team.

1 *Prepare detailed tutor notes for every session that they will oversee*. Tutors will appreciate guidance on their weekly activities. In these notes you might suggest useful questions they might pose, ideas about the session structure, and possible outcomes they should monitor.

2 *Meet with your tutors before classes start*. Some universities pay for tutors to attend a planning session. This meeting allows you to review roles and responsibilities, explore the learning philosophy and goals, and discuss plagiarism and cheating.

3 *Meet with your tutors halfway through the semester*. An interim meeting will identify any issues that must be addressed. It is important to encourage your tutors to give you feedback if they see problems occurring.

4 *Meet with your team prior to assessments being marked to review expectations and standards*. Review your marking key and discuss the purpose and nature of the assessment. Set three common sample pieces of student work for each marker to evaluate. Review the assessments, and discuss the differences that are evident. This moderation encourages a consistent standard across all markers.

5 *Communicate regularly with your tutors and markers via email*. A weekly email is an essential means of keeping tutors engaged and committed. It is also an important mechanism for sharing what you have conveyed to students in your sessions with them, and exploring any emergent issues that have been identified.

6 *Encourage your tutors and markers to contribute to the student learning management system and course materials*. Some coordinators insist that tutors should not generate anything that would be seen as giving one group more of an advantage. However, this will guarantee the course remains targeted towards the lowest common denominator. Instead, try encouraging your tutors to share any ideas, handouts, or templates that they might generate for their own students. Recognize and acknowledge these contributions.

7 *Conclude your semester with a final meeting and review of the course*. Your tutors will have many observations about the design, assessments, threshold concepts, and student response overall. This review session can offer you important feedback to guide the next iteration of the same course.

Teaching transnationally

You may experience a work context where you teach on your home campus, at other campuses, or possibly, in other countries. Lost time through travelling can be very frustrating and may impact on other roles and opportunities that you would like to explore. On the other hand, the different learning settings can offer many interesting experiences and avenues for development, particularly if you are working transnationally.

Different cultures and time zones, straddling home campus demands and the exigencies of teaching, living out of suitcase in a barren hotel room, and operating as a remote parent are but some of the challenges we experience when teaching transnationally. Some universities recognize the challenges of working offshore and provide effective induction and professional development for their academic staff. Many, however, leave their staff to sink or swim (Smith, 2009).

The actual learning context overseas can be amazingly different. In some Muslim countries you may be teaching single gender classes, required to wear different clothing, or to teach in a more constrained way. You may need to work with a translator: another barrier between you and your students (Debowski, 2005). However, the greatest challenge is perhaps the creation of an effective learning experience that mirrors the home university outcomes and requirements while reflecting the learning needs of your offshore students. The material that you taught locally may not mesh as easily with these students, given their different backgrounds, prior experience, and likely graduate destinations. This disconnection between your broader curriculum and their learning needs can cause you some difficulties. In preparing your original curriculum, think carefully about the learning goals you wish to emphasize. For example, considering these diverse contexts may encourage you to scope your assessment practices differently, so that the students can integrate their own contexts more readily. Simple adaptations of this nature can make a real difference to the quality of the student experience. Finding suitable resources may prove challenging, necessitating alternative readings and guidance on how students might interpret particular segments of the text that perhaps clash with their own cultural or national understandings.

In some countries your students will be practised in surface learning. If you are hoping to encourage them to think differently, take the time to explain your pedagogy and principles, and assure them that there is no single right answer. Be aware that this in itself could be a threshold concept that students will take some time to accommodate. If you do experience this challenge, you may also find it necessary to engage with other instructors in the discipline stream to discuss the key principles of learning and how the process of instruction might be improved to better emphasize these critical outcomes.

A challenge when teaching transnationally is that you may not see your students very often, relying on occasional intensive visits. In this situation, it is particularly important to think about your bridging role of linking this group with your other students. The development of online communication, learning communities, and perhaps group exercises across the national divides, can offer more intensive and engaging internationalized learning experiences. Clearly, this is going to require more effort on your part to build an effective learning platform where those interactions may occur.

One of the challenges in teaching transnationally is building your own understanding of the international context. As you establish a relationship with your students, consider visiting their workplaces or other relevant settings. They will be delighted to host you and to support your interaction with their key representatives. In some instances you may need to stay in your overseas location for a sustained period of time. This is an ideal opportunity to broaden your perspective and increase your capacity to offer an internationalized learning curriculum. Alumni who are located in the region would also value an opportunity to have you share your current research, or to simply meet and exchange perspectives. This opportunity could be the start of some interesting research and scholarship around the cross-national perspectives relating to your field of knowledge.

Clarifying your teaching performance expectations

It can be very hard to know what standard of performance is acceptable for a new teacher. Without some sense of the required performance expectations, you will be likely to set an unreasonably high benchmark that will demand much more of you than you should commit. A challenge in clarifying these expectations may be that the university's criteria and particular indicators of success are fairly poorly defined. If you cannot find clear guidelines on your required standards, go back to Chapter 7 and use the Quality Teaching criteria as your guide.

Your university is likely to have some guidelines about its performance expectations for your level of appointment. These are commonly found with promotions information. Discussions with your supervisor or discipline chair might clarify relevant expectations. Another source of advice might be the institutional data generated from the student feedback evaluation system. This might offer a better sense of the normative performance levels, allowing you to monitor your performance relative to others. It is important to recognize you will not be perfect. The critical thing is being able to show that you are working towards better performance.

Having said this, if you can see there are some challenges with your teaching, take action early. Don't wait until you have complaints from students or high student withdrawals. Seek help to see if you can identify and then address the problem.

These simple tips will hopefully make your transition into teaching a lot smoother. It can be a challenging time that will make you occasionally feel overwhelmed. Recognize you are not the first person to feel this way – and you won't be the last. Secure a teaching mentor who is experienced in working with similar contexts to those you are facing, and share perspectives with colleagues working in a similar role. Don't forget too, that developers in your university will be pleased to offer additional guidance.

Most importantly, don't lose your passion. Remember why you are teaching in the first place: you chose to be an academic to share your enjoyment of the pursuit of knowledge. Keep this in the front of your mind, and don't let administrative issues distract you from the main goal you are seeking to achieve. You will get more efficient, and it will get easier. Just have faith, keep focused, and recognize that you are on a major learning curve – just like your students!

10 Scholarship and research of learning and teaching

Your teaching is like other elements of your academic practice: it requires careful assessment and review on a regular basis to ensure you are on track, meeting the expectations of your university, and contributing to the ongoing development of your professional community. As a reflective practitioner it is important to integrate a regular process of evaluation, critique, research and scholarship around your educational practice. This chapter therefore explores the principles relating to research and scholarship in teaching and learning, offering you some practical guidance on how to develop an effective and rigorous approach to these important processes.

Reflective practice

Reflective practice is an increasingly important part of the core behaviours expected of professionals, and indeed, of students (Brockbank and McGill, 1998). It is now recognized that people who remain entrenched in long-standing practices and belief structures will have limited capacity to respond to their changing setting. This is certainly a major challenge for our sector, where we are faced with rapidly evolving contexts, pedagogies, student needs, and our own gradual move towards being an academic 'expert'. Barnett (1997) notes academics need to regularly critique their practice, problem solve, engage in educational debate, and critically review the development of the field. Although there may be limited opportunity to reflect on your effectiveness while you are in the throes of teaching, it is important to take time after the event to evaluate how successfully it operated and what you have learned from the process.

The concept of 'reflection' has been evolving over the last few years, particularly in the area of teaching and learning (Brew, 2010b). At a basic level, you might explore your technical capabilities in managing and overseeing the class setting. This will be particularly important in the initial years as you learn how to switch between different activities, question students, monitor group dynamics, and manage your time. However, as you develop your confidence and skills, you will move towards a freer, more open exploration of your teaching that encourages you to challenge your own assumptions, test new ideas, and consider innovative approaches. Reflection helps explore your practice from a number of different angles: How effective is my teaching?

What are students gaining from the experience? Was that new intervention successful? How can I improve it? Are my assumptions about my students correct? How else might I use this learning opportunity?

When employing reflective practice, you might draw evidence from a number of sources: your own insights, the students and their perceived experience, colleagues' views, and/or drawing on theoretical sources (Brookfield, 1995). These perspectives may all operate concurrently to offer different views of the teaching experience and its effectiveness.

Teaching portfolios as reflective practice

Teaching portfolios promote a more scholarly approach to the understanding of our own teaching (FitzPatrick and Spiller, 2010). Many institutions encourage the development of portfolios to instil a scholarly and reflective approach to educational practice. As noted in Chapter 3, the teaching portfolio normally comprises statements regarding your teaching philosophy, achievements, leadership and associated evidence. Portfolios offer an additional benefit: providing a structured framework to monitor your progress in mastering your professional teaching role. The discipline of documenting your insights from the various actions you have taken helps to make sense of the learning context. In a similar vein, the process of reflection encourages the regular identification of new goals, lines of enquiry, and learning points to flesh out your growing understanding of your role and impact. This scholarly approach matches the same care you would take with your research work.

Teaching portfolios can be particularly challenging when they are first under development. You will need to consider many things: Why do you teach? What are your broad learning purposes? What do you hope to encourage in your students? How have you sought to achieve those goals? These are critical questions that effective teachers need to address. The philosophy statement will change as you grow and learn. Like a photograph, it is a snapshot at a specific point in time. When it is next examined it will require revision to reflect further learning from new experiences. However, after the initial angst of trying to explain your key principles, you will find it becomes easier to overlay your new insights and pedagogy.

You may find that your university treats portfolios as a fairly blunt source of evidence, regarding their use as a reflective tool and a dossier of evidence as one and the same. The two purposes are quite different, with one emphasizing your incremental development, while the other is intended to support critical career decisions, such as tenure or promotion (Trevitt et al., 2011).

The development portfolio is a personal document, exploring your progress and monitoring your achievements or improvements. It may be read by a mentor or by peers if you so choose. To get the most from this portfolio, it usefully documents your emotions, your failures and errors, and the learning that came from those formative experiences. The process of writing can be highly influential in taking you to a more developed reflective state with heightened understanding of your role and impact

(Kligyte, 2011). It will include an outline of the development goals you wish to pursue and help you to monitor their achievement.

A summative portfolio, on the other hand, is a dossier of evidence to assist career-related assessments that evaluate your effectiveness. You would not share your failures unless you can show how you have converted them into successes. This is quite a different orientation to the developmental portfolio. Universities that recommend they be one and the same have failed to recognize that reflective practice can be messy, confusing, emotional and challenging (FitzPatrick and Spiller, 2010; Trevitt et al., 2011).

Excellence in teaching awards

Universities and national education systems often host awards for excellent teachers. In many cases, there are specific categories for new teachers. Many schemes require nominees to be suggested by students, although some may also encourage self-nomination. If you have the opportunity to participate in these processes, make the effort! They will offer considerable benefit in helping to clarify your teaching philosophy, tidy up the evidence base, and identify your next learning goals. The discipline of putting the dossier together will stand you in good stead as you continue to reflect on your outcomes and processes. Many universities provide support to nominees in the portfolio preparation process (Layton and Brown, 2011). This close guidance offers an invaluable learning experience. Be aware that excellent teachers must often put themselves forward several times before achieving a profile that is deemed to be outstanding.

Scholarship of teaching and learning (SOTL)

Self-evaluation serves an important purpose, but is insufficient for those who wish to be effective professional educators. A more scholarly approach to your teaching offers richer guidance and the opportunity to critique your practice against established scholarship and research. Trigwell et al. (2000) suggest six levels of scholarship that you might integrate into your professional practice, ranging from self-assessment, through to the highest level that comprises drawing on the known research to reshape your practice, undertaking research on the efficacy of that approach, and then publishing your findings.

Since Boyer (1990) first promoted the scholarship of teaching and learning as one of the key functions of the professoriate, there have been some shifts in emphasis. The early focus on assessing outcomes has moved to a greater emphasis on teaching processes and their impact on student learning and outcomes (Vardi, 2011). Cranton (2011) suggests that it is now time to take an even more expansive view to explore the broader socio-political context: a critical stance that questions the assumptions and principles on which higher education learning and teaching operates. An emerging focus explores the changing environment in which academic work operates, particularly with respect to how teaching and learning is valued and recognized (Räsänen, 2009).

Teaching and learning scholarship has helped to reshape policy and practice across the international sector (Brew and Sachs, 2007); however, it is still relatively young, having emerged just a few decades ago. The field largely operates across a broad framework, with limited disciplinary research being undertaken. Some countries have moved into research on learning and teaching far more vigorously. and have a larger body of literature around this area. The influence of national societies for learning and teaching in stimulating this focus and publishing research findings has been significant. University and national recognition of scholarship as an indicator of teaching and learning expertise and excellence (Chalmers, 2011) has encouraged SOTL in many institutions (Laird and Ribera, 2011): academics seeking recognition for their teaching excellence must now demonstrate a track record in their practice and their scholarship.

There are many useful sources that can assist the development of your ideas and strategies (e.g. Healey, 2000; Brew and Sachs, 2007; McKinney, 2007; Seldin and Miller, 2009). Conferences are an important way to learn about the evolving teaching and learning environment. Most national learning and teaching societies hold an annual conference, or your discipline may include a stream on educational practice as part of its forums. Sharing your own good practice, and interacting with colleagues who are discussing their innovations, can generate new opportunities for collaboration, and at the least will open up important chances for reflection.

As the field has matured, it has become more challenging to write for publication in some of the leading learning and teaching journals. This is particularly so if you are simply describing your own professional practice, without anchoring those observations to the evidence of student outcomes and rigorous research. When writing about your instructional practices, consider how you might link your insights to the broader domain of published knowledge. You may wish to focus on your discipline and its educational context when considering your SOTL approach. It can be useful to collaborate with other teachers to trial new methodologies or test impact across several class groups or universities.

Researching your teaching effectiveness and impact

An important part of being an effective higher education teacher is the building of rigorous methodologies to assess your impact, student engagement, and overall effectiveness. There has been considerable growth in our understanding of educational research for higher education, although this is still evolving and open to some criticism from traditional educationalists – often with good reason (Foreman-Peck and Winch, 2010). The challenge has been that many people come to the sector as discipline specialists, and operate as teaching enthusiasts rather than teaching professionals. Their notion of teaching research is often naive and fails to build on past research. In many cases, their research demonstrates many of the fatal flaws that would lead to rejection in other disciplines if they submitted a similar paper for publication. Effective research about your teaching requires a sound knowledge of the foundational literature, established concepts, and potential methodologies. This learning process can take some time and may prove challenging if your disciplinary paradigm is quite different (Hubball et al., 2010; Nsibande and Garraway, 2011). Your entry into this new professional domain can be more efficiently managed by attending a course on teaching and learning, working with more experienced academics, or requesting assistance from your faculty or academic developers.

As you review the literature you will see that there is shift in the way the research is being reported. New research methods, the capacity to access institutional data sources, and the use of digital research techniques have opened up new and exciting possibilities to explore causal effects, trends, policy matters, and the impact of teaching on students. The use of quantitative metrics and triangulation of data from various sources has become more common. Collaborative or peer-based research is also on the increase (Barnard et al., 2011), particularly as a result of external grants to undertake teaching and learning projects (Willcoxson et al., 2011).

Research on teaching and learning (ROTL) can be challenging, given the absence of robust measures, established constructs, and accepted methodologies (Hubball et al., 2010). For many academics, it also requires the development of a new language, literature base, and conceptual framing. On the positive side, this emergent field opens up considerable opportunity to make a significant contribution. It is sensible, however, to seek collaborative avenues – both for the stimulation and exchange, and because the process of documenting and disseminating the research can require considerable tenacity (Haigh, 2011). The increasing formalization of ROTL activity, and its growing presence as a collaborative endeavour, has required more careful consideration of ethics and integrity issues. If you wish to publish about your teaching, you will need to seek ethics approval and protect the rights of your students.

Some useful sources of research and scholarship

There are many benefits in joining a scholarly society that supports post-secondary teaching and learning. You will be able to keep abreast of new innovations, participate in networks and learning opportunities, and benefit from hearing of new efforts to share scholarship and research excellence. Table 10.1 lists some international sources of guidance that you might access to further explore learning and teaching research and scholarship.

Your teaching is a major responsibility. It can influence thousands of students and inspire them to achieve new goals, gain deeper insights as to their individual potential, and better prepare them for their role in society. These chapters have offered a brief insight into the world of teaching and learning, no doubt opening up many

Table 10.1 National and international societies supporting scholarship and research in teaching and learning

Agency, country and web link	Description
Ako Atearoa: National Centre for Tertiary Teaching Excellence New Zealand Government http://akoaotearoa.ac.nz/	This government agency sponsors research on tertiary teaching and offers a useful repository for project reports and research outcomes. A useful source of discipline information.
Higher Education Academy Subject Centres United Kingdom http://www.heacademy.ac.uk/subjectcentres	For many years the United Kingdom led the way in its development of discipline-based subject centres to support scholarship and research on learning and teaching. While the funding for research has ceased, the sites are still available for you to access and review.
Higher Education Research and Development Society of Australasia (HERDSA) Australia http://www.herdsa.org.au/	HERDSA has been established for over 30 years and is the primary scholarly society for Australian and New Zealand learning and teaching. Its website includes links to practical HERDSA guides and refereed conference papers. HERDSA also publishes the prestigious *Higher Education Research and Development* journal.
International Society for the Scholarship of Teaching and Learning (ISSOTL) International http://www.issotl.org/	Founded in 2004, ISSOTL is an international society that encourages faculty members, students and other advocates of post-secondary teaching and learning to explore the emergent issues and ideas. It holds annual conferences, hosts interest groups, and produces a regular newsletter. This is more suited to building collaboration than publishing your research.
Office for Learning and Teaching (OLT) Australian Government http://www.olt.gov.au/	Newly established in 2011, the OLT captures all of the SOTL outcomes of its predecessor, the Australian Learning and Teaching Council. A substantial number of projects are to be found on the website, along with guidance on Excellence in Teaching Initiatives.
Professional and Organizational Development Network (POD) United States http://www.podnetwork.org/	POD is a long-standing network that has greatly contributed to the development of SOTL. It offers useful resources and information, including the titles of some journals familiar to POD members. Its annual conference attracts large numbers to explore SOTL and related issues. *To Improve the Academy* is published annually.
Society for Teaching and Learning in Higher Education (STLHE) Canada http://www.stlhe.ca/	STLHE has been hosting the 3M Teaching Fellowship scheme for over 20 years. It also hosts an annual conference and publishes helpful guides for academics and *The Canadian Journal for the Scholarship of Teaching and Learning*.
Staff and Educational Development Association (SEDA) Great Britain http://www.seda.ac.uk/	SEDA supports the promotion of teaching and learning in the United Kingdom, and more broadly across the world. It offers seminars, professional recognition, conferences, and other forms of professional development.

new questions, rather than resolving them. This key element of your role will continue to consolidate and build as you explore it further – hopefully in partnership with other learners and models. They have shown that teaching excellence requires three main emphases: a clear sense of purpose and understanding of your students; a scholastic approach to your role and methodologies; and embedded critique and reflection to explore how your strategies and impact might be further enhanced.

Section 3

Building an effective research track record

11 What makes a successful researcher?

A successful research career doesn't happen by chance. It requires careful planning, hard work, ideally some good sponsorship, and a strong sense of strategy. Each researcher needs to be clear about their strengths, and be willing to act on opportunities available to them. Careful judgement about which options are going to reap the best benefits will be important when considering diverging paths and available capacity.

While a doctorate is a very useful platform to build a research career, it is not necessarily a guarantee of success. Equally, not having a higher degree does not preclude you from being a successful researcher. However, its absence may mean that you have to work a little harder on establishing your credentials and worth in a very competitive sector. While it won't fully prepare you for a research role, doctoral study does provide an opportunity to think, write, and establish some research frameworks and principles. If you do not have this grounding, the basic skills of writing and obtaining grants may take longer to consolidate.

This chapter explores the concepts of research success, indicators of accomplished research performance, and the development of an effective research strategy. A number of the elements introduced here will be further explored in the following chapters.

Research track records

A successful track record normally comprises a number of different elements.

Publications are a critical building block for most research careers. Over time you will need to build a clear thread of publications exploring particular themes or issues relating to your research area. The goal is to create a concentrated focus that establishes your credentials as an expert in that area. As you develop strong depth of expertise you will have a good basis for writing a range of papers on your preferred area – including literature reviews, theoretical papers, critical commentaries, or state-of-the-art reviews.

Your research may follow several themes relating to your area of expertise. This may happen accidentally or be purposefully orchestrated. Sometimes, the opportunity to write a paper that is a little peripheral to your main focus may arise. These opportunities can often lead to some very interesting tangential avenues of research, and may ultimately prove to be far more profitable than the initial research you thought you might emphasize. However, a risk in this process is that you may end up using a scattergun approach: following any interesting avenue that happens to arise. Your publications track record will need to demonstrate coherence and a logical growth in expertise. Chapter 12 explores some useful tips for getting published.

Citations illustrate the power of your research track record. As your research becomes published you will start to be cited by other writers. This will vary according to the discipline with which you are associated. The medical and science disciplines, for example, are more likely to have high levels of citations compared with the humanities. Specialist disciplines also have a smaller pool of people who will be accessing and citing your research outputs. Thus citations will carry greater weight in certain disciplines compared with others. Where it is an important measure for your track record, it will be necessary to include evidence as to how well you are being cited to justify your research profile.

Grants are another core foundation of a good successful career. In many disciplines, a track record of successful grants will be seen as one of the essential requirements to demonstrate research success. They signify that others see the research to be worthy of investment and that the outcomes will be regarded with good favour. There are many researchers who argue they don't need funding to do good research. However, this often limits their potential to take their research a quantum leap forward. Funding can offer many benefits. For example, it can provide extra resources in the form of research students, funding to go to meetings and conferences, assistance to buy new equipment or software, and many other opportunities to put more strength into your research plan. Above all, it can assist you in finding concentrated time to better plan and manage the research. If you are in a discipline where grants are not regarded as necessary, but you have actually gained research funding from external sources, you will stand out as someone who is a cut above the norm. Chapter 13 explores writing persuasive funding proposals.

Research student supervision is the third primary activity of a research role. Over the course of your career you will hopefully build a history of successful students who have achieved a credible piece of research under your tutelage. While you may initially commence this process as a co-supervisor, you will gradually move to the role of chief supervisor. This is a large responsibility – and one that needs to be given very careful attention. Poor supervisors gain a bad reputation as colleagues are forced to pick up the shattered remains of students who are failing. A track record that demonstrates successful completion of students in a timely fashion is important evidence of your capacity to shape research, guide novice researchers, and contribute to the growing body of knowledge in your discipline. This important process is explored in Chapter 14.

Patents may be an important outcome if you are in a science-based discipline. Patents acknowledge that you have created an original piece of work that will be used and deployed in other research, and possibly commercialized. To gain a patent is no small feat, as the cost of licensing patents is significant. The willingness of your university to register your outcomes in this way sends a clear message that you are on a significant path to success. It does need to be noted that, for most people, patents will not be part of their overall track record. Further, those who finally achieve a patent may have laboured for many years with little visible progress before reaching this definitive stage.

Fellowships, awards and recognition are another avenue that can be used to demonstrate research success. Many early career academics benefit from a commencing fellowship. For some academics, a long and successful career is sustained by competitive fellowships. There are various types of fellowships on offer, ranging from those that assist you to travel or pursue your research activities, through to large-scale prestigious schemes that include the researcher's salary, funding for staff, and long-term projects. The opportunity to be recognized through a fellowship offers many advantages. Fellowships and awards are normally very competitive. You may not be successful the first time you apply for support or recognition. However, the process of applying is in itself a learning journey. Don't give up if you're unsuccessful. Keep trying, and think about where you might strengthen your track record. These processes of external review greatly assist in building a balanced portfolio.

Keynotes and addresses are invitations to feature your research as an important speaker at a conference or seminar. Keynote speakers are normally selected because they will both inform and entertain. They are invited as recognition of their sustained and impressive track record – reflecting their publications and other documented research outputs. However, selection of keynotes is also somewhat dependent on the visibility and relationships that the candidate has achieved across the sector. Your public speaking and engagement capabilities may greatly assist in providing these sorts of opportunities, particularly if the organizers are scanning for talented early career presenters. It will be important to meet and engage with the key influencing people in your discipline. Use your conference attendances to maximum effect: not just to attend and listen to presentations, but also to become better known by others, and to learn more about where they are trying to take the discipline. Contributions to national committees can also assist in increasing people's awareness of your research.

Collaborations are also recognized as an indicator of research strength. They affirm that the research community deems you to be someone worth investing time and effort into. By working with other colleagues on publications or grants you can build considerably more strength in your research and greater diversity in your overall track record. The opportunity to collaborate with other researchers normally takes some time to develop. Potential collaborators will look very carefully at your capabilities, your reputation, your personality, and your future potential to be a creative and productive partner, before they will extend an invitation for you to join them as a research partner. Collaborations take considerable work. You will need to be ready to invest the amount of time that is required, and to ensure that you add value to the relationship. The benefits of collaboration are enormous. Importantly, they will increase your productivity, the quality of your outcomes, and your enjoyment of work. Some early career researchers feel they can't spare the time to socialize and talk with others. However, this undersells the importance of collaboration as another cornerstone of success. Sponsorship, as mentioned in Chapter 5, can be an important way of moving into valuable collaborations. Collaboration is explored in Chapters 16 and 17.

Impact measures and their implications for academics

A key goal of your research is to have your output recognized and valued by the broader disciplinary community. This enables your research to be integrated into the work of other researchers and ensures it contributes to the ongoing development of ideas and enhanced practice. However, we also aim to generate even more impact from the work we undertake than simply having it recognized and adopted within the narrow academic community. Ideally, our work will influence societal policies and practices.

There has been considerable debate across the international sector as to what we mean by impact. Table 11.1 offers a brief summary of the key elements that tend to be identified when considering the impact of higher education activity on broader societal outcomes.

Table 11.1 Defining impact

Impact facet	Examples
Economic or commercial benefit	• Commercialization • Licenses • Royalty agreements • Patents • New products or services • Joint ventures • Spin off companies • Increased competitiveness • Increased employment • Adoption of new practices
Social benefit	• Increased productivity • Increased well-being • Improved processes • Changed community attitudes • Public debate on issues that have surfaced
Environmental benefit	• Resource savings • Reduced risk • Changed practices to reduce environmental impact • Influence on community attitudes to the environment • New or enhanced government policy • Reduced consumption
Cultural benefit	• Improved understanding of societal issues • Greater inclusion of marginalized groups • Enhanced leadership within target groups • Public discussion of cultural issues

One of the notable points about impact is that the diffusion of your knowledge can take many paths. The influencing of broader public good and community practice will be picked up again in Chapters 16 and 17 when we explore engagement. However, at this stage, it is important to commence thinking about how your research might translate in this way.

Evaluating your track record

One of the biggest challenges in working as a researcher is that the pace can never be allowed to slacken. As one goal is achieved, another needs to be pursued. To review your comparability and competitiveness you will need to assess your track record regularly. There are many ways in which you can benchmark your performance. For example, your university may have a metric system that monitors the performance of all researchers. Make sure you are familiar with the process, and review its report of your outcomes on a regular basis. The university metrics may offer an opportunity to benchmark against comparable colleagues, those working in your discipline, and the University at large. This can be an important way to assess your level of performance. Ensure that all of your outputs and successes are being correctly listed: not all systems operate perfectly.

A useful tool to check your level of citations and your credibility in relation to this criterion is the free programme: *Publish or Perish* (see http://www.harzing.com/pop.htm). Upload the software on your computer, and regularly check your status in terms of the degree to which you are being recognized. This is widely used by many researchers. Google Scholar also offers a similar check.

Another way to benchmark your performance is to identify a colleague in the discipline who you see as a possible competitor, or demonstrating the level of performance to which you aspire. Search their profile on the web, and consider how you both compare. Would you be seen as competitive if compared with them? This level of self-assessment can be very useful and highly informative. Further mechanism to assess your competitiveness is to seek feedback from others who are expert in the discipline. While your supervisor should be providing regular feedback on your progress, advice from colleagues can offer valuable cross-checking.

Research capability framework

An important source of guidance that can assist you in your research strategy planning is to think carefully about the skills you require as you move into more advanced research roles. One of the more valuable sources of guidance now available is the Vitae Researcher Development Framework (see: http://www.vitae.ac.uk/researchers/429351/Introducing-the-Researcher-Development-Framework.html).

This comprehensive overview of the many skills that underpin successful research leadership and management will clarify your existing strengths and capabilities and the new skills and capabilities required to move to more senior research roles. Take the time to review the framework so that you are well positioned to be a leading researcher, and ultimately an excellent research leader. (This is an extremely comprehensive framework, so you will need to be selective as to which skills and capabilities you believe are most critical. Discussions with your mentor can assist in this clarification.)

Documenting your research strategy

An important technique to help you maintain your impetus is to develop your research plan. The research portfolio outlined in Chapter 3 illustrated the value of specifically documenting your research philosophy and then reviewing the goals and strategies you will target to achieve your ultimate intentions. This process of formally reviewing and documenting your research strategy has many benefits. For example, you can use your strategy plan in your discussions with your mentors, to monitor your annual performance and set new goals, identify gaps and areas that are not as productive as other elements of your track record, and consider new avenues that you might explore. Strategic research requires careful planning and evaluation. The process of regularly documenting and reviewing goals and strategies ensures that you are conscious of your strategy, rather than merely responding to opportunities that are immediately apparent in your environment. Figure 11.1 offers you a sample research plan that might assist you in starting to build your own version.

As you can see, the research plan does not need to be long or complex, but it does offer a clear sense of direction and purpose. In this example, the researcher has a clear sense of priorities, recognizing the critical necessity of continuing to build a publication track record. Goal 4, however, identifies the need to look ahead and to commence the process of building a stronger presence to socialize the research. The process of engaging the community will take some years, but there is a very clear sense of direction as to how this might be accomplished. Note too, the start of a collaborative focus.

Research strategy is an essential foundation for a good research career. Without a good plan, the months can trickle by with very little to show at the end of it. A good time to evaluate and set new goals is at the start of each year. You will feel fresh and invigorated, and can see that there is a good 12 months ahead where some key outcomes can be accomplished. Every researcher's strategy will be different. Each plan needs to be informed by an understanding of the discipline context, the researcher's strengths and capabilities, and an understanding of what is valued and recognized by the broader research community. As can be seen, this creates a strong strategic focus that would increase the level of outcome each year.

To further illustrate the importance of setting clear research priorities, Figure 11.2 offers three vignettes – drawing on the real experiences of three early career academics.

Sam and Pauline illustrate the value of setting clear priorities and staying focused on building a good career strategy. Time goes quickly when research outcomes are being pursued. It is especially important to seek both quality and quantity in research outputs in the early years, particularly where continuing employment is contingent on demonstrable performance. It can be seen that the plan needs to change and adapt

Research context   I am affiliated with the Centre for Ocean Research and am currently working as a postdoctoral researcher. While I am accountable to Prof Fish for my overall outcomes, I also have responsibility for three Masters students who are completing projects relating to marine species preservation. Prof Fish expects me to complete three publications per year, and at the end of my three years I am also going to need to secure additional funding for my ongoing role as a researcher. My work takes me offshore for around three to six months a year, which I greatly enjoy, but it does reduce my capacity to attend conferences and meetings. I feel my profile has remained largely hidden as Prof Fish tends to be the main speaker relating to our projects.

Research philosophy   I am passionate about preserving our fish and marine life for the future benefit of coming generations. As a result, my goal is to be an expert in the preservation of marine species. I would like to run my own research laboratory within five years and to lead a team of research students and postdoctoral staff. I wish to be a leading commentator on environmental matters that affect marine species, and to gain some collaborative grants with other industry groups that are interested in this same issue. Ultimately I would like to write a book on this issue, but at present my main priority is to build a large number of research publications that are highly cited and recognized for their common-sense approach to preservation matters. I can also see the potential to produce some media footage from the ocean research excursions that we undertake. I believe there is potential for me to socialize my research to engage the community much more strongly.

Research goals and strategies   For the next three years I aim to:

1   Obtain a mentor who can assist me in developing my laboratory leadership skills.
2   Develop a strong publications record:

     2.1   Publish five papers per year as first author.
     2.2   Ensure each graduate student publishes one paper from their thesis.
     2.3   Collaborate with the Centre for Marine Life and develop a joint project and associated papers.
     2.4   Submit three refereed conference papers for presentation in the coming year.

3   Seek funding:

     3.1   Attend workshops relating to successful grant writing.
     3.2   Secure a grant mentor.
     3.3   Obtain a university grant to seed a side project on community engagement with marine life preservation issues.

Figure 11.1   Sample research strategy

3.4 Discuss communal interests with the Department of Fisheries with a view to building some common research interests.

3.5 Prepare a proposal relating to possible projects for consideration by community groups that support marine preservation.

3.6 Commence planning for a national grant next year in conjunction with other colleagues in the centre.

4 Build an engagement strategy to promote my research to the broader community:

4.1 Attend media training workshops to build skills in public presentations.

4.2 Publish one newspaper feature per year on the preservation of marine life.

4.3 Discuss the video concept with university media experts to identify the skills and technologies that would be required to create a quality production.

4.4 Identify some potential collaborative partners with media and communication expertise.

Figure 11.1 (*Continued*)

to both opportunity and demands. The first example, Shelley, shows the risks that can occur if the career strategy relies on one source of support: the supervisor.

The vignettes illustrate the importance of monitoring your research needs and the avenues you can explore to address any gaps in capability that might be emerging. It is important to plan ahead and anticipate the next stage of your career so that you are setting up appropriate building blocks to move yourself forward. If, for example, you are in a discipline where managing a research laboratory will be an important element of your role, you will need to target particular activities that will give you an opportunity to build those skills. You might seek to work with one of the more successful researchers to learn how he or she guides a large successful team. You might seek a mentor who can give you some assistance in this area. Reading about leadership, management of teams, and knowledge workers, could also assist in increasing your understanding of yourself as the leader and the role you might play. Each of these elements needs to be consciously integrated into your research strategy. Relying on trial, error, or intuition, will reduce your level of performance and effectiveness.

Staying strategic

It is very easy as a researcher to lose track of what is happening in your broader community. The exigencies of completing research can encourage tunnel vision: ignoring

Shelley completed her PhD and was successful in gaining a postdoctoral fellowship for three years. She had not published extensively from her doctoral studies, but chose instead to move into a new field of research that her fellowship supervisor was exploring. This required considerable learning around a new discipline, and a new methodology. Shelley worked hard to draft papers with some guidance from her new supervisor and prepared a number of grant applications. Because she lacked a track record she was unable to be listed in the grants. Despite having written the applications, she had no capacity to be recognized for that work. At the end of three years she had one co-authored paper and little else to show for three years of frustrating hard work. Dispirited, Shelley decided that she would join the public service as a research officer and has not pursued a research career.

Sam had worked as an academic for five years and built a credible track record in his discipline of sports science. As a previous physical education teacher, he had a keen interest in helping the profession move forward. He had started to work on interesting side projects relating to retention of teachers and moved into some strong collaborative projects around mentorship and sponsoring new generations of teachers. His discipline head was quite ambivalent about this shifting focus, suggesting that it was diluting his research credibility. Sam felt quite anxious about this feedback and concerned that it was perhaps an indication of him losing his way. However, in talks with a mentor he realized that his research focus would be best advised to shift towards this new interest and build on his collaborative opportunities. He started to work more intensively on gaining funding to support his interest, built a strong media profile around the topic, and became much more passionately associated with guiding the profession towards stronger leadership and mentorship practices. His work has now been recognized, and resulted in some fascinating new career and research opportunities that he did not envisage four years ago. The important point about Sam was his willingness to review, evaluate and adapt to changing opportunities and to better understand his passions and interests.

Figure 11.2 Building the research strategy

Pauline was fortunate in having strong sponsorship from the moment she commenced her PhD. Her supervisor was a constructive mentor who ensured she had many opportunities to seek fellowships, travel grants, opportunities to present at conferences, and supervise undergraduate students and research teams. After working with her supervisor for another six years after completing her PhD., and having received a bank of awards, she now faces the challenge of moving into an independent research space while maintaining her collaborative partnership with her ex-supervisor. She has been well set up to continue a strong research career, but now faces the challenge of maintaining that strong impetus. Fortunately, Pauline is very strategic and has a plan that has prepared her well for the coming years. She has mapped out opportunities to work overseas, and has also built some emerging partnerships with other collaborators across the world.

Figure 11.2 (*Continued*)

the long-term in favour of short-term outcomes. However, researchers should not operate in a vacuum. It is very important to keep track of what is happening both within your university and beyond. Monitoring media publications, subscribing to university digests, and joining online networks are all critical to being an informed, connected and engaged researcher. This interaction will greatly assist in building your political awareness and your understanding of the new opportunities and expectations that can assist your research strategy. As the game changes, you will need to be agile in weighing up options and consequences.

12 Getting published

Most academics are expected to publish. Most of us hope to produce a body of work that confirms our expertise and credibility in our chosen field and, hopefully, that others will cite as an influential source. Unfortunately, many academics will never reach that pinnacle of success. It isn't necessarily because they are not worthy, or have little to say. Instead, it may relate to the way they approach their writing and, in many cases, a lack of awareness as to how the academic publishing context operates. This chapter will therefore outline some useful techniques that successful academics employ to successfully build their publication strategy.

About writing

The sooner you learn to write confidently, articulately and coherently, the better. If you have undertaken doctoral studies, you will hopefully have a good basis to build a body of work that will be accepted by your colleagues. However, even then, you will find that each year sees a growth in your writing skills. If you have not had that grounding, you may need to dedicate more time to building your analytic and communication skills to the necessary level.

Don't be afraid to write. This is one of the key pitfalls of inexperienced academics: they feel inadequate, so they avoid exposing themselves to criticism. As time progresses, the fear of failure becomes so strong that it becomes almost impossible to see a way out of the impasse. Writing is essential and must be part of your regular routine. It is equivalent to exercising your body to keep healthy. It is the lifeblood of academic work.

Recognize that the process of writing is, in itself, an important academic outcome (Kamler and Thomson, 2006; Aitchison, 2010). By writing, you will find that your ideas coalesce and cohere. You will see the gaps in your understanding and the areas that need more strengthening. The discipline of working on your ideas and getting them documented will encourage you to dig deeper and set new challenges to research and explore.

The world of academic publishing is predicated on peer review and competition – an environment that many academics fear. Most of us feel anxious about receiving negative feedback. Many see reviewer comments as an indication of failure, and in some cases people give up and refuse to continue working on their papers. Let's take a different spin on the issue: how fortunate are we to have access to regular, careful evaluative feedback that can help us improve our success rate? Reviewer comments offer a wealth of guidance on areas that need to be targeted for learning and enhancement. They provide feedback on structural, stylistic, scientific and intellectual components that need to be improved. In effect, they offer a road map for the next stage of the writing journey. If you can see writing as your core foundation for academic work, and a lifelong journey of growth and experimentation, you will discover an immense pleasure that will sustain you throughout your career.

Developing your publication focus

Academics sometimes operate on 'automatic pilot' in developing their careers, particularly in determining what they will publish and where they will position their research efforts. Ideally, the foundational building blocks of doctoral research will lead to new lines of investigation that reinvigorate your research focus and stimulate allied areas of interest. It is important to think carefully about how your initial publications will advance your knowledge base and provide fruitful new avenues to strengthen and expand your research. Interdisciplinary collaborations may offer some rich perspectives and ongoing learning. Alternatively you may choose some parallel areas to develop concurrently, including publishing about your educational practice and teaching research.

It is important to be consciously aware of how your profile is growing. Think of it as a tree: is it growing into a nice shape that has some interesting branches and good solid density? Does it have some interesting texture and fruit? If it resembles a single trunk with little character, then it is unlikely to sustain you. On the other hand, if it is unwieldy and uncontrolled, it will be very difficult to create a strong academic identity from the matted offerings that are evident. You will need to regularly prune and guide your focus to keep that purposeful but organic approach.

Defining publishing success

Why do you write? Is it to meet your university's expectations? To get tenure? To build your track record? To share your passion and learning with other like-minded souls? It is important to be clear about your motivations and what you seek to achieve from your efforts (Delamont and Atkinson, 2004). This can help to keep you focused while you develop your strategy.

Publishing success can be defined in many ways, but may include:

- papers published in top-tier journals
- a body of publications that demonstrate your expertise across a period of time
- highly cited papers that have been mentioned by other writers

- the number of times your paper is downloaded by others to read (which is closely monitored by journal editors and publishers)
- invitations to speak at conferences or universities, as a result of your publications
- prizes or awards for your papers
- selection of your paper to be included in a best paper series
- communication from people who have read your paper and been interested/inspired by your ideas, or
- translation of your work into policy and practical applications.

Table 12.1 offers a quick overview of some of the ways that journals and authors are evaluated. As can be seen, there is a very strong focus on peer recognition as a measure of publishing success.

You may have other criteria that you perceive to be important. Keep monitoring how well you are reaching these goals.

Table 12.1 Journal and author metrics

Impact factor	The impact factor measures the average number of citations for articles published in a journal over the preceding two years. Higher scores = higher impact. In general this is most relevant to science and social science publications.
Eigenfactor	This scoring is used to measure the importance of the journal as evidenced by the number of citations it receives from papers in other journals. High-impact journals are weighted more heavily.
h-index	The h-index was first proposed by Hirsch (2005) and gives more weight to highly cited papers by an author. Scoring is based on how many of your papers have been cited at least that many times. For example, a score of 8 means at least eight papers have been cited eight times.
Egghe's g-index	This index adapts the h-index to give greater weighting to highly cited papers.

Choosing your publication channel

With clarity as to why you are writing, you can better judge which publication channels will best assist you. Authored or edited books, book chapters, academic articles, conference papers, reports, discussion documents, newspaper features and magazine articles are but some of the options that you have at your disposal. Your choice of where to feature your work will be partly dependent on the expectations of your discipline. However, it may also relate to how efficiently that channel connects with your desired audience to get your message across. If you are still trying to build a strong foundational track record, you will want to develop some strong papers that quickly establish your presence. A series of good papers on a focused area of research can help to establish you as a person of authority. Delamont and Atkinson (2004) and Sadler (2009) are particularly helpful in discussing the pros and cons of traditional publishing avenues and how each can assist your profile building.

For most disciplines, articles published in academic journals are the preferred mode of publication. One of the reasons for their popularity is the immediacy and accessibility of the paper after publication. High- to medium-quality science or social science journals are generally well indexed through international online databases and will often be accessible upon acceptance through online repositories. Books and book chapters, on the other hand, may require more tenacity to obtain a copy, although digital copies are becoming more prevalent. Unfortunately, high-quality journals are increasingly hard to crack: many have 5–20 per cent acceptance rates and the time taken to write, revise and then hopefully publish can require several years of patient, dedicated work. While it is easier to publish in less reputable journals, there will be less likelihood of the paper being picked up and cited by others or recognized as worthwhile (Rochon et al., 2002). Given the time it takes to produce a paper, you want to optimize the return. On the other hand, you need to recognize that if the paper is not seen as sufficiently sophisticated, it is better published in a mid-tier source than not at all.

You will need to think carefully about where you invest your time and ideas. The channels you choose need to optimize the time expended and maximize the return for you. Emergent or specialized disciplines may be minimally represented in journal ranking processes, as publications must meet a number of criteria before they are considered suitable for inclusion as ranked journals. Regional journals also find it more challenging to be recognized as worthy publications, and yet they may be a critical avenue for your specialist writing.

Books could be an important outcome for your particular discipline. Authored books can be very satisfying to write, but they are a big commitment and consume all of your focus. This can be very detrimental to your track record in the early years. Edited works can be quite effective in mapping new terrain: drawing key thinkers together around a theme and then publishing a topical set of papers can be an efficient way of setting your name as a thought leader. However, many edited works pass unnoticed by the broader discipline and may be seen as having little value. So you may invest considerable effort to little avail if the book does not capture the attention of those who you wish to influence. In some artistic disciplines creative works may be valued more highly.

It is important to recognize that the different forms of publication are not mutually exclusive. A refereed conference paper can be a building block for a more substantive published paper. Conference presentations operate as advanced organizers for your thoughts, helping to clarify the key concepts you wish to share and to check that there is sufficient weight in your material to be of interest to others. The feedback and questions from audience members can identify possible issues that will need further consideration before you publish. If your presentation is refereed and published, you will have an output that is publicly available and citable, while you beaver away on your more substantive paper. You may also find that your paper stimulates some useful contacts and relationships that will assist with developing collaborations and, ultimately, additional papers.

Getting published: tips for success

There are some basic principles that can greatly assist you in getting a paper published.

1   Make sure your targeted journal's aims and scope fit with your intended paper. Editors will reject your paper if it is outside the journal's parameters. You might consider sending the editor a brief abstract of your proposed paper to see if it is of interest.

2   Most journals offer clear guidance on the style, referencing requirements, word limits and expectations of authors. Read these guidelines carefully and make sure you conform.

3   Read the reviewer guidelines for your selected journal. These are the criteria by which your paper will be judged. Download some sample papers that have recently been published to gain a sense of the style and approaches that have been successful. These models will greatly assist in thinking about your paper design.

4   Think about your contribution to the field. What makes your topic special? It is important to be clear about where you are positioned and why your paper needs to be published. What unique message does it offer? You need to put a compelling case as to why your paper should be chosen. In particular, consider how your paper contributes to the field and moves it forward.

5   When developing your paper, consider the implications of your research for theory, research and practice. Operating across these three dimensions will ensure you are capturing the attention of academics, researchers and practitioners. You are, in effect, offering something of value to all likely readers.

Designing a quality research paper

As a novice writer you will need to work harder on building some of the foundational skills that will help you get published. Studies of expert versus novice authors have found that experts expend *more* time, effort and practice to improve their academic products (Alexander, 2004; Reio, 2011). While they have better integration and richer domain-specific knowledge, they also undertake more planning and analysis to ensure the paper's focus and argument is appropriate. Novices, keen to get their paper submitted and done, may find this perfectionistic approach frustrating. However, premature submission can be problematic, as it may jeopardize ultimate acceptance. Once an editor has rejected a publication, there is little chance of seeking a 'retrial'. Take the time to edit, re-edit and hone your paper before you send it out. Despite feeling vulnerable, make sure someone else has read the draft, and listen carefully to any feedback. It is much better to anticipate any challenges the reviewers may experience and address them before submission.

You will no doubt agree that many academic papers are almost impenetrable. Reviewers and editors look for papers that the readership will find useful, informative, well researched and strongly argued. If you can develop a paper that meets these expectations and is easy to read, engaging and well designed, you are more likely to be published. In recent years, there has been a push to change the formal language and style of academic writing so that the barriers between writer and reader are reduced (Sword, 2011). This summary draws on those ideas and may assist you in creating that successful paper.

1 ***Design your title carefully:*** Your title will be the most frequently read component of your paper. It will appear on websites and abstracting services, and will be the factor that leads people to read or dismiss you. Aim for an enticing title that helps the reader understand the main message of your paper. Make sure you include the critical keywords in your title to ensure search engines identify your paper. 'A good title is like a well chosen hat: it makes you look visible from a distance' (Sword, 2009: 324).

2 ***Create a powerful abstract:*** The second most widely read part of your paper will be your abstract. In effect, this is your paper writ small. It needs to offer a compelling case for why the reader should take the effort to read the paper. Developing a strong voice and authoritative identity helps to position your work (see Kamler and Thomson, 2006: 85–90). The abstract should describe the research problem being addressed, and set out why the paper is significant, how it supplements prior research and the main findings that you identified. Readers will want to know what you discovered or argued so that they can judge the paper's relevance. Release enough information to make the reader want to delve deeper. This is your key marketing tool to attract readers.

3 ***Build your story:*** Papers are stories: they explain the antecedents to your research challenge and then lead the reader through your tale of how you addressed that issue. If you think of yourself as a narrator and check that the flow of the ideas works smoothly, you will find that the cohesion will be much improved. In some cases, you may need to follow a stipulated structure and strong traditional protocols as to what is covered and how outcomes are reported. Even then, think about the logical ways in which you lead the reader through. The use of clear topic sentences at the start of each paragraph and headings to guide the reader are important signposts as to what is being shared. (See Cargill (2009) for some very helpful tips.)

4 ***Create a readable paper:*** 'Bland, strung out, abstract sentences are much, much easier to write than tight, active, concrete ones!' (Sword, 2009: 333). The readability of your writing is very important. Academics are being encouraged to write more freely, using a range of writing techniques to create more accessible works. For example, readers appreciate clear explanation of

concepts, limited use of jargon, examples to show how concepts work, visual guides, illustrations, and, if appropriate, metaphors, anecdotes and an engaging style of writing. Well structured, short sentences keep the reader's attention. Active, not passive, writing is desirable (see Sword (2009) for some helpful examples). Your style of writing can also be enhanced by defining constructs early and avoiding jargon and acronyms. Your voice will depend on the particular journal and the paper concerned. Reflective pieces may offer more opportunity to integrate a more individualistic, humorous approach. Even in more formal journals, however, aim to reflect your passion, commitment and engagement.

5　***Keep the audience in mind:*** Be aware of who you are writing for. If your journal is for a general audience, ensure that readers are carefully led through your argument. If it is for a more informed, specialized readership, you will need to demonstrate a knowledgeable stance, while also keeping novice readers in mind.

6　***Build a strong introduction:*** Your opening paragraph needs to be engaging. Traditionally, authors aim to set out the need for the study and introduce the questions that need to be addressed. Consider hooking the reader in by offering a story, an anecdote, an intriguing question. This can help to differentiate the paper from the hundreds of ponderous submissions that land on the editor's desk. It will also grab the attention of the audience and encourage them to continue reading. Avoid sweeping generalizations or naïve statements that will open the paper up for criticism.

7　***Ensure your paper reflects high standards of scholarship and research:*** A very important element of your preparation is ensuring the literature is effectively reviewed, integrated, cited and referenced. Aim for a confident voice that offers an expert view of the field and the need for your paper.

Coping with rejection

Academics need to build resilience when seeking to publish. Risk and rejection is part of the process and needs to be recognized as an important learning journey. It is extremely rare for a paper to be accepted following the first submission. Instead, the editor is likely to send back the reviewer comments and an outline of what will require redesign and further development. It can be very disheartening to read the comments that have been received. In the first instance, read the feedback and then put it away for a time until some distance and perspective has been gained. Then review the statements again. You will have had time to think through the comments and come to terms with them. Importantly, recognize that the opportunity to resubmit is a step in the right direction. It is a successful milestone on your publication quest.

In general, editors offer very helpful summaries of the issues that will need to be addressed. Their goal is to guide the resubmission process so that the paper will ultimately be accepted. A resubmission does not necessarily guarantee publication, however. Papers generally go back out to reviewers for a second consideration. Despite meeting the criticisms from the first round, it may be that the paper is still not sufficiently developed for acceptance, or new issues arise as a result of the revamp. The editor may also end up with diametrically opposed viewpoints from different reviewers and may need to mediate between the two perspectives. In some cases, there may be three or more reviewers whose views need to be respected and reflected in the changes. In revising the paper, it is important to consider each criticism carefully. If the comments are ill-advised, consider how they might be addressed in the paper. If one person sees the paper in this way, readers may also respond similarly. If the reviewer's assumptions are incorrect, look at how the paper can address those misunderstandings. If they suggest additional literature (which may include their own papers!), take the time to review and integrate this where possible. When you feel the paper is ready to resubmit, take some more time to critically read and review the flow, structure and argument. In making the revisions, inconsistencies and poor writing can sometimes creep in. The paper will be critically analysed by the initial reviewers to see if it has been suitably enhanced. Don't leave any areas underdeveloped.

If your paper is rejected for publication, read the feedback carefully. Was the journal a good fit for the paper? Was the document ready for submission? Were there grammatical and editorial errors that reflected poorly? Was the argument clear? Was it enticing? In some instances, the paper may require further development before it is ready for resubmission to another journal.

Submissions to prestigious journals may be rejected because the research or body of work is insufficient. In this case, there are two choices: do more research and resubmit when the gaps are addressed, or seek a less illustrious journal in which to publish. Both decisions have a cost. In the first instance, more time will be required to rewrite the paper. In the second, the research may have lower impact in the long term.

The most essential message about being rejected is to ensure the paper is not left to languish. Most academics have 'paper carcasses': submissions that did not get published because they were put aside when rejected. This is a tragic loss of good effort. Persevere and look for alternative publishing avenues. Don't let good work go to waste. On the other hand, if the paper is failing to engage editors, you may need to recognize it as a lost cause and move on. Before you do abandon it, review the reasons for failure to avoid repeating these errors in the future.

Book publishing

Most academics see book writing as a goal they would like to pursue at some time in their career. As a new academic, it is not necessarily the optimal use of your time. Books take at least a year to write – often two – and absorb the majority of your time during that period. Although you may be working furiously to get it completed, that work is largely invisible. It is a little like doing another doctoral thesis – but without the support crew!

There are many different forms of books, each possessing particular characteristics.

- An authored book is designed and written by the author(s). The content draws on the expertise of the author(s) and generally seeks to position their ideas as foremost in the field. Books of this nature take one to two years to develop and may not have the impact one would hope. They require strong organizational skills and focus. There are two possible tracks that might be followed: writing a popular work that will attract a general readership, or developing an academic work that may be more specialized and less widely read. Academic publishers are moving towards online and digital printing to reduce their exposure from low sales of academic publications. Shared or self-publishing is also an option, but may have less status in the eyes of traditionalists (Plate, 2006).
- An edited work brings in co-writers who develop different chapters. The editor needs to create a strong 'story' around the chapters and has the role of ensuring that the quality and cohesion is high. Part of the secret is carefully choosing the contributors for their expertise, writing calibre and capacity to meet deadlines. The editor would normally write an introductory chapter positioning the work and a concluding commentary, which count as outputs. The actual editing is less highly regarded in some disciplines.
- Textbooks are the least well regarded academic book output, with many people seeing them as summaries of the field, not original work. In fact, they can be very innovative, offering original and creative thought – particularly for new fields of knowledge. 'Hybrid' works, that explore new concepts and ideas in a textbook format (Delamont and Atkinson, 2004), can increase your exposure, reach a wide readership and lead to new research opportunities, but are unlikely to be valued by your colleagues as you would wish. In some countries, they will not be counted as a research output at all. Textbooks can also be quite demanding, as they require careful consideration of the student learning needs, and may require additional illustrative material, reflective activities, teaching resources and, in some cases, a databank of test items. But as authors normally receive royalties from each sale, they can be lucrative!

The cardinal rule with book publishing is: do NOT start writing a book until you have a publisher lined up. Reputable publishers normally offer guidelines on their websites as to the types of proposals they will consider. They often request a proposal that outlines:

- the market audience
- the proposed content
- length
- timetable
- existing works that either complement or compete for the same market
- why you are the author of choice.

It takes time to write a proposal, as you will need to provide a brief synopsis of each chapter, and possibly sample chapters – particularly if your track record is less well established. In that situation, choose chapters that you could also convert to papers if the proposal is not accepted.

Once accepted, you will receive a contract. Check carefully the expectations and agreements, particularly timelines. Some publishers will have more rigid accountabilities. In the case of textbooks, for example, you may be asked to regularly submit the next chapter so that technical editors can review the quality – a great way to keep to schedule.

Fast tracking publishing

An important issue to consider is your method of developing papers. Take time at the start of each year to plan your writing schedule for the year. Identify any conferences that are critical places where you should be featured, and identify what is required. Put together the sequence and scheduling that you believe is achievable and try to keep to it. Most reputable journals use electronic submission, so you can track your paper's progress. Even so, a response can take a long time to come back. When you have submitted a paper, move to the next goal rather than waiting for the outcome of the review. You might also consider a mix of modes: a book chapter, articles, a review article, a newspaper feature. Each offers different benefits and helps to build your presence in the broader community.

You can benefit from working with a more experienced writer – they will have a good understanding of the nuances of getting published and see the writing as a project that needs good management. If you are working as a sole author, it is likely that your publication rate will be lower and your rejection rate will be higher. It is harder to keep on task and to maintain the focus when you are the only person keeping track. Successful researchers with highly prolific track records note the value of working on papers in collaboration with other colleagues. They highlight the advantages of bringing in fresh perspectives and creating a stronger sense of urgency through working together. The range of papers they produce as co-authors is greater and the collaboration also sparks other research opportunities because they become better known. In effect, the collaboration operates as a peer-learning circle that encourages, stimulates and challenges each participant. These successful collaborations generally stem from a base of mutual respect and liking, thereby creating a strong sense of well-being and achievement through the association. In some situations, you may find that you have picked a collaborator who is difficult or ineffectual. Finish the agreed task and then move on to new relationships. Your time is too precious to waste, and stressful collaborations will not be a healthy addition to your professional activities.

When working with others, make sure the intellectual property issues are discussed and agreed before commencing. Who will be first author? What are the contributions each should make? It is critical to resolve these issues before they become contentious.

Increasing your publishing productivity and output

It is important to recognize that academic writing is a craft that takes discipline and practice. Experts recommend that you exercise your skill every day rather than wait for the optimal conditions that would make it easy to write (Gardiner and Kearns, 2010). This will increase your annual output markedly, even if the time you have available is quite short. Even 15 minutes will generate another paragraph. The best time of day to write will vary for each individual. For some, a fresh new morning is alluring, while others find they work best later in the day. Whatever your preference, try to build a regular habit of putting time into your writing *every day*, no matter how busy you feel. The biggest risk for academics is to fall into a writing void, as the momentum, self-confidence and capacity to write become increasingly hard to regenerate.

While self-discipline is important, solitary writing can be hard – particularly for a novice who is still working out what a suitable standard and voice should be. There are various ways in which support can be built in to keep you stimulated and energized.

- *Courses on writing academic papers* can be very helpful in highlighting key principles, protocols and successful models. These are usually presented by experienced and well regarded authors and may be intensive or more extended programmes. Publisher seminars or faculty discussions of publishing will assist you. Learned societies often offer a workshop or seminar on getting published in their journal at their annual conferences. These are a must to attend as you will hear from the editors, meet them, learn about their thematic priorities and pick up more tips to consider. You may also be able to canvass an idea for a paper to see if it will be of interest.
- *Writing support groups or circles* meet regularly to offer encouragement, feedback and, in some cases, time to write (McGrail et al., 2006). They often run fortnightly or monthly and last around one to two hours. While some universities sponsor facilitated circles, they can operate successfully as self-organizing groups. Successful groups have found that goal-setting and agreed deadlines for completing a component can keep the motivation high. Some institutions also offer writing retreats, where participants can fully immerse themselves into the writing experience, draw on feedback and support, and build additional skills (Jackson, 2009; Murray and Newton, 2009).
- *Coaching* has been less intensively employed by academics. In this approach, an expert guides the writer towards better outcomes and a higher standard of work. In many ways, academics regularly access coaching: doctoral supervisors, mentors and more experienced colleagues all contribute to the learning process. Reviewers also provide critical guidance on how the paper has shaped up.

Each of these avenues for learning requires a willingness to accept feedback and to share your work. It is important to open yourself to these experiences, as the quality of your work will improve greatly.

At this stage in your career you can also nominate to review papers in one or two key journals that you respect and aspire towards. Journals need good reviewers and would welcome your involvement. Most journals now offer an online enrolment process where you would upload your profile and areas of research interest. Your profile will then be matched to an incoming paper and you will at some stage in the future be invited to review a paper. The process of intensively reading and critiquing other people's papers is a very informative learning process. More experienced colleagues will be happy to evaluate your first few reviews to ensure they are at the right level.

Building your publishing presence

Getting something published is not the end of the process. It is also valuable to share it with your network to make sure people are aware of it. Many universities now operate online repositories where you can upload your submitted paper for public access. Your journal may also offer a prepublication online service so that the paper is available for purchase prior to its official release. Make sure you share news of your new paper with your collegial network. Online communities are a further option. Look, for example, at http://academia.edu/. Your university may also have guidance on other networks that can assist you in building your profile and presence. The goal is to have people citing that paper as soon as possible!

Recently an Australian academic sent out a twitter message about his new book. Within weeks it was a bestselling work in Australia, much to the bemusement of the wider fraternity. It was a clear message that social media also has an important role in sharing our outputs. This is a growing area of engagement that is still emerging.

Writing is a professional craft: it requires practice, discipline and tenacity. As a new researcher, make sure you commit regular time to write. It is the secret to a successful career.

13 Getting funded

An important part of building an academic track record is the securing of funding through external sources. This element of academic work is often little developed through the PhD, as postgraduate students are normally not required to seek funding for their projects (Kubler and Western, 2007). After graduation it is generally anticipated that new academics will commence the process of securing some funding to support their research activities, and in some cases their own employment as full-time researchers.

In some settings, the techniques for getting funding are jealously protected, as it is seen as competitive edge or a craft that is developed over many years (Blaxter et al., 1998). In fact, securing funding is like other elements of academic work: it requires dedication, practice and a sensible strategy that builds on your strengths and assets. It is possible to achieve successful research funding if you follow some simple, widely accepted principles.

Why seek funding?

There are many reasons for seeking research funding. First, it is a significant scholastic achievement that recognizes your ongoing progress in building a body of scholarly work. Second, it offers important sponsorship of your research activities, so that they can be more efficiently and effectively executed. Third, each process of seeking funding encourages ongoing growth in research and scholarship as the concepts and goals are more finely articulated. Successful fund-seeking also affirms that the focus and design of the research are of interest to a broader community. The achievement of funding also acts as an important scaffold for future sponsorship: success begets success. Finally, external funding encourages original research and creative activity, stimulating researchers to push their boundaries and stretch their capabilities.

There are downsides to seeking funding that also need to be recognized. For the most part, funding is hard to obtain, with many worthy proposals unsupported. This can be disheartening and may lead to some researchers giving up. The limited opportunities can be particularly challenging for those who require funding to retain their positions as researchers, as it can generate considerable anxiety and insecurity. Finding funding is perhaps the hardest element of building a research profile – but one of the most critical to pursue – despite likely setbacks.

Various disciplines place a different priority on securing funding. Academics in the humanities and creative arts, for example, sometimes argue that they don't require funding as they predominantly rely on their own talents or knowledge base. However, there are many ways that funds can assist even an individual researcher: for travel, to work on a novel project, to join with other like researchers to build more generalized approaches, or to hire an assistant to escalate the rate of output. The quest for funds can also encourage some different research orientations that stimulate creative bridging across to new disciplines, forms of thinking, operating or interacting.

Assessing funding options

The decision to seek funding should be a calculated step towards the broader research goals that have been identified. Funding focuses the likely direction of research and assists in building depth of outcomes and expertise in that area. There is no single strategy that will work for all researchers. While those working in experimental/scientific research may seek funding from competitive grants, recognition and support for the creative arts and humanities might take the form of fellowships, prizes and awards.

An important outcome of research funding has been the encouragement of interdisciplinary collaboration. The building of a diverse research group to address complex issues is a particularly exciting benefit of research. Many of these collaborations have been stimulated by the quest for external funding. New researchers with skills in using particular methodologies or who have explored an innovative area may be invited to work with an established research group so that they can enrich the existing profile. For others, it will be necessary to first build some profile and credibility as a single researcher. For now, we will explore the process of gaining funding as an individual applicant.

Submissions for funding take considerable effort. It is important, then, to work on approaches that will be likely to reap a good outcome. The decision to work on a proposal needs to be based on good judgement as to the likelihood of success. This can be a complex evaluation, based on the merits of the proposal, the track record of the researcher(s) and the history of the funding body. It may also be important to consider whether a proposal would be more successful in collaboration with others or as a sole researcher. In many cases, your funding trail may comprise a progression of grants that initially operate as small-scale investigations before moving into larger, more complex projects.

Research funding normally works in close synergy with the specific research specialism that the researcher has identified and consciously pursued. Researchers may sometimes choose to follow conjoint paths as various funding opportunities open up. Responsive research, for example, is set by the funding body to support its particular priorities and goals. In this instance the successful candidate(s) must fulfil the predetermined research brief. While responsive research can be alluring and well recompensed, it may also reduce the capacity to undertake more strategic research that will help build long-term reputation and impact.

There are other contextual considerations that may influence the building of each individual's research identity. With the increasing competition for funding, many research institutions have chosen to identify research priorities that support their areas of strength. Researchers are encouraged to affiliate with those identified foci and to build collaborations with other like colleagues. This can require some subtle shifting of emphasis in the research strategy. Similarly, over time the research strategy may become broader rather than more specialized as new possibilities and lateral areas of investigation open up. A key message here is that flexibility, openness to opportunities and a willingness to venture into allied fields can be helpful in building a robust and future-oriented research strategy. Collaboration with others is a valuable way of continuing to challenge and enrich the initial research focus.

When to seek funding

The decision to seek funding should be based on a careful assessment of your competitiveness against the likely field. Most funding sources will see each candidate's track record, as it relates to the proposed field of study, as a predetermining hurdle. A credible history may include a good record of cited publications, a history of published papers and, preferably, achievement of funding from other sources. If the track record also shows a depth of experience in investigating the proposed field of research and applying the described methodology, you stand a greater chance of being judged an acceptable candidate.

Be realistic about your likelihood of success. It may be better to put the time into another paper or a less competitive funding option if the chance of gaining funding through a more competitive scheme is minimal. Advice from university experts, mentors and peers can help in judging whether the timing is right at a particular stage of your career development.

Funding sources

There are many ways in which research may be funded. You might, for example, access support to undertake research, attend conferences, participate in exchange programmes, gain research posts, studentships or fellowships, take research leave to visit a hosting research institution, gain awards or seek broader recognition. Think carefully about the benefits to be generated by the opportunity before investing time and energy in gaining the funding.

Some of the key sources you might access are briefly described below.

- *Start-up grants:* There are few times in your career where you can negotiate extra support or better conditions. However, the offer of a position at a new university or research group is one of those opportunities that should be leveraged. Many employers will provide a start-up grant to help get your research moving. You might seek initial funding, a laboratory space, research assistance, or other forms of support that suit your needs.

- *University funding:* Most universities now offer specific grants for early career researchers. In many cases, these allow sufficient support to demonstrate the feasibility of a concept or follow-up studies, clarify a research problem or refine the necessary methodologies. Funding of this nature can be very useful for undertaking pilot projects, demonstrating that you are capable of executing and finishing projects and publishing the outcomes in a timely manner. They also contribute to a proven track record in gaining funded support.
- *Competitive grants:* The primary source of funding for research is through competitive grant schemes. Generally peer-reviewed and critiqued, they are the principal avenues of funding for experimental or exploratory research. Grants can originate from a range of agencies: regional, federal, state or philanthropic sources. For the most part, these operate on predictable annual cycles. Within these grant schemes, there are likely to be different emphases, including support to build research capacity through centres of excellence as well as project-based funding. The increasing pressure to publish and build an international reputation has stimulated a marked growth in submissions for funding. The likelihood for success may be around 25 per cent for nationally competitive schemes, although other grant schemes may be less difficult to access.
- *Foundations:* Research foundations are often driven by a desire to further a particular research area. Funding will need to be tailored to their specific area of interest, but they are likely to be much more accessible if your research matches their primary focus.
- *Commissioned research/developmental projects:* There may be opportunities to tender for specific nominated projects, such as evaluation studies or mapping of existing practice in a field. These projects will be strongly influenced by the funding body's mission and goals. The income generated from this work can help to supplement other research projects.
- *Consultancies:* Industry and other organizational groups often seek research experts to investigate particular issues they need to address. In this instance, the researcher acts as their vehicle to provide the evidence and know-how to resolve their challenge. These research activities are generally well recompensed, but may limit what can be later published.
- *Learned societies and groups:* These funding sources can be particularly helpful in gaining support for travel grants, awards, small-scale studies and specific scholarships.

As part of your research strategy, invest the time to identify which sources are best suited to your current profile and needs. Most universities now offer a regular update service on upcoming funding opportunities to assist. There will be many opportunities – the challenge is choosing the right ones to build a track record of successful sponsorship.

Preparing the proposal

Preparing funding proposals takes time. Effective researchers commence grant proposals up to one year ahead of the deadline. This allows sufficient time for the necessary drafting, costing, reviewing, refining and seeking of approvals through their host institution. If you are working with collaborators who are located in other institutions, industries or regions, you will need to allow additional time to compensate for the longer communication and negotiations that may be necessary. It may also be necessary to seek ethics approval or discuss legal implications before a submission can be lodged. If your proposal isn't ready for the required deadline, keep working on it for the next cycle. Grant bodies keep records of submissions and you may be building a history of unsuccessful grants that will not necessarily benefit you.

In preparing your proposal:

- Review the funding agency guidelines to clarify whether you are eligible or not. See if you can find information on previous funding rounds and the profiles of successful applicants, as this will clarify what areas of research are encouraged. At this stage, check that your proposal is clearly appropriate for this funding source. If not, consider whether you should: a) adapt your focus, or b) seek a different funding avenue.
- Check the deadlines for submission and ensure you have enough time to develop your proposal. In many cases, your university may have earlier lodgement deadlines so they can review the completeness and suitability of the bids.
- Find out what support is available from your university research services. You may be in the fortunate position of having access to professional grant writers who can work with you. Other possible support might include guidelines on your specific funding scheme, workshops and seminars to explore the issues you need to address, costing templates to estimate your funding requirements, or the opportunity to request feedback on the proposal from expert research officers in your university.
- Before commencing your submission, read the guidelines several times to ensure you clearly understand the required format, length, content and evaluation criteria.
- Identify who will be assessing your proposal. If your request will be read by colleagues who are specialists in your field, you can write to an informed audience. If you are seeking support from a grant body where reviewers are drawn from many disciplines, ensure your proposal offers sufficient information for a lay person to interpret and understand the research.
- A well prepared and edited submission attests to your capacity to develop and manage good research. Poor editing, on the other hand, can undermine the reviewer's confidence in your skills and execution. Take time to ensure all required elements are effectively covered and clearly presented. Check that your document is clear and well written. Avoid sweeping generalizations,

unclear reasoning, repetition or bad grammar. Check that your bibliography is absolutely accurate. The reviewer could very well be the author you have cited wrongly!

- If you are working with other researchers, collect and document their CVs well ahead of time to ensure all necessary information is available.
- Be kind to the reviewer! A risk is the intense desire to pack the proposal with as much information as possible. With restrictions on page limits, many researchers resort to small print, narrow margins and other tricks to increase the content. However, reviewers greatly appreciate a submission that is clear, well laid out, easy to read and concise. Make sure your submission is an oasis of reading pleasure for a tired reviewer. Keep some white spaces and consider using some diagrams to illustrate your points and approach. These all help to keep the reader engaged and make your proposal stand out.

Typical proposal elements

When developing a funding proposal the ultimate goal is to demonstrate that the project:

1 is achievable, given your skills, expertise, concepts and design
2 is worth doing: even more than others being proposed
3 stands out as a unique, exciting and special idea that really needs to be funded, and
4 will lead to ongoing research opportunities and development.

Try to integrate the funding source criteria, intentions and philosophy in your discussion where applicable. Your job as the submission developer is to entice and excite the reader, to make them feel that this particular proposal is calling for support. To achieve this outcome, focus carefully on the following key areas.

Summary statement

In a short space of 100–200 words, you may be asked to encapsulate your project idea. The statement offers a concise and clear overview of the need for the project, what it will deliver, and why it stands out from the crowd. Ideally, it should whet the appetite of the audience and encourage them to read on. While short in length, this is your marketing for the project and needs to be carefully edited and re-edited to achieve maximum impact. It will determine whether your proposal passes first base.

Introduction

The introduction offers a similar overview of the project and some context as to how it fits into the existing discipline(s) and economic or policy context. It is here that you might introduce how it links to the priorities of the funding agency. Your introduction also needs to clearly outline what the project will achieve, why it should be funded at this time, why you are the person to do it, and how the results will assist in furthering the funding agency's goals. After reading the introduction, the reader should have a clear sense of what the proposal will explore.

Aims

Your aims should be clearly stated, documenting the main outcomes you hope to achieve from the project. These may relate to the project development and implementation, the methodology, the deliverables and/or dissemination activities that will be executed. Each of these aims will need to be fully justified and readily tracked throughout the rest of the proposal.

Literature review

You are likely to have expert reviewers critiquing your proposal. A key area they will evaluate is the positioning of your proposal within the broader disciplinary knowledge base. The reviewers will expect to see a succinct, sophisticated review of prior research that sets up the project as the next logical step in moving that issue forward. Take care in highlighting the deficiencies of prior research, as the author of that research may be a reviewer. Make sure key writers are cited and the full terrain is covered in the review. In preparing the literature review, consider the audience and their likely level of knowledge of your topic. Where the reviewers may come from a range of backgrounds, provide some background information on basic concepts and terms.

Methodology

The reviewers will focus particularly on the described methods and procedures in assessing each proposal. This is an area that commonly lets candidates down. In this section, you need to provide a clear outline of the data collection process: what will be collected, how, from whom, where and when. Ensure the intended design and procedures are suitable to the study aims, well articulated, rigorous and well justified. They should lead logically to the intended outcomes. Each applicant will be expected to be thoroughly familiar with the latest techniques and applications that are employed in the field of study. If you have innovative methods as well as an innovative research concept, this will be a further benefit. Also consider in this section how you will address any ethical requirements.

Analysis

Outline clearly how you intend to analyse the data you will collect. This description may include information about the transcription, data entry, data checking and coding techniques you will employ. Ensure the analytical techniques are appropriate for the research being undertaken, and that they are achievable in the time and funding available. If you have undertaken similar studies before, it is helpful to mention this as evidence of your capabilities.

Timelines

Your proposal should offer clear and sensible timelines that effectively capture the key milestones and activities that need to be integrated. Document each element of the project, including obtaining initial ethics approvals, data collection, analysis, writing up the results, good project management (see Chapter 14) and evaluation and dissemination strategies. This offers a very clear indication that the project will be well executed throughout.

Evaluation and dissemination

You will need to demonstrate that you have a good awareness of quality assurance practices. Some key questions you should address include: How will you know that your project is successful? What are the key milestones you will need to meet, and how will you know you have reached them? How will you measure success? What will you do if you are not reaching those standards? A clear strategy as to how the project will be evaluated with regard to its effectiveness and achievement of the stated aims also demonstrates a strong focus on delivering the best outcomes.

A dissemination plan to promote the project outcomes may also be required. Various strategies may be employed: reports, conference presentations, workshops, seminars and other modes. The main issue here is to show that you understand the need to spread the word about the outcomes and to link to the key stakeholders who are likely to be interested. Consider including regular communication with stakeholders throughout your project to ensure effective dissemination. Web-based and social media technologies may also be part of your dissemination strategies.

Budget

A common risk to projects is their consistent underfunding through poor estimation of costs and time requirements. A useful technique for accurately estimating the time a project may take is called Work Breakdown Structure (WBS). This process encourages detailed analysis of the necessary tasks to complete the project and effective estimates of the actual costs associated with undertaking the tasks. Cost estimates may also need to include facilities, travel, administrative support, resources, research staff time or postgraduate student stipends. Include any overheads that the project must cover when estimating costs. In many universities, for example, an infrastructure overhead may be integrated into grants to help defray the costs of the research office, library, information technology and other key services. If the funding includes staff costs, increased salary costs may need to be anticipated over the course of several years. University funding templates can help with these calculations.

The budget needs to be realistic and cost-effective with respect to the estimates provided. Any costs that are included will need to be fully justified and well linked to the study being planned. The reviewers will be looking for 'fat' that can be removed. Your goal is to show that every item has been carefully assessed.

Your track record

As previously noted, a first hurdle is whether you can sufficiently demonstrate that you have the experience, skills, capabilities, training and available resources to execute the project. Put particular care into explaining how you have built up the credentials to do this work. You may need to create a cogent story as to what you have been doing and how it relates. If you have had time away from research, don't hesitate to outline this. There is increasing understanding of the need to judge achievement relative to opportunity.

The Grant Proposal Checklist (Figure 13.1) offers a quick review of whether the proposal is ready.

Rejoinders and rejection

The world of research funding is highly competitive and can be quite demoralizing in the early stages. It is very important to recognize that critical review and commentary comes with the territory. It is likely that the first proposals submitted may be unsuccessful. Don't throw the rejected proposal in the bin and consider it wasted. Carefully read any comments that are provided. After you have had a tantrum and declared the reviewers to be totally lacking in any wisdom or insight, come back to the feedback several days later and read it again. Then redevelop the proposal to take account of the commentary and resubmit in the next round. In the meantime, you might consider undertaking some further investigation of the topic, publishing a preliminary paper on the need for the research, or looking for alternative funding sources.

You may be fortunate in passing the initial hurdle of mass culling and move to the second stage. In some competitive grant processes, you may be asked to write a rejoinder that enables you to address the comments and criticisms from your reviewer. It is important in this case to set a tone of confident assurance and humility! You need to show that you have a good grasp of the issue(s), that you have addressed their concerns and that you respect their judgement. At the same time, you need to be seen as a competent operator in this area, who is flexible enough to integrate good suggestions and ideas.

In some cases you may receive partial funding that will not fully support the proposed project. You then face several options: redevelop the project and seek approval

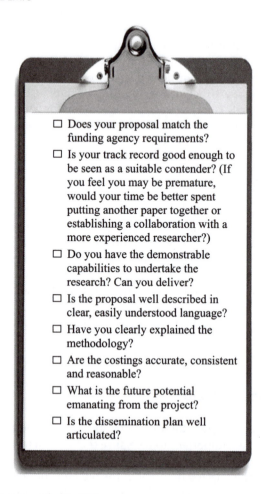

Does your proposal match the funding agency requirements?

Is your track record good enough to be seen as a suitable contender? (If you feel you may be premature, would your time be better spent putting another paper together or establishing a collaboration with a more experienced researcher?)

Do you have the demonstrable capabilities to undertake the research? Can you deliver?

Is the proposal well described in clear, easily understood language?

Have you clearly explained the methodology?

Are the costings accurate, consistent and reasonable?

What is the future potential emanating from the project?

Is the dissemination plan well articulated?

Figure 13.1 Grant proposal checklist

for the changes; operate more leanly and carefully within the reduced funding; seek alternative sources to top up the budget; or reduce the time frame of the project.

Resilience, reflection and reality checks

The process of fund-seeking is likely to require resilience, fortitude and tenacity. Success will come with patience, practice and through the process of trial and error. There can be major benefits in seeking a grants mentor to assist you in the early stages. Look for someone who is expert in the field you are moving into and who has a generous nature. A helpful approach is to obtain a successful proposal they have developed and discuss their particular approach and principles. This modelling offers a very valuable learning experience and may also open up further opportunities for collaboration. Hopefully your mentor will also agree to review and provide feedback on your proposal draft.

Interim feedback on your proposal will increase your likelihood of success. Fund-seeking is similar to publishing, in that formative feedback is critically helpful in identifying likely issues that could preclude your success. Be active in seeking advice from university experts, research officers, peers and mentors. They can assist you in clarifying the public (and less public) requirements of the funding agency, accessing unpublished knowledge, and possibly past grant proposals. Valuable insights as to the coherence, effectiveness and attractiveness of the proposal can ensure particular inconsistencies or gaps are addressed prior to submission.

If you are requesting feedback, ensure you have allowed sufficient time for the review, feedback and revision cycle.

Working with industry

Some grants are directed towards supporting research partnerships with industry. The goal of industry-based research is to build a relationship that will continue through a number of projects and over considerable time. Successful partnerships are often built up from smaller consultancies or investigative projects that establish trust and knowledge about each partner. These relationships need to be nurtured and regularly refreshed. The expectations of each partner will benefit from clear discussion and rapid addressing of any concerns.

The invisible grant writer

Some early career researchers face a particular challenge that can vex and frustrate them: where they are writing proposals to fund their ongoing employment, but unable to be listed on the grant as a Principal Investigator. This can seem unfair, but it does make sense, as the granting body needs to be assured that there will be checks and balances in overseeing the proposed project. The new researcher needs to recognize that there are benefits that offset that invisibility. Apart from continuing employment, the development of grant-writing skills under expert supervision will provide a valuable apprenticeship for the future. Once the grant is awarded, a strong focus on developing sufficient publications to later seek funding as an independent researcher should be the primary goal.

Grant-seeking operates in partnership with publishing. It is best integrated once a credible track record has been established. As with other elements of research strategy, it relies on careful planning and sufficient time to ensure a high-quality product. Above all else, resilience and tenacity will be essential to long-term success.

14 Supervising research students

There are few things more rewarding than guiding new generations of students through their research apprenticeship. The opportunity to explore new areas of research, share your existing expertise and sponsor protégés into the scholarly community offers significant satisfaction. Effective supervision is another component of academic work that is recognized as the mark of a good performer – particularly if the students publish during their candidature and complete their degrees in a timely fashion. This chapter offers a brief overview of some of the core practices that can set you up to be a very successful and valued supervisor.

Research students

Being a successful supervisor is not necessarily easy. Students come with their own agendas, personal capabilities and expectations (King et al., 2003; Martinsuo and Turku-lainen, 2011). They may have emotional, physical, financial and personal pressures that influence their capacity to perform (Denholm, 2006). If they are international students, they may also feel homesick, carry onerous family expectations as to their expected outcomes and be grappling with huge debts to fund their study. Students writing in a second language may find it difficult to work with sophisticated concepts and a more academic style of writing. Students may also have different expectations as to the supervisory relationship and its enactment (Watts, 2009; Wang, 2011). Doctoral candidates also come from many backgrounds and are increasingly older, with families and other complications.

Despite a student's strong motivation to undertake a research degree, the success rates are not high (Taylor and Carter, 2005). Many students lose their way or are guided out of the programme as they fail to thrive. This is disappointing for all concerned. While sometimes the reasons relate to issues that are outside the control of the supervisor, in many cases there are supervision strategies that could have greatly helped. In the last few years there has been strong consideration of how the research supervision process could be better managed. We have moved from a process of intuitive personal style to much greater understanding of good supervision practices.

The goals of a research degree

There has been considerable debate about the purpose and design of graduate research degrees (Boud and Tennant, 2006; Lee, 2008; Halse and Malfroy, 2010). Many institutions now encourage a more structured learning experience in the first year of candidature to make sure students are well prepared for their research. While all agree that students should pursue an original line of research enquiry, there are also increasing expectations that they will enhance their work-related skills, personal capabilities and career strategies (Maxwell and Smyth, 2010). Many graduates complete their doctorates with minimal experience of teamwork, project management, grant-seeking skills (Kubler and Western, 2007), university teaching, student supervision or university engagement (King et al., 2003: 18–19). If they wish to move into academic roles, they are poorly prepared for the work they will undertake. These emergent studies highlight the importance of thinking carefully about the full learning experience students should encounter while undertaking their degrees.

The structures of research degrees vary greatly, ranging from the traditional doctor of philosophy, to professional doctorates or more applied industry partnerships (Borrell-Damian et al., 2010). The Bologna model of moving to a uniform structure has had repercussions across many parts of the world. The harmonization process has encouraged stronger consideration of what constitutes an ideal experience for students and how long the candidature should last. While three years has been commonly set as a reasonable time frame for succesful completion, many students take considerably longer. These generalized expectations can create challenges for different models of supervision, particularly where there is increasing accountability for supervision outcomes (Sampson and Comer, 2010).

The rise of graduate schools has reflected a formalization of expectations and concerns for encouraging the best outcomes for students. Many of these schools have developed structured programmes that require students to demonstrate preliminary suitability to undertake their degrees. In addition, they offer developmental courses for students, effective policies, guidelines and supervisor training. It is sensible to build a good relationship with the school and to take advantage of their expertise – particularly if a student proves to be challenging. Accessing their support is a fast track to success, preventing many of the errors that new supervisors commonly make (Amundsen and McAlpine, 2009).

It is possible that in your university you will work in partnership with co-supervisors. This is extremely helpful and educative. The workload will be no less, as you will still read each piece of work and meet with the student as regularly, but multiple supervisors do protect the student and provide an important support for new supervisors.

Supervision models

To some extent supervisory models are disciplinary-based, although interdisciplinary projects are becoming common (Adkins, 2009). The sciences have a strong history of experimental, laboratory research where students will join a research group and follow a particular line of enquiry that complements other work being undertaken. Students benefit from regular social interaction and group learning opportunities. In many cases, the student will be recruited to undertake a research study funded by the supervisor through a grant. The student may also be offered support through an advisory committee that reviews progress and offers an independent assessment of the student's outcomes (King et al., 2003)

The other dominant model is that of a sole student working with their supervisor(s) on a topic or project that has been proposed by the student. Ideally, the topic and supervisor's expertise will align. The student in this situation follows a largely solitary path of exploration and learning, meeting with the supervisor(s) on a regular basis to discuss progress. They are more at risk in this model, as there is such high dependence on the supervisor(s) to provide encouragement, guidance, support and the necessary scaffolding.

Whatever the broad framework, the key expectation of a supervisory relationship is that the student and supervisor will work effectively together. Essentially, the goal is to build a robust, resilient relationship that is based on trust and mutual respect. The deliverables from the partnership are both a product (the thesis and a related body of work) and a process (moving from novice to independent, expert researcher; building confidence and a range of academic skills for a future career). To achieve this, the relationship needs to be dynamic, with the supervisor initially offering significant direction and support, and gradually shifting the power to the student as they assume ownership of their knowledge and outcomes (National Academy of Sciences (US) et al., 1997). In very successful relationships this partnership may continue into the future as a collaborative venture. The supervisor also offers considerable support in helping the student develop a scholarly mind and better understanding of the discipline and research community (Halse and Malfroy, 2010).

In addition to these broad structural frameworks, there is now much greater understanding of the impact of supervisory style (Gatfield, 2005). Supervisors employ various approaches to guide their students, including laissez-faire, pastoral and directive approaches. However, these have been found to be far less effective than a contractual style, where the student is offered high structure, high support and encouraged to move towards independence (Gatfield, 2005). While there is more formal interaction between the supervisor and student with this style, it leads the student towards independence with a much higher degree of success. This will be the framework that is explored in this chapter.

Underpinning these processes are some personal qualities that have been found to be more evident in highly successful supervisors. Enthusiasm, sensitivity, appreciation of individual differences, generosity, accessibility and a willingness to listen and question have been found to be important (Lee et al., 2007). Encouragement and celebration of each milestone and achievement is a very important part of building the student's confidence. Celebratory cake and chocolate biscuits feature strongly in many student accounts of good research communities!

The supervisory cycle

It is useful to picture the supervisory cycle as a process of recruiting good students, providing suitable guidance to ensure they are clear about their goals and related tasks, creating the right environment to see them thrive and then launching their career through sponsorship and mentoring.

Finding the right student

Recruitment of students can be challenging. Students are often required to identify suitable supervisors when they apply. As a junior academic, you may not be the supervisor of choice for students. It takes time to build the profile that attracts candidates. You will need to market yourself to highlight the areas that you are capable of supervising. In some cases, students may be appointed to your supervision without your active involvement in the selection. This can be particularly challenging, as the student's background, skills and topic may not be as well matched to your capabilities as you would like. As you become more expert and known, this is less likely to occur.

An important method to recruit desirable students is to identify and mentor them during their undergraduate studies. Share your research interests with students; talk to talented potential candidates about their goals and future intentions or build opportunities for them to work on research projects. Early exposure to both research and yourself as a potential supervisor is a very productive approach to recruitment.

Getting started

The first meeting with the student sets the scene and establishes important principles for a successful candidature. Before starting into the business of supervision, take the time to learn a little about your student, their background, ambitions and motivations. Share a little about yourself and your journey to date. This exchange sets a good basis for future interchange and highlights that you value the student as an individual. Then clarify the roles you will each play and clearly outline the performance and accountability expectations.

A discussion about the overall goals of the candidature is most helpful. What does your student hope to gain by the end of the degree: a successful thesis; to be confidently presenting at key conferences; to have published two or three academic papers; to have gained teaching experience and developed a number of other skills? This preliminary discussion helps to set up the framework for your supervision to ensure you offer the right career guidance. It is useful to discuss the apprenticeship model at this point: that the student will initially need considerable direction and guidance, but this will decrease as the programme progresses towards completion and they move to independent researcher status. Of course, this also depends on the student's experience and capabilities, and may need to be negotiated.

As your student progresses, you will be guiding them towards research production: the thesis, papers, conference presentations, media commentary... These processes and university publishing protocols need to be clearly discussed before publications start emerging. Students should be first author on any papers and outputs from the research, with the supervisor(s) also listed as co-author(s). Given the time and energy (and angst) that supervision entails, this is a very important point to clarify early in the relationship. Of course, if you have been an engaged and highly effective supervisor, they will see the merit and worthiness of your inclusion. If you are a laissez-faire or absent overseer, they have good reason to resent you benefiting from the fruits of their unsupervised labours.

On a practical level, agree on the frequency of meetings and review the broad principles of how these will operate. Do you expect a written summary from each meeting? Will you establish agreed goals to be achieved? If you are supervising other students, are there opportunities to meet collectively? You will also need to discuss the courses that the student would benefit from attending, their office space, equipment needs, and how the administrative side of your faculty works. This scene-setting is essential, as it ensures that all obligations and understandings are clearly discussed. You will need to undertake a similar discussion on a periodic basis to review progress and context.

Finding the right topic

Topics need to engage the student and ensure their long-term career goals are supported through the research that will emerge. As the expert, the supervisor has a responsibility to guide the student through their preliminary foray into the area of knowledge that has been chosen. Sometimes topics just don't work – the area of study becomes less appropriate, or the research approach is risky... or the student loses their passion and is unlikely to keep focused for the necessary time. The exploratory phase is an important period, where the supervisor learns what will work for the student, both parties grow into the topic and its complexities together, and they build a joint agreement as to how the plan will move forward. At this stage, the knowledge and expertise of the supervisor is critical, as the framing of the research will determine the next few years' work. In many cases, it may take two or three attempts to get the focus correctly calibrated. A key principle is to make sure the topic is not too broad. Students need highly focused, very specific projects. Inexperienced supervisors often encourage large, ambitious studies that can increase the risk of burnout by the student (Mullins and Kiley, 2002). Keep the topic as tight and focused as possible. It may also be necessary to bring in additional experts from other disciplines to support cross-disciplinary research (Adkins, 2009).

Ongoing supervision

There are now many sources of guidance on good supervisory practices (e.g. Delamont, 1997; King et al., 2003; Denholm, 2006; Lee et al., 2007; Buller, 2010). They all affirm the need to provide effective pastoral care. Key principles are to: be sensitive to the student and their needs; provide effective guidance and scaffolding to keep the student focused; encourage and build confidence; offer regular and constructive feedback; provide exposure to the broader academic discipline/research community; meet regularly to keep the momentum going.

An essential element of successful supervision is good communication. This starts at the basic level of meeting regularly and treating those meetings as a high priority. Fortnightly meetings work well for many. Communication also relates to setting clear expectations and making sure goals and agreed outcomes are clearly understood. The role of the supervisor is to build the student's confidence in managing and negotiating the regular interchange. This requires sensitivity, providing spaces for students to take ownership, and possibly setting up a meeting structure that guides those interactions. At the start of the student's project, you are the expert and should be offering clear guidance and perspectives. By the end of the project, you will be hoping to have a confident, articulate new expert graduating. There is a delicate line between providing direction and encouraging self-direction.

The next chapter on research project management outlines a number of useful techniques in relation to managing a research team. Many of these principles also relate well to research student supervision. It is important to recognize that the process of developing a thesis is a project – it needs good planning, effective management of each stage and clear milestones to be accomplished. Students work better with clear goals and deadlines. Their time-management skills are generally recognized as being insufficiently developed to anticipate the time and demands that the process will take (Cryer, 1996; Kearns, 2006). As their supervisor, you will be monitoring progress across several sets of expectations: the thesis; meeting university requirements (including ethics approvals); setting up a research presence through conferences and publications; and career management. This requires considerable foresight and some expert guidance on how to manage multiple demands at the same time. In addition, it is important to monitor the student's well-being. There needs to be a balanced approach to achieving these goals and keeping some time for personal relationships and physical health.

Student writing

Writing is one of the bigger challenges that a student faces. It is not merely a process of documenting the research that has been undertaken, but is, in fact, the core practice that the candidate needs to consolidate and build (Kamler and Thomson, 2006; White, 2011). Pay attention to writing from the very beginning: encourage small pieces to be written for each meeting and provide regular feedback on the writing (Phillips and Pugh, 2010). Experience in writing for a number of audiences will help your student. However, if the process remains a private exchange between you and the student, you are limiting their growth and readiness to deal with the robust world of academic feedback when they later encounter it.

Try, then, to build a number of different forums for your students to interact with others in a writing context. A learning circle can help to build confidence in talking about research, sharing writing and receiving feedback (Cuthbert et al., 2009; Parker, 2009; White, 2011). Some supervisors encourage a weekly meeting where a publication is reviewed and discussed. These models assist in viewing good writing and understanding how research is critiqued. Students can also be encouraged to review manuscripts and grant applications, and as they become more experienced, move into sharing their writing with the group. The opportunity to critique published works in a group setting is a powerful learning tool, as it encourages interaction with peers, regularly demonstrates the key principles of good writing, and guides more sophisticated understandings of the research community and its expectations.

While this model is more prevalent in science learning communities, it can also be established in other disciplines. The group might comprise different supervisors and their students, rather than a sole supervisor as the host/teacher. This in itself opens some stimulating opportunities to explore the broader disciplinary domain for all concerned.

Students should also be actively engaged in the various writing skill workshops that are made available to them. Keep an eye on the offerings from the Graduate Research School and make sure your students use these services to their full potential. If they have particular writing deficits, you might offer some preliminary guidance, with the expectation that they will develop from that modelling and feedback. Unfortunately, this is not always the case. If your student has particular challenges that are not shifting, encourage them to seek professional help. Your priority is to explore the research and its ultimate analysis and documentation. It is the student's responsibility to learn from the feedback and shift their skills to a higher plane. In some instances, they may need to seek additional tutoring and coaching to reach that level.

Examination

The examination process also requires careful guidance. There is evidence that more experienced examiners are far more forbearing than their junior counterparts (Mullins and Kiley, 2002). Choosing examiners is an important part of the role, and one that can take considerable thought – particularly if the research is interdisciplinary or contentious. It can be very helpful to identify a pool of potential examiners early in the candidature. This will allow for some careful consideration of each examiner's research work and careful treatment of any issues that may arise in critiquing their ideas.

In some institutions, students will also be required to present to an interview panel (Cryer, 1996). The viva can be a very confronting experience for some students. Encouraging them to regularly present on their research can reduce the anxiety attached to meeting an expert panel. Preparation, identification of likely questions and careful review of the paper are critical functions of the supervisor. Exploring any issues that arose in the viva is also an important perspective that the supervisor can offer.

Despite your best efforts, your student will generally receive examiner reports that require some amendments to the thesis before it is passed. The student is likely to see these as quite devastating, particularly if there is considerable work to be done. Many will have moved by then to a new role or reintegrated into a full life. It can be hard to reignite the motivation and determination that will be needed to complete the revisions. As the supervisor, you may need to remotivate them and be firm about getting the task completed. Your enthusiasm and positivity will be critical.

Tough love: giving feedback

One of your key supervisory responsibilities will be to offer regular feedback, both verbal and written. From the first meetings, your questioning and guidance on how to think and write about research will be the critical factor in successful supervision.

There are some key principles in giving (and receiving) feedback:

- Provide regular and timely feedback. This increases the student's capacity to learn.
- Think about the learning outcomes you are seeking. If you are currently scoping out the research topic, fine-grained feedback on writing style or structure will impede the student's creativity and reduce their focus on ideas. It also creates considerable work that will not be evident in the final product.
- Ensure your feedback is specific and offers a model as to how the student could improve that work. Set clear guidelines on what is needed and develop small tasks to help the student improve. Consider setting that focus as the next meeting's priority: ask the student to rewrite a segment to reflect the principles discussed.
- Do not rewrite the student's work and hand it back as a repackaged product. Instead, work with them on their script and discuss how it can be improved. This can be productively done at a computer screen, and has been termed 'joint texting' (Kamler and Thomson, 2006: 53). After modelling the process, encourage the student to apply the principles in another piece of their writing.
- Seek feedback from the student. Encourage them to discuss whether your supervision style is working for them, to explore if they are receiving enough guidance – or too much. If your university offers supervision assessment tools, use them regularly to gain feedback. Be open to new ways of working that better match your student's own style. This will be particularly important for students who bring more experience into the relationship. Most critically, do not be defensive if you are given feedback on your effectiveness.

Addressing students at risk

A particularly challenging situation is where a student is not thriving (Delamont, 1997; King et al., 2003). Many supervisors battle on, hoping the issue will resolve itself. They may send positive progress reports through, in the belief that this is helping the student. However, if there is little likelihood of a successful completion, self-deluding practices harm all concerned. The student suffers, as they will spend years of their life with little outcome other than a sense of failure. As a supervisor, you may be viewed as delinquent or incompetent in not picking up the issues. There is also an impact on the university or faculty statistics, which will show long-standing enrolments that did not reach fulfilment.

If you have a student who is starting to lose their way, the following steps may help.

- Speak to your Graduate Research School advisers and seek guidance on university policy and expectations.
- Meet with the student and explore how they feel about their current progress. This can be very illuminating: they may be very anxious about the situation, or blissfully unaware! Their perceptions will help you to determine how you approach the problem. In many cases, the student will articulate the issues you wished to raise and will assist in moving the discussion forward proactively.
- Talk to them honestly and openly about your concerns. Provide a clear outline of the issues you can see emerging. Link this to the performance expectations that students must meet. Give examples of critical incidents to illustrate your points. Be calm and factual, and focus on the big issues, not everything. If the student is emotionally distraught about the feedback, reconvene the meeting for a later date to allow them to digest and think about the issues.
- The student will have several options available: address the issue(s), take time out to think about their desires and intentions, or withdraw. Each of these is a big decision and will benefit from discussions with the Graduate Research School and other key advisers. Suspension can be a good option, as it keeps the student in the pool, but offers space to work through the issues that are compromising their progress.
- If the issue is resolvable, set clear performance goals to get the student back on track. Encourage them to seek specialist support from the university. Meet weekly: this is a student at risk, who will need extra attention. Review the achievement of those goals regularly – at least every two months or so, to see if progress is evident.
- If you cannot see progress, you will need to have further discussions about possible deferral or withdrawal. Undertake these discussions in conjunction with your specialist support services.

You may feel like this is a failure. However, it is a responsible enactment of your role and a better investment of your time than continuing to persevere. Graduate study does not work for everyone.

The supervisor as mentor and sponsor

Supervision incorporates three key roles: overseeing the research production process and its successful completion; mentoring the student, ensuring they reach their full potential (Sambrook et al., 2008); and sponsoring the student into the wider research community. These three roles each require a slightly different relationship with the student. While the first operates in a similar way to a contractual, employment relationship, the others are more collegial in nature (Deuchar, 2008).

Mentorship is an important element of your supervisory role, focusing on the student's growth and potential. When students enter their research programme, they will encounter a large new world where they will be learning a myriad of skills, exploring new frontiers and learning more about themselves as individuals. Mentorship helps to build the student's confidence, encourages self-reflection, offers an evolving picture of future possibilities, affirms the growth that is occurring and supports risk-taking.

An important area of development is the student's growth in self-awareness and research self-efficacy (Overall et al., 2011). They will need to become more conscious of their strengths and possible areas of growth, to seek opportunities to challenge themselves, and to learn from those experiences. When they fail, they will need you to work through those disappointments and to bring out the positives from the experience. Resilience is an important quality for all academics, but can be hard to acquire initially.

While you may mentor your student regularly, it is also useful to set aside a specific time once a year (or more frequently) to take a broader view of the student and their directions. This sits comfortably in tandem with a review of the achievement of annual goals and discussion of new targets for the coming year. Importantly, good mentorship looks beyond the completion of the thesis to explore the student's career and life goals. The student will benefit from opportunities to undertake a personal stocktake: considering what new skills have been added to their repertoire, identifying achievements that can be cited and reviewing the emerging profile. Towards the end of the candidature, discussions about career paths and directions and a review of the dossier and CV can all assist in building a confident way forward. An important role for the supervisor is to make sure personal and production goals operate compatibly and don't become imbalanced towards one set of priorities. Students who get involved in teaching, for example, may reduce their productive research activities considerably to meet the demands of a teaching schedule and students.

As a sponsor, your role relates more strongly to advocacy, focusing on introducing your student to the broader research community and making sure those encounters are successful foundations for future associations. Conference and poster presentations are valuable mechanisms to help students profile their research, gain feedback and build some connections. Because they are learning their craft, they will need to prepare well ahead and be carefully guided through the necessary processes. Practice and supportive critique will be essential preparation. Students who have regularly attended faculty research forums will have a better sense of what is expected, but may still suffer from a desire to present the full thesis in 15 minutes. You will be an important guide as to what needs to be said, and how to present it attractively and coherently. The practice sessions also offer experience in responding to questions – particularly those that are hard to address. It is important to debrief following the presentation, and to explore how it might be improved and what issues arose from the audience discussion. The student may also need to be counselled about the possibility of having a very small audience – a real risk at many conferences, but a bonus for those starting out and learning how to present.

When attending conferences or professional meetings with students, successful supervisors showcase their students. They introduce them to key people, talk about their research to possible collaborators and draw them into conversations. Networking can be a difficult skill to acquire, and your modelling of those skills can greatly assist.

There are many other forms of sponsorship that a supervisor can offer. As the research develops, you may identify other colleagues who can assist in providing more expert information or feedback on drafts. Keep watching out for doctoral forums, competitions and funding opportunities that will help the student stand out or gain more experience. Encourage the student to take on some broader professional roles that will introduce them to the research community. Sitting on regional committees as the student representative, participating as a conference paper reviewer and other forms of engagement can be most valuable mechanisms to build a larger presence.

Within the university, there will also be opportunities to sponsor your student. Selective leadership programmes, representation on committees, involvement in faculty or school meetings all assist in building a bigger view of the academic context. If the student is less concerned with being an academic, and more interested in a professional path, opportunities to meet with external collaborators or to join professional networks may be very beneficial. Shadowing a person in a desirable role may also be of interest. Again, the networks and knowledge of the supervisor are critical in this sponsoring process. Additional sponsorship might relate to sending your student overseas to research or present, or bringing experts in. Students don't always get to meet world experts when they visit universities. If they can meet and present their research to those luminaries, they will gain insights into how leaders view the field and their work.

Many graduates move to different career paths (King et al., 2003: 20; Denholm and Evans, 2009: Section 2). It is important to recognize that students seeking an alternative to academic work may require mentors who can offer different perspectives and insights. Supervisors can best assist by helping to identify suitable contacts and supporting the student's efforts to create those new connections. It is very important to understand your own limitations and expertise.

Supervision is a gift. It allows you to guide and support the new generation of researchers, offers opportunities to think about your own craft and skills, encourages ongoing learning about allied fields of knowledge, and helps you to grow the discipline and sponsor new talent. It is also a responsibility. Your students have entrusted their future and their dreams to your care. Fortunately, we now better understand how to make optimal conditions for students to flourish and succeed.

15 Research project management

Receiving funding to undertake a research project is a great achievement. The next challenge is to execute the project successfully to ensure it achieves its full potential. While many researchers just 'jump in' to start their project, this can generate many risks to the project. Research projects often suffer from insufficient planning, poor forethought and minimal anticipation of likely risks. This can lead to suboptimal outcomes, insufficient funds to complete the project, and, in the worst scenarios, no outcomes at all.

For many years there was little understanding of the need for good research project management. The PhD graduate was assumed to have gained sufficient exposure in working through their research project to translate this expertise to further activities. In reality, these apprenticeships have been found to offer limited grounding in relation to initiating and managing projects (Kubler and Western, 2007). Fortunately, the last few years have seen a growing recognition of the need to build a more rigorous and disciplined approach to managing research projects. In Australia, for example, universities have developed a series of courses to guide researchers towards better project management practices (see: http://www.frlp.edu.au/). In the United Kingdom, the Vitae project has identified capabilities that researchers need to develop as they move towards independent research. Many of these relate to research project management (see: http://www.vitae.ac.uk/). These adapted models and frameworks draw on broader project management principles, but with recognition of the specific challenges that are inherent in research projects.

In this chapter you will be offered a comprehensive overview of how research projects can be better managed. The methodology that is described can be adapted to large or small projects, with or without team members. It offers a scientific approach to project management that has been developed and tested with thousands of researchers.

What makes research projects challenging?

There are a number of characteristics of research projects that make them more complex than many other forms of projects. Firstly, they are constrained by the funding that is initially allocated, with little or no capacity to seek additional resources. The funds need to be very carefully managed to make them stretch. Second, the projects may draw on the expertise of a range of staff, from very experienced people to novices. This means that some people will require considerable training and supervision, while others may be able to operate with minimal guidance. Third, research projects often draw on methodologies and practices that are experimental or developmental in nature. This means that established routines and processes are less likely. Fourth, research projects may have associations with many different stakeholders, including funding bodies, the university, collaborators, industry partners and possibly the wider community. These relationships must all be managed throughout the project. A further complication is that the final outputs from the project may need to be generated after the funding has been expended and members of the team have moved on. Additionally, research projects may be primarily intellectual tasks that are focused on knowledge building. Their progress may be erratic and unpredictable, possibly stymied by unexpected issues or results. With these challenges, it is even more important to establish logical and well managed practices that will reduce any risks and ensure the investigations can be undertaken with confidence and due diligence.

Some typical research project challenges

There are many pitfalls that can occur during a research project. Some of the common challenges identified by researchers are listed in Table 15.1. You can see that these challenges can easily occur when people are busy and trying to focus on the process of doing research. There needs to be some overall coordination to ensure that everyone understands their role, direction and required contribution and the expected outcomes. Good project management can avoid most of these pitfalls.

Managing research projects

Project management is an important technique for managing the timing, integration of tasks and overall flows of work that occur. While it was originally introduced to manage technical projects, project management is of great benefit when complex intellectual processes and inputs require careful coordination. The use of some simple principles from project management methodology can greatly assist in bringing your project to a quality conclusion with the desired outcomes that you initially defined. It helps to keep you on track and to clarify the critical tasks that should be completed.

Project management will add value by:

- assisting you to logically manage the project to its successful completion
- systematically planning all components of the research
- effectively planning for project stages, tasks, time, people, funds and facilities
- effectively managing stakeholder relationships, particularly through regular communication and interaction
- identifying and managing risks.

Table 15.1 Potential research project challenges

Planning and scope control	• Insufficient pre-planning • Overambitious projects • Lack of priority-setting
Process management	• Adding new elements into the project as new ideas occur ('project creep') • Procrastination or indecision • Poor follow-through on decisions and agreed tasks • The systems and processes are inconsistent, poorly developed or misunderstood • Failure to monitor outcomes and progress • Data is lost, misplaced or incorrectly recorded • Poor-quality outcomes
Leadership	• The leader is too busy to meet with or guide the team • Ineffective or time-wasting meetings
Team engagement	• The team has little sense of direction or understanding of their roles and project goals • Team members are distracted by other projects and activities • Poor coordination of interdependent activities across team members • The team is untrained in required systems and protocols

Good project management operates across the entire project life cycle to clarify the major tasks to be accomplished and ensure the necessary processes are clearly costed, planned, executed and monitored. Research project management can also monitor the intellectual outcomes of the project and check that the intent of the research is reflected in the outcomes.

Use of some basic project management techniques will ensure your research project achieves its defined objectives and that costs and delivery times are controlled. These methods also assist less experienced members of your team, as they clearly define and communicate the expected outcomes and contributions. The process helps to make sure the project is managed logically to a successful completion. It encourages systematic planning, integration of the critical processes and stronger oversight of the project team, relationships, risks, resources and time management.

Research project management principles

The PMBOK model (Project Management Body of Knowledge) (Project Management Institute, 2008) offers a clear and commonly accepted guide to project management (see http://www.pmi.org/PMBOK-Guide-and-Standards/Standards-Library-of-PMI-Global-Standards.aspx). It reflects the main issues that are likely to emerge and require management during a research project. The basic framework of the model is to see a project in terms of four distinct development phases (design, planning, implementation and closeout) and nine knowledge areas that require planning and control across those four phases. The nine PMBOK knowledge areas are briefly described below, along with research management and stakeholder management, two important additional elements that must be considered when managing research projects.

Scope management

Scope management ensures the project keeps to its agreed framework and focus. It ensures there is strong clarity about what the project will or will not do. While the initial scope is defined as part of the proposal, regular reviews need to be undertaken to ensure the project remains on track. It is very easy for research projects to evolve into something different as interesting new paths emerge. Scope management helps maintain a tight control over what is done, so that any changes of direction are intentional and considered, not unplanned. It helps the researcher maintain an awareness of the agreed outcomes.

Time management

Time management estimates and monitors the times taken for each of the project activities or stages. Key activities need to be defined, sequenced, estimated and then monitored.

In a research project it is harder to estimate the time that a particular activity will require to reach completion. However, the process of thinking about a task and what may be required helps to anticipate any likely blowouts in scheduling. Milestones are monitored to check they are happening in a timely manner.

Cost management

Cost management involves estimating the costs of the research activities and then monitoring those costs to ensure the research project stays within budget – or, alternatively, determining what is required to bring costs under control.

This may sound obvious, but in research projects it can be far from easy. A research project normally operates from an agreed funding allocation. The project is then required to operate within those parameters. But unanticipated project costs can emerge over time: the cost of supplies for experiments may rise; there may be an increase in staffing costs; an experiment might go horribly wrong and need to be redone – or the project may simply escalate above the agreed budget. Regular reviews of the budget and prompt action to address likely funding concerns encourage more careful oversight of costs.

Research management

You will have certain requirements that need to be fulfilled to meet the contractual requirements of your university or the funding agency. They may relate to legal, ethical or reporting requirements. They will require ongoing oversight and management throughout the project life cycle. Scheduling these expectations into the project plan ensures you do not forget critical obligations.

Quality management

Quality management ensures the project activities support the aims of your research and reflect the sponsor's expectations. It also measures the consistency of delivery of outcomes. Quality management is largely achieved by specifying processes required to deliver results, identifying the cause of any problems, dealing with the root causes rather than the symptoms of the inconsistent outcome, and building a common understanding across the research team of the quality expectations.

It is important to ensure that: all members of the research team clearly understand what standards should be followed, consistent data and history are captured, regular review processes are followed, and quality assurance principles are implemented. If regular reviews of project progress are included in the project oversight, issues relating to poor quality outcomes or delivery can be quickly addressed.

Risk management

A risk is a possible future event that may harm your research project. It is important to identify potential threats to the success of the research project and develop a treatment plan to help reduce or eliminate any hazards. This goes well beyond the safety and health issues in laboratories. It can relate to reputational or relational risks, the loss of critical researchers, experimental failure and many other potential issues.

A good way to approach risk management is to consider what might go wrong with respect to reputation, deliverables, the team composition, budget, quality, project creep and any other element that makes the project vulnerable. By anticipating any likely problems, you can introduce contingency planning to reduce the likelihood of that issue emerging. As part of your planning, you will benefit from periodic reviews of things that have gone wrong so that there is a record of what should be avoided in subsequent projects. This is best accepted as a whole-team responsibility, as many risks can remain invisible to the leader but can still undermine the project's progress.

Human resources management

Managing human resources involves defining the roles and responsibilities of your research team members, managing the university's obligations to the team members and leading your team to achieve (or exceed) the project goals. Project management assists in checking for underload and overload and clarifies the interdependencies of different members. It also clarifies who is responsible for certain project elements.

The planning relating to human resources management may include elements relating to recruitment and employment of new staff as well as building an effective team. The research team requires careful nurturing as effective systems are established and a positive and inclusive culture is promoted. Mentorship systems and sponsorship of junior researchers may be factored into your planning. You will also need to consider how to communicate with, coordinate and monitor team members. A highly competent, experienced researcher would be greatly offended at being closely monitored as to performance and task completion. A very junior researcher would find it very useful in the commencement stage, but may require less supervision over time – particularly if a good project plan is operating. Good project management can assist with these delicate processes by allowing latitude within a clear framework of performance expectations, role delineation and clear outcomes.

Stakeholder management

Research is strongly reliant on good relationships with stakeholders. There are many different groups that may have expectations about the research, or possibly have invested their own resources into the venture. Stakeholders can include research agencies, ethics committees, your school or faculty, the university research service agencies, industry partners, overseas collaborators, the wider community that will benefit from your research, and many others. As part of your project management strategies you should integrate regular communication and interaction with these parties. You might also review the ways you involve them in the research planning and development, and what types of reporting will be required.

Communication management

To ensure the dissemination of relevant project outcomes and updates, you need to develop and oversee delivery of a communication plan for your research project. Communication management includes developing a plan to keep research team members and interested parties informed of the progress of the research and emerging issues. You are also advised to think of ways in which information about your project can be promoted. A website, media releases and social media strategies are just some of the approaches you might consider.

Procurement management

Your project will have various supplies and equipment to be sourced up front, and possibly on a regular basis for the ongoing research. Planning for procurement ensures there is enough time allowed for the sourcing and supply of materials. It also encourages consideration of the processes that your university may require to purchase or lease. You may need to train the team in using the necessary systems – all of these issues need to be anticipated in your project planning.

Procurement management therefore encompasses the acquisition of any resources you need for the research project, including the organization of outsourcing where relevant. Procurement may also include negotiating agreements, acquiring equipment (purchased or leased), and sourcing consumables. It also addresses what will happen to fittings and resources after the research project is completed.

Integration management

Integration management monitors the coordination of the other ten knowledge areas to ensure the different elements are sequenced appropriately. This is a very critical part of the project process, particularly in a research team, where different people may be working interdependently. Integration management ensures that people have a sense of what each team member is doing, when elements need to be completed, where blowouts are likely to occur, and how the project components mesh. It also guides the scheduling of progress meetings to ensure interdependent processes are effectively coordinated.

While these principles no doubt make sense, a checklist can make the process much easier to follow and review. The research project management checklist presented in Table 15.2 was developed in consultation with hundreds of researchers and university experts. It offers an invaluable tool for thinking ahead to ensure that any potential issues are addressed in a strategic manner. When managing your project, take the time to plan and review on a regular basis. Researchers who simply plummet into the project are likely to experience many more mishaps than those who consider the 11 associated areas of good research project management.

Table 15.2 Research project management checklist

Phase 1: Designing the project proposal	
Knoswledge areas	*Design phase checklist*
Scope management	• Has the project scope been defined? Does it match your research capacity? • What is the evidence for the project need and likely value? • What are the project objectives and deliverables? • Are your deliverables realistic? • What are the requirements of your stakeholders? • Can you seek input from other parties? • Is the idea feasible or the best option? Are the proposed time frames achievable?
Time management	• Identify the broad timelines to be integrated into your project. • Estimate the total time for the research by developing a high-level breakdown of the tasks to identify all likely processes and major demands. • Identify any milestones to be achieved. • Do you have sufficient ease for unexpected contingencies?
Cost management	• Estimate all costs of the major research activities, including likely staff costs, equipment, travel, rental of offices, etc. • Are there supplemental funding opportunities you might access? • Have you allowed for university overheads in your estimates?
Quality management	• Do you need to seek ethics approval? • What quality management processes and systems should you establish? • Do you need an advisory group? Who should you invite?
Research management	• Develop a broad project plan showing the key stages, outcomes and main relationships between the contributors. • Have you covered all elements of your project? • Seek expert help to check your research plan.
Risk management	• Is there sufficient capacity to undertake, lead and manage the project? • Is the budget sufficient? • Are you reliant on others? How will you ensure they deliver and stay engaged?
Human resources management	• Develop profiles of each researcher in your team and place them on your website. • Establish who else might contribute to your project. Can you include research students? • Establish your project management team as soon as possible. • Set up a regular meeting schedule. • Develop a policy on authoring publications. • Ensure all team members are aware of the project design and goals. • What training will your team require? • Is there sufficient capacity to support high demand project periods?

Table 15.2 (*Continued*)

Phase 1: Designing the project proposal	
Knoswledge areas	*Design phase checklist*
Stakeholder management	• Who are the stakeholders? What do they expect of the project?
	• If you are seeking an industry partner, how will the project operate? How can you build or strengthen those relationships?
	• Do you need support from the faculty or university? Prepare a one-page project overview to assist with discussions.
	• Have you marketed the benefits of the project and the talents of your research team to your collaborators?
	• Have you defined roles, expectations and contributions?
	• Has intellectual property (IP) and research dissemination been clearly agreed?
	• Do research collaborators understand research student needs?
	• Has confidentiality been satisfactorily addressed?
Communication management	• Develop a communication plan, including a media strategy.
	• Schedule regular meetings with your research team, partners and stakeholders.
	• Develop a plan to keep virtual team members engaged with the project.
	• How will reporting be managed?
Procurement management	• Do you have somewhere to do the research? Can the research be accommodated in existing facilities?
	• What equipment do you need? What is already available in your faculty/university? If you plan to share available equipment, how will that be managed?
	• Are you better to buy in bulk for the whole project?
	• Who will be responsible for managing the resources?
Integration management	• Who is involved in the project? How will you coordinate their efforts?
	• Where are the likely pressure points for the research project?
	• Are you reliant on others to perform elements of the research? How will you liaise and ensure they are ready to support your research when you need it?
Phase 2: Planning the project once funding has been received	
Knowledge areas	*Planning phase checklist*
Scope management	• Review the scope and objectives of the research and confirm they are still appropriate. Revise your project plan accordingly.
	• Prepare a detailed breakdown of the project, outlining the key tasks, contributors and roles.
	• Review and confirm your milestones and deliverables.

Table 15.2 (*Continued*)

Phase 2: Planning the project once funding has been received

Knoswledge areas	Planning phase checklist
Time management	<ul><li>Estimate the total time for the research.</li><li>Identify any milestones that should be included in the plan.</li><li>Review the scheduling to identify any pressure points.</li></ul>
Cost management	<ul><li>Review the project costs and prepare a preliminary budget.</li><li>Set up the project fund account and allocate the budget to each category.</li><li>Establish protocols for expenditure, with one or two people maintaining oversight of expenditure.</li><li>Plan for regular reports on expenditure and project costs.</li></ul>
Quality management	<ul><li>Identify quality assurance requirements and develop strategies to monitor quality and risk.</li><li>Develop a process for team members to follow.</li><li>Train research team members to follow the process.</li><li>Establish a protocol to deal with incomplete/unsatisfactory or unsuccessful outcomes.</li></ul>
Research management	<ul><li>Review the conditions of the grant and ensure any reporting or deliverables are included in your project planning.</li><li>Ensure all necessary contracts and grant documents are signed off.</li><li>Obtain all ethical clearances.</li><li>If your research includes students, liaise with the graduate student office to identify any requirements.</li></ul>
Risk management	<ul><li>If your research uses dangerous processes or chemicals, or involves fieldwork, integrate the required protocols and safety checks.</li><li>Establish a risk log and encourage all members to identify potential risks that require consideration.</li></ul>
Human resources management	<ul><li>Recruit and appoint staff based on university policies and protocols. Ensure you are appointing your researchers at the right level and to the correct roles.</li><li>Organize contracts for research team members.</li><li>Conduct team induction, orientation and planning sessions to explore the team/project processes.</li><li>Clarify project goals and outcomes.</li><li>Confirm principles for constructive team culture, interaction, support and quality control.</li><li>Conduct meetings with each individual team member to explore their strengths and development needs.</li><li>Confirm relative contributions, expectations and roles of each member.</li><li>Clarify IP understanding with all members.</li><li>Establish reporting and timeline expectations.</li><li>Agree on timelines, procedures and protocols.</li><li>Confirm budgeting processes, expectations and controls.</li><li>Celebrate the project start-up with team members and stakeholders.</li></ul>

Table 15.2 (*Continued*)

Phase 2: Planning the project once funding has been received	
Knoswledge areas	*Planning phase checklist*
Stakeholder management	• Confirm the project scope, milestones and deliverables. • Finalize expectations regarding meetings, reporting and outcomes. • Confirm the processes for dissemination of findings and IP management. • If you need a steering or advisory group, determine terms of reference, roles and responsibilities of members. Appoint an executive officer to work with the group. • Finalize issues relating to ownership of IP and outcomes of the project.
Communication management	• Maintain a file of email correspondence. • Document all conversations with the granting body and keep on file. • Set up your website for the project, including staff profiles, an overview of the project and contact details. • Schedule relevant meetings and milestones in the calendars of each team member.
Procurement management	• Check the university's systems for procurement. • Consider whether computers should be hired or leased. • Seek support from your school/department manager with respect to procurement.
Integration management	• Maintain a centralized and consistent record of the research project. • Set up templates for reports, progress logs and other processes. • Set up regular meetings with your junior staff and students to ensure they receive appropriate guidance and supervision. • Finalize your project management systems and processes, e.g. for tracking, timelines and accountabilities.

Phase 3: Project implementation	
Knowledge areas	*Implementation phase checklist*
Scope management	• Maintain control over the project scope. • Set up a system for recording interesting/new research possibilities that are beyond the project scope. • Address issues as they arise. • Regularly affirm the desired outcomes and milestones to the research team. • Review the out-of-scope areas that have emerged and consider whether these are areas suitable for new grant submissions. • Revise your schedule and project plan if the scope has changed.

Table 15.2 (*Continued*)

Phase 3: Project implementation	
Knowledge areas	*Implementation phase checklist*
Time management	• Monitor progress against timelines and milestone completions. • Meet with groups and individuals to explore whether the timeline is reasonable. • Review the timeline if necessary and outline the changes to the team. • Implement corrective actions if slippage is evident. • Adjust the project plan to reflect revised timelines.
Cost management	• Monitor the budget regularly, particularly with respect to staffing costs (including leave entitlements). • Ensure all funds are spent according to the agreed budget and conditions of award. • Address budget overruns promptly. • Ensure financial statements are prepared and reflect the necessary requirements of the funding body. • Monitor that full expenditure of the funding has occurred prior to grant closure.
Quality management	• Are quality assurance processes being followed (e.g. reports, research practice, team communication)? • Are project changes being addressed or logged?
Research management	• Plan for publication and presentation as part of the project cycle. Acknowledge industry partners/sponsors in any publications. • Ensure students are progressing with their theses and reporting. • Is the research on track? Does it still match the grant agreement? • If the study is not prospering, how should this be addressed?
Risk management	• Monitor emerging risks and address them. • Are safety and health requirements being met? • Is the project conforming to the ethics requirements? • Is the project team working as a cohesive and productive work group? • If a problem arises, review the issue, why it occurred and how to avoid it next time. Document this discussion in the risks log to ensure the same mistake is not repeated again. Consider whether additional training may be needed. Do you need to cover this in future induction processes?
Human resources management	• Celebrate milestones. • Acknowledge team member contributions/achievements. • Ensure all team members are contributing to quality assurance. • Mentor young researchers and ensure they receive opportunities to publish, present, shadow and take responsibility. • Discuss postdoctoral fellowships with students and identify the goals they need to achieve to be well placed for these opportunities. • Conduct regular performance review meetings with each individual. • Set development goals as well as project goals. • Explore how the team can be rewarded for major achievements. • Are staff taking their annual leave? (You can't afford a leave liability at the end of the project and members need time out to renew their energy.)

Table 15.2 (*Continued*)

Phase 3: Project implementation

Knowledge areas	Implementation phase checklist
Stakeholder management	• Be clear about accountabilities and what is expected. • Treat stakeholder relationships as a high priority. • Schedule regular meetings with the stakeholders. • Prepare stakeholder progress reports. • Meet with stakeholders to review progress and provide regular updates on process, publications and outcomes. • Monitor stakeholder satisfaction with the progressive outcomes. • Explore and identify the potential for further investment into new areas of research with stakeholders. • Commence planning for follow-on projects with the stakeholders.
Communication management	• Contact your public affairs/media arm to promote breakthrough outcomes – involve the stakeholders in this process. • Maintain a record of media releases.
Procurement management	• Monitor supplies and ensure resources are sufficient to support the research. • Check for equipment maintenance/upkeep.
Integration management	• Maintain regular meetings with the team. • Check work flows for highly integrated activities: is there a bottleneck that is holding up the research or a potential risk evident? Address it urgently! • Review the project plan at meetings to affirm completed activities and highlight coming project requirements.

Phase 4: Closing the project

Knowledge areas	Evaluation/closeout phase checklist
Scope management	• Evaluate the achievement of the project milestones. What work is still to be completed? • Is there an opportunity to further collaborate with your partners?
Time management	• Review the timeline and plan and ensure all necessary tasks will be completed prior to project closure.
Cost management	• Update the budget summary. Aim for full expenditure of the grant by the conclusion of the funding period.
Quality management	• Prepare the final report for the granting body. • Prepare a final summary of the project, lessons learned, expenditure, time management and other observations to apply to subsequent projects.

Table 15.2 (*Continued*)

	Phase 4: Closing the project
Knowledge areas	*Evaluation/closeout phase checklist*
Research management	• Copy all data files to storage devices. • Ensure confidential records are secure. • Continue writing publications from the project – keep your stakeholders apprised of these. • Monitor project impact over the coming years. • Clean up records and prepare an archival file to be stored in the university.
Risk management	• Summarize lessons learned from the project. Share with other researchers.
Human resources management	• Celebrate the project's successes. • Review the project and identify learning that has been drawn from the project experience. • Ensure staff have expended their leave allocation prior to project closure. • Assist team members in planning for transition to new roles. • Plan for redeployment or transfer of team members to other projects or roles. • Interview project team members on their project experience and suggestions for future projects. • Conduct an exit interview for each team member to review their contributions, affirm their achievements and assist in exiting the project.
Stakeholder management	• Celebrate the project successes. Invite relevant local colleagues and stakeholders. • Canvass stakeholder feedback on the benefits of the project and its potential impact.
Communication management	• Present a seminar on the project outcomes to interested parties and peers. • Develop a media release on the project and its value. • Update your website to profile the outcomes. • Continue to maintain your media archive. • Communicate the project closure to all stakeholders and provide a forwarding contact address.
Procurement management	• Dispose of equipment and resources. • Ensure confidential material is not accessible by subsequent users of any equipment.
Integration management	• Ensure the final stages of the project are understood by all team members and assist them in completing their agreed commitments.

Section 4

Effective engagement

16 The engaged academic

In the early years of academe it can be challenging to know where to put your energy: teaching and research will take top priority as they are the core foundations on which your career will be built (and judged). Engagement is the third pillar of academic work, offering an opportunity to creatively interpret your role and its broader influence. This chapter therefore explores the notion of engagement, encouraging you to build a clear sense of your own strategy and focus. Chapter 17 will offer more practical guidance on engagement strategies to support your identified priorities.

Higher education engagement and academic work

Over the last decades, higher education's relationship with society and other public institutions has shifted towards a stronger partnership based around mutual benefit and obligation. A significant signal for the changing recognition of this interrelationship was the Carnegie Foundation's inclusion of 'Community Engagement' in its classification of universities and colleges (see: http://classifications.carnegiefoundation.org/descriptions/community_engagement.php/).

Academic communities play a key role in shaping society, and in turn are shaped by it. This recognition of mutual reciprocity is increasing as the separation between university and the wider community further diminishes. The term 'engagement' recognizes that the relationship is two-way and based on mutual respect (Sandmann, 2008). Academics have moved from the role of 'expert' to a stronger appreciation that their work complements that of many other knowledge workers in society. In addition to undertaking theoretical work, their scholarly practice is increasingly directed towards supporting applied research and applications of that knowledge to resolve real-world issues or to increase the connectedness of the university with society. Practitioners have become a more vocal force in helping to shape professional practice and the knowledge base that guides future learning and research (Sandmann et al., 2008), operating more overtly as partners in knowledge production. This shift in relationship and dynamics has become better recognized, encouraging a more considered discussion around the role that academics play in translating their teaching and/or research into a wider sphere of influence and applications (Giles, 2008; Thoma, 2011) and, in turn, learning from those interactions.

The concept of *engagement* has been applied to a number of different phenomena in higher education. Until recently the primary emphases related to encouraging student engagement with their learning (Kuh, 2003) and establishing stronger linkages between universities and their broader communities. Many institutions have now established executive roles to guide the development of their corporate identities and engagement strategies. Interesting approaches to establishing connections between 'town and gown' are now being mapped. However, it is only recently that the critical role academics play in achieving engagement has been examined (Sandmann et al., 2011).

Sandmann (2008) identifies various stages that have guided our developing understanding of academic engagement. These can be briefly described as:

- The recognition and progressive definition of engagement as an important academic function.
- The integration of engagement into teaching and research (e.g. service learning, work-integrated learning, applied research, community and participatory-based research).
- The valuing of engagement as scholarly practice (reflecting appropriate scholastic approaches to the role, clear and consistent methodologies, and critical reflection).
- The embedding of engagement as an institutionalized strategy within and across academic settings (recognizing the critical impact that institutional practices have on encouraging academic engagement).

Academic engagement

Engagement is a powerful term that describes a conscious and willing decision to enact roles that increase our impact and influence on the world around us. In the past, engagement was labelled 'service' (Buller, 2010; McBeath, 2010), reflecting a belief that roles additional to teaching and research were primarily an obligation or duty that contributed to the development of the university or its interface with the broader community. This limited view of the function and outcomes of engagement has been a disservice to our sector and to academics in their personal career strategy. Institutional undervaluing of academic engagement has been cited as a strong disincentive for many academics when determining potential roles (Holland, 1999; O'Meara, 2003; Sandmann et al., 2008). O'Meara (2003) identifies a number of factors that impede or encourage academic engagement, including reward systems, workloads, working conditions, a supportive community and perceived impact of the activity. Academics who devote time to outreach and service activities note that they are strongly motivated by their personal values and intrinsic motivation to make a difference (Holland, 1999; O'Meara, 2008).

Why engage?

You may encounter suggestions from colleagues that engagement and service need to be avoided at all costs. This attitude has partly been driven by the sector's long-established practices of judging individuals as sole performers rather than as part of a larger intellectual collective. It also reflects the long-standing prioritizing of research over teaching and engagement – possibly because they are harder to measure and evaluate. This tension between the different academic facets still remains. In this chapter we explore how to employ engagement as an enrichment and enhancement strategy, rather than an additional burden that is disconnected from your other activities. It should be complementary, adding value to your capacity to perform your role.

Effective engagement offers many benefits, including:

- ensuring the work environment operates in a way that supports quality teaching and research
- providing opportunities to interact with colleagues and other worthwhile individuals, thereby offering social and intellectual benefits
- opening up new opportunities to further enrich our teaching and research
- increasing overall meaningfulness and work-related satisfaction
- expanding our social capital, which in turn increases our well-being
- encouraging personal growth in relationship management skills or other relevant capabilities
- enriching the learning experience offered to students, and
- broadening our reach and influence across the university, the sector or society as a whole.

Strategic academic engagement

There will be many times in your career when you will have to make choices as to what activities you will emphasize. As there is only limited discretionary time to devote to engagement activities, think about which options will offer the most benefit and impact. *Strategic engagement* relates to the *conscious* decision to pursue particular engagement activities to benefit society, the university, your academic role, and, ideally, your progressive career enhancement. To some extent your choice may be driven by recognition that you have skills and talents that are best deployed in certain ways. However it can also be useful to view engagement as a way of extending yourself to reach your full potential. Table 16.1 illustrates the main forms of engagement in which academics might participate.

Engaged academics commonly perform two kinds of service to their communities: *university-based service* that supports the core activities of the institution, and *external engagement* comprising interactions with external groups that include industry, community or discipline representatives. The most readily accessible forms of engagement are within the university, offering an opportunity to build networks, learn how the university operates, and establish a profile. You will be expected to contribute to your school or department through being actively engaged in core activities (such as staff meetings, student information sessions, graduation ceremonies and social events) as well as more specific roles that contribute to the development of your department. As your capabilities become better known it is likely you will be invited to assume some

Table 16.1 Types of engagement

Focus	Examples
School or department	• Student support • Course coordination
Faculty or college	• Committees • Working parties • Events coordination
University	• Working parties • Boards • Project teams • Selection panels • Presenting workshops or seminars
Industry	• Teaching projects • Work-integrated learning • Consultancies
Community	• Service learning projects • Consultancies • Board membership • Giving public lectures • Providing development workshops for groups • Supporting community bodies or agencies
Media interaction	• Newspaper features • Documentaries • YouTube features • Website development
Discipline/national/ international roles	• Industry groups • Professional societies • Reviewer roles • Contributing to journal editing • Chairing or assisting a conference committee
Collaborative research with community, government or industry groups	• Targeted, applied research • Collaboration with commerce, industry or the public • Commercialization of research • Research consultancies

more sophisticated roles, such as chairing or contributing to committees and working parties. These are all valuable forms of engagement and will be positively recognized when you seek promotion or tenure. Participation in university activities also increases your visibility and involvement with key people. An established presence as an academic who is willing to support the university can be an important asset when seeking sponsorship for certain initiatives at a later date.

You will need to complement your internal university contributions with an expanding profile beyond the university. Over time, engagement beyond the university will assume greater importance, reflecting your growth in academic stature through more experience and confidence (Sandmann, 2008). The focus of this external interaction may relate to supporting student learning in an authentic setting (such as work-integrated learning or community service) or professional outreach, where research or professional skills support the needs of a community, reflecting Boyer's (1990) recognition of the scholarship of engagement.

External engagement can take many forms, requiring you to think about where you can best position your energies and talents. Do you wish, for example, to build greater engagement with your professional research network? Or possibly you might be working with an innovative teaching programme that relies on strong industry engagement. In that case, it would be necessary to put considerable effort into building your industry contacts and relationships to ensure the programme is a wild success. If you are seeking sources of funding for a research project, your emphasis might be around potential collaborators and increasing your media presence to build interest across the broader community. These are but a few examples.

The win-win-win principle

When weighing up various contribution options it is important to think about the win-win-win principle. This simple concept suggests that any activities you undertake should also benefit one of your key academic roles in teaching or research, and/or assist you in developing further competencies and capabilities that will serve you well into the future. In other words, your engagement strategy should ideally offer long-term career and professional benefits, while also supporting the university's engagement goals and benefiting the community.

When choosing your engagement focus, then, carefully weigh up how this opportunity will assist in:

- developing your skills and capabilities
- strengthening your teaching or research
- providing opportunities to enhance your leadership skills
- increasing the reputation of the university, your programme, your school and yourself, and
- providing an enjoyable and meaningful opportunity for you to interact with people who are interesting and worthwhile.

Engagement is more easily accomplished if the experience offers enjoyment, growth and personal benefits. We are in a very fortunate position as academics to have so many choices from which we can select. The secret is to be highly strategic and to acknowledge the long-term and professional gains we will derive from contributing to others. Engagement is, perhaps, the most complex work of the three academic functions, as it remains at a very formative stage of development. (See The University of Texas Intellectual Entrepreneurship website for a range of fascinating papers relating to academic engagement and its implications: https://webspace.utexas.edu/cherwitz/www/ie/engagement.html#focus).

Translating your work into broader community policy and practice

The growing integration of impact measures to assess academic work reflects the increasing value placed on engagement as a core academic practice (see Table 16.1 above). While it would be most unlikely that anyone would have an impact across all of these domains, it is certainly possible for us to influence at least one of these areas. It is important, then, to think carefully about how your work might ultimately benefit society at large, and to keep this firmly in mind as you build your engagement practices. Notably, the definition and measurement of engagement and impact remains both fluid and negotiable. An important task will be the development of your definition of engagement and the impact you wish to achieve. Where might you focus: Broader public practice? Industry support? A small niche related to cultural understanding? Or the opening of public debate around critical issues that are not yet in the public domain? To some extent, these considerations bring us back full circle to your understanding of your role and identity, and the part you wish to play in linking and translating higher education practice back to the broader community in which you are located.

You might engage with the community for a number of reasons. The most common purpose might relate to your research, with the goal of translating the findings and learning into broader public policy and practice (Duncan and Spicer, 2010). However there are other motivations for interacting with the community. For example, if you are coordinating a work-integrated learning strategy, you would be seeking to build strong linkages and partnerships with likely employers or community groups who could host students (Bolden et al., 2010). Your engagement with these members could lead to further collaborations and interchange around the profession and its development, possible research opportunities and, potentially, discussion as to emergent issues facing the profession. Your engagement with these groups will also create opportunities for you to present to their professional networks, and possibly undertake some consulting or continuing education programmes on their behalf. You will find that many other opportunities will emerge as people get to know you. The challenge is to stay focused on the key priorities, as it is easy to become totally engrossed, reducing time to undertake your ongoing research and other roles. In some cases, you may find that this is work you enjoy much more. If this happens, consider whether your career perhaps needs to be reorientated. A secondment, for example, might be an attractive way to test whether this is a future direction for your career. These are but two examples of the way in which you might interact with the public and broader community. In planning your engagement strategy you will need to identify the particular target groups that best match your expertise and long-term goals.

Getting established as an engaged academic

As Table 16.1 illustrated, there are different forms of engagement, with some requiring initiation by yourself while others will be by invitation. You will operate in two main engagement settings: within the university and beyond. Each requires a slightly different approach to establishing your interactions.

University-based engagement

Universities offer boundless opportunities for staff to be engaged in their activities. In the early stages of an academic career it is important to build a presence and identity within your own school or department. This sounds obvious, but it can be easy to get into the ritual of focusing on the daily teaching and research routines, not the broader work context. Your interactions with colleagues will open up new opportunities and offer deep enjoyment in working with similarly committed people. When volunteering for selected service roles, remember to be strategic: short-term but high profile commitments are very productive uses of your time. Coordinating the student orientation day, taking students on a discipline camp, acting as executive officer for an industry advisory group or coordinating an accreditation panel visit are highly valued activities that will build good recognition from other colleagues. They will give you a chance to meet a number of people, build your reputation for being an effective contributor and provide you with many personal benefits in the process. Ensure the scope of engagement activity remains manageable. This will require careful prioritization and consideration of career implications. It can be useful to take on something that is tired or needs some attention. Aim for a maximum of three years on any particular contribution. This allows sufficient time to demonstrate you have made a difference and enhanced the previous practices, but reduces the risk of being pigeonholed as someone who only has one talent.

Your visibility in the school will reap many benefits, as you will be identified as a newcomer with high potential who can contribute effectively to broader university initiatives. You may be invited to participate on committees or working groups. If you are not getting picked for these opportunities, signal your interest to your head or the convenor by dropping them an email or visiting them. People can require prodding sometimes! Once you are looking for opportunities you will see them in all sorts of contexts.

Beyond the university

There will be many paths you can follow outside the university. It may be that your discipline welcomes new talent on committees, working parties or various other activities. You may enjoy working with industry or other community groups. A media profile where you create a presence through blogs, commentary and topical features could be your path of choice. Others might choose to be more focused on working collaboratively with research colleagues from across the world. While you have many choices, the key challenge will be choosing just a few that best complement your capabilities and will achieve the greatest impact and benefit from your involvement. Engagement with the public, for example, will not suit everyone's personality and capabilities (Holland, 1999). Your mentor could assist in working through these considerations.

Getting known outside your university will take time, energy and focus. There are different approaches you can take:

- Seek assistance from a sponsor who is well established with that particular community.
- Become a member of the appropriate professional groups that you are interested in moving into. You will receive newsletters and other sources of information that will give you an idea about their activities.
- Do your research on the group that you are interested in joining. Attend a meeting or functions to identify the key identities. Make a point of introducing yourself at these functions as someone who is interested in contributing.

As this chapter has illustrated, you will find many different opportunities that might attract you towards wider engagement and scholastic practice. Take the time to map the options and consider which ones attract you and/or will support your career strategy. You should feel both cognitive and emotional attachment, which will encourage full participation and the willingness to expend considerable energy and focus on building those relationships and impact.

The first step is to identify your engagement strategy. The next step, explored in Chapter 17, is to build your engagement practices.

17 External engagement and relationship management

As Chapter 16 illustrated, engagement is an important part of translating our work into the broader community. It is as essential to our academic effectiveness as the other core roles of teaching and research. Successful engagement takes time to develop: it relies on the many skills and capabilities that we build over time. In her study of academic engagement, Holland (1999: 39) noted that many academics find it hard to move into external engagement activities as they lack the skill and confidence to participate. This chapter therefore offers a practical guide on building your academic profile to enable increased visibility, impact and effectiveness in working in this translational space. It emphasizes the goal of establishing long-term and respectful associations where people are keen to continue working with you, explores engagement in terms of relationship management, and identifies some of the key engagement activities you might integrate.

Establishing your professional presence

An important part of generating opportunities for engagement is to make sure that you are visible to the wider community. As an academic it is important to build an effective profile that effectively showcases your talents, capabilities and track record. Some ways in which you can build your presence include:

- Develop a one-page profile that outlines your research interests: why your work is important, how it contributes to the broader community of knowledge, and what particular issues you are addressing. Make sure this profile is easy to interpret by someone who is not expert in your area. Keep this handy for use as required and integrate it into your web profile.
- Create your personal web page as a high priority. Aim for three to four paragraphs that outline your history, interests and areas of expertise. Include a photograph, but make sure it is one you would be happy to have someone use if they are trying to profile you. (It is worthwhile thinking about obtaining some professional photos to have at hand for this purpose.) Your web page should include a link to your publications and a profile of your research and teaching interests. If you are creating useful handouts for your

students that you think have wider value to the larger community, take the time to develop the material into a document that can be shared, either through the university repository or a general creative commons website (see: http://creativecommons.org). The more you profile your intellectual outputs, the greater the chance that they will impact on others. Leaving them languishing on your laptop will generate no gain at all. In effect, your web page and links are your main advertisement, and will be reviewed by people both inside and outside the university. Take the time to keep them fresh and interesting.

- If your university has a research repository, make sure your publications are listed there for external access.
- Your university is likely to offer access to a number of online research communities. Take the time to set up your profiles carefully as these networks can generate some very interesting opportunities. Make a point of updating these on an annual basis as your interests and experience grow.
- Set up a facebook page that relates to your research and/or teaching. Be aware that whatever is on facebook is likely to be visible to others. As an academic, you will need to carefully guard your reputation. Be very conservative about what you profile. Check who is linked from your page and consider how their pages reflect on you. Keep tight control over who accesses what on your page and edit it occasionally to ensure it retains the right message about your character and interests.
- Join key online communities such as LinkedIn and Academia.edu as they will open up some interesting possibilities for collaboration, particularly through their community forums. You might also consider starting a special interest group of your own.
- Twitter feeds, blogs and other forms of social media may also form part of your strategy to influence (Thoma, 2011). They enable ready communication with colleagues around the world. If you commence these forms of engagement, make sure that you can sustain them with regular, interesting updates.
- Newspaper features can be an important way of socializing your research. This requires a very different style of writing from what you would be accustomed to. It needs to be engaging, written in short paragraphs, and readily understood by those who are not expert in your field. Writing in this medium can lead to some interesting opportunities and associations that would not occur if you remained focused on academic dissemination alone.
- Writing for professional magazines is another way of translating your academic interests for a wider audience. Again, this form of writing needs to be informative, conversational and practical, offering guidance on how professionals might adapt your knowledge to their working needs.
- Your university is likely to have a public affairs section that seeks to promote university interests more broadly. They can offer useful advice on building your profile and may have a register to identify specialists who can assist with media enquiries.

- You may also see an opportunity to engage television stations. Make contact with the producer of a current affairs programme that might be interested in your story about your work, community engagement, teaching or students' activities. This won't always work, but it is only a phone call, after all.
- Local community newspapers sometimes feature popular interest stories. Provide good notice, offer a short, accessible written piece to ensure the right information is conveyed, and cross your fingers! Whether you are featured will depend on what else emerges closer to the day, but it can be worth a try.
- All of these strategies are useful, but they need to be integrated into your ongoing profile development. If you generate something of interest, make sure you let your wider network know. A simple message with a hyperlink to the source of information will increase the impact of your strategy.
- Every now and then, check your profile development by searching your name on Google.
- Keep note of your successes in your CV under a heading called 'Engagement'. As noted in Chapter 3, it is also useful to develop a clear and focused strategy as to what you are hoping to accomplish and to document this in your engagement portfolio. Keep evidence of your impact – including emails and other commentaries that have been generated from your efforts (Driscoll and Lynton, 1999).

Networking

Profile building is greatly enhanced by networking. You will have many opportunities to network, ranging from conferences and seminars to more formal meetings with significant people. Many of your professional collaborations will commence as a social interchange at a conference or similar event. While you may then work virtually with your peers thereafter, that first encounter will have a profound impact on their assessment of your potential suitability as a colleague and collaborator. It is important, then, to make the utmost use of any opportunities that arise.

Many of us feel quite tentative about approaching strangers and introducing ourselves at events. Fortunately, there is considerable knowledge as to how to successfully network to maximize the interactive value and minimize the anxiety – as Table 17.1 illustrates.

Treat networking and profile building as core business. It is an essential part of increasing your reach and influence. It will open up significant opportunities and new avenues of collaboration that will take your career forward.

Effective collaboration with other academic colleagues

There will be many opportunities to collaborate with academic colleagues who are located both within and beyond your university. In any one year you might be involved in a number of different collaborations relating to your teaching or research.

Table 17.1 Ten tips for successful networking

1	**Do your homework**	<ul><li>Who is likely to be there?</li><li>Who do you want to meet?</li><li>What do you already know about them?</li><li>What will you tell them about your work?</li></ul>
2	**Pre-prepare some useful topics**	<ul><li>Your role at the university.</li><li>A one-minute sound bite on your research and/or teaching.</li><li>Reflections on the conference or meeting.</li><li>Recent travel or sabbaticals.</li><li>Commentary on current issues (carefully!).</li><li>The weather.</li></ul>
3	**Find someone to talk to**	<ul><li>Someone standing on their own will be grateful for a new companion.</li><li>People you have heard speak.</li><li>People you know (but don't stay with them the whole time).</li><li>People you would like to meet.</li><li>Interesting or positive-looking people.</li><li>Trade fair representatives.</li></ul>
4	**Select a group that will welcome you**	<ul><li>Choose a group that is small enough to include you: fewer than four people is ideal.</li><li>Avoid groups that are tightly huddled: they are sending a message that you are not welcome.</li><li>Look for a space between individuals that you can move into.</li><li>Ask permission to join the group: this may be with a smile or a gesture rather than words.</li><li>Listen for a while before commenting or introducing yourself.</li></ul>
5	**Introduce yourself confidently**	<ul><li>Take the initiative to start conversations by introducing yourself. Useful starting sentences are:</li><li>*Hello, I'm X from Y. I'm so pleased to be here today because...*</li><li>Smile, offering full eye contact.</li><li>Practice your handshake. Extend your full hand; grip firmly without crushing their hand; ensure your hand is clean and not sweaty, and release after two to three seconds.</li></ul>
6	**Ask open-ended questions**	<ul><li>*What did you think about the keynote speaker?*</li><li>*Have you applied these ideas in your research?*</li><li>*If you could change X, what would you do?*</li><li>*What challenges have you experienced in...?*</li></ul>
7	**50–50 interchange**	<ul><li>Aim for a fair interchange between you and other members of the group. Don't dominate: aim to listen instead, interspersing occasional useful contributions.</li></ul>

Table 17.1 (*Continued*)

		• Contribute a maximum of three sentences before inviting someone else to continue the conversation. • Don't talk over the top of other people. • Go with the flow of the conversation rather than trying to direct it to your interests.
8	**Leave gracefully when the conversation is over**	• Exit politely and move to a new group. • Some useful exit lines include: • *It's been great to meet you all.* • *I'm glad we've spoken.* • *I'll be in touch.* • *Good luck with your...*
9	**Stay in contact**	• Take your business cards and have them readily accessible. • If you meet a useful contact, make a note on their business card about the topic you were discussing. • Take the initiative to schedule a coffee or a phone call if you wish to make a strong connection. • Send a follow-up email acknowledging the conversation and discussion you had. • Identify the key people you wish to reconnect with. • If you promised to send something, make sure you do. • Record the person's details into your email contacts directory. Include a note as to what you discussed and how you might work with them in the future. • If you agreed to follow up with a new contact, schedule the task into your diary so that you don't forget. • Invite your network targets to a related event where your work is being profiled or that may be of interest to them. • Send them interesting information about your work if it is relevant to them. • Create a list of people you've met who have similar interests. Put this into your email directory as a themed group. Send them articles/papers/news items that may be of interest to them. Encourage them to share items of similar interest.
10	**Maintain your profile**	• Keep a one-page profile current and ready for dissemination as required. It can be scoped for different purposes. • Prepare an abridged CV that profiles your strengths and achievements. • Develop an outline of possible topics/presentations you might present when visiting another university. Send this to possible hosts, with your abridged CV, if you are going to be in the area.

(*continued*)

Table 17.1 (*Continued*)

- Look for future conferences that are coming up and make contact with the organizers to see if they would be interested in having your papers featured in a guest slot. Make contact as early as possible so that discussions can be had before they publish the final schedule. (While they may not feature you, they will remember you for next time! You will, at the least, be asked to chair a session or fulfil some helpful role.)
- Seek assistance from your mentors and sponsors to gain access to key people.
- Attend professional events regularly.
- Volunteer to serve on state or national communities to become better known by the broader community.
- Schedule key events into your calendar early so that you don't end up double-booked.

Successful collaborations anticipate that:

1   Everyone will contribute to their optimal capacity.
2   Quality outcomes will be achieved.
3   The experience will be meaningful, enjoyable and constructive.

With the limited time available, seek collaborators who can offer a 'multiplier' effect. That is, the time invested in the collaboration generates greater returns than you could achieve by yourself. In most cases this will certainly be evident. Creativity and innovation is greatly stimulated when exploring different perspectives and ideas with a variety of colleagues. They will challenge some of your assumptions and offer new ideas and perspectives. In working with other individuals who come from different backgrounds and contexts you are likely to reach a higher order of thinking that takes you to another stage of conceptual development. Working with colleagues in this way can be both exciting and highly engaging. People who collaborate generally find the interactions generate even more opportunities for productive partnerships and innovation.

Your choice as to who to collaborate with will partly determine how effective those partnerships will be. Relying on those in close proximity will result in lower levels of influence and impact. Collaborations that extend across the world, and perhaps across disciplines, will significantly increase your reach. This broader network will enable productive international exchanges that may become very influential over time. Choose collaborators who bring a diversity of backgrounds and experience. Working with someone who is more experienced will offer considerable advantage. Similarly, identifying someone with complementary skills and expertise will enrich and expand your innovative capacity.

Formal academic collaborations require careful deliberation, particularly if they involve research grants or contractual arrangements. Mutual agreements as to author ascription, roles to be played and management of the collaboration need to be clearly established. The concept of reciprocal obligation will need to be discussed: that is, each academic anticipates benefiting from the association, but in return must contribute to a suitable level. Clarifying what that level entails will avoid many difficult moments in the future. Setting up clear quality assurance arrangements to address poor quality or non-delivery of agreed commitments is a sensible approach to be taken early in the relationship, before it becomes personal.

In some instances the partnership won't work. People who are laggard in their contributions, providing poor quality outcomes, or undermining the group's well-being will be detrimental to the long-term viability of the collaboration. There will be several choices here. If the collaboration comprises a number of people, the group may choose to carry that person, particularly if their name opens important doors. But this could eventually lead to the group's demise. Commence by discussing the issue with other affected members to determine their level of concern. It is much better to raise the issue, explore how protocols are not being followed and discuss how the problem might be addressed. At the worst extreme the group may fade away and then reform without that difficult person. While a cowardly way to address the issue, it is often quite effective, although there will be considerable lost opportunity and potential reputational damage during the traumatic disestablishment period.

Teaching collaborations are another form of collegial engagement. Watch for opportunities to connect with colleagues who are interested in similar areas of teaching scholarship or practice. Likely individuals can be identified at conferences, or through the web or literature searches. These collaborations can generate significant benefits, including joint development of online resources, shared unit materials, textbook authoring, research collaboration on teaching issues and many other opportunities. The process of working with colleagues from different institutions can be particularly helpful in challenging assumptions about how teaching is done and why the subject is taught a certain way.

The principles of collaboration remain consistent across each of these contexts. Mutual obligation, trust and a willingness to learn from each other underpin effective relationships. Developing and regularly reviewing collaborative goals can also assist in building a common understanding of the potential outcomes.

Virtual collaboration

Collaborations often commence because one individual had an inspirational idea that drew others to the partnership. That sense of vision and direction needs to be sustained over time. Ideally, collaborators will be able to meet face to face to establish a strong bond, trust and a clear and coherent understanding of the collaborative focus. With technological advances, most collaborations primarily continue as virtual communities after their initial formation. It is particularly important to keep strong oversight of the group's functioning, as it can lose shape and identity very quickly once the connections are ethereal.

No matter what your role in this virtual collaboration, you can play a significant part in keeping it active and engaged. A risk with virtual collaboration is that members lose connectedness with the group. Unless there is regular interchange with colleagues, the collaboration will assume a lower priority as people tend to focus on what is in front of them. Regular email updates, sharing of new innovations and reminders about looming deadlines are but some of the strategies that can assist in maintaining good flow across the group. Sharing of successes and maintaining regular interactions help to sustain a productive virtual community.

Look for likely forums where the group might reconvene for a face-to-face meeting. These might include conferences where the group has a common interest or, as part of the agreed commitment to the group, an annual meeting where the agenda for the coming year is explored. The cost of travelling to the agreed meeting will be well recompensed in the productive work that is accomplished through the face-to-face interchange. This might also be a good time to bring in future collaborators, stimulating speakers or other sources that might help the group continue to generate innovative ideas. The opportunity to meet might also coincide with visits to each other's work settings.

Given that communications will be primarily via electronic means, keep careful track of them through good record keeping. Set up an email folder and drop any communications straight in so that they can be readily retrieved as required. Online conferencing will be an important part of the group's collective practice, encouraging the engagement of all members. Assigning a specific individual responsibility for maintaining a regular communication process is an important strategy for success.

Virtual collaborations benefit these days from free, accessible cloud-based technologies where documents can be stored for group use. This process ensures that the latest document is sourced while still protecting the intellectual property of the group. Establishment of some core practices, systems and protocols early in the collaboration will also assist in building a common understanding of what is expected from each member.

Working with community groups

When working with members of the public you will need to build sustainable relationships that are based around mutual understanding and respect (Bringle and Hatcher, 2002; Fitzgerald et al., 2010). The following principles will assist in building effective community engagement and relationship management.

- Your work with practitioners and members of the community needs to be based on trust, open communication and an understanding of the mutual obligations the relationship generates. Reciprocity and mutual benefit will be expected, particularly in recognizing the intelligence and expertise that non-academic colleagues bring to the partnership (Holland, 1999).

- Ensure contributing members are publicly acknowledged and recognized.
- Learn about them and their world. Get to know the politics, who makes decisions, how the protocols work and any other contextual information that will assist you in avoiding critical mistakes or misinterpretations.
- Develop an understanding of their language, key concepts and protocols. Avoid speaking academic jargon or words they will not find familiar. Write in a way that reflects their expectations, not yours.
- Explore the questions and issues that are pertinent to this community. Don't make assumptions about what you think they need. Aim, instead, to explore their perspectives and lived experiences. You will find that you gain a much richer understanding of the authentic context and will be better able to relate your work to the solutions they wish to generate. Some of the areas you may find helpful to investigate include:
  - What is the history relating to the issue?
  - How have things changed over time?
  - What is the current opinion around the issue?
  - Who are the key players in this particular area?
  - What has been tried in the past?
  - What impact have past initiatives had on this group's experience?
  - Are there particular 'wins' that the group would like to see achieved?
- Build a core of partners who are keen and capable of providing the necessary support and advice to effectively manage the interactions and overall project.
- Identify the key policymakers or practitioners who are likely to influence the final outcome. Seek their advice and provide information on the project. They may ultimately operate as sponsors.
- Identify the common ground between your preliminary work and the needs of this target community. You will have a range of ideas, but you will only be able to focus on one or two. What is the potential point of connection that will engage this group?
- Prepare well for any meetings or interactions. You'll only get one chance to make a first impression and it needs to be a good one. Avoid coming across as superior. While you may be the expert in your research area, those you are meeting will offer considerable expertise in the real setting, and may see you as remote and ignorant about how things really work. You will find that this is a rich and challenging learning experience. You may, in fact, be the person most changed by the encounter.
- When presenting your ideas and arguments, aim for clear and coherent messages that enable your audience to think about how your ideas relate to their particular experience and needs. Make sure your message is simple and streamlined, and clearly tailored to their particular context and requirements.

You may need to use a variety of communication channels to work with various members of the community. Building a communication plan can be a good approach. This requires you to think about the different audiences you will need to connect with and how they might best be broached. For example, if you are trying to work with a larger group, an open meeting could be a good first step. If you are trying to influence and engage a leadership group, a more interactive session to explore issues and perspectives would be useful.

Relationship management operates strongly from an understanding that the parties need to gain mutual benefit from the association. It will be important that you remember this and create opportunities for regular interaction. Your collaborators will be more enthusiastic and committed if they experience regular communications, opportunities to explore emerging issues and involvement in the development of the collaboration and interchange. A failing of many academics is that they work hard to build a relationship, then ignore the other parties until they have completed the final report, leading to disengaged and disenchanted contributors. This is an extremely risky strategy as it alienates people who might have continued their support for many years if they felt the process was a mutual, respectful partnership. Potentially, that dismissive approach to collaborators may also impede the efforts of other academics seeking to establish similar relationships in the future.

Despite all your best efforts, you may find that your ideas and insights are not yet of interest to the target audience. Some reasons for this lack of engagement might include the political climate, a lack of resources, poor mobilizing of the group, infighting at the leadership level, insufficient development of the necessary infrastructure or many other factors. Don't despair. You may find that people will make contact with you later as their ideas mature or the context changes. In the meantime, you might put your efforts more firmly into building stronger translation of your ideas into the public domain, and further testing those preliminary concepts.

Working as a consultant

As you build your reputation for being a highly knowledgeable and credible expert, you will be offered opportunities to work as a consultant. Some types of consultancies include conducting reviews, evaluations of impact or effectiveness, assessments of business processes or proofs of concepts. You might also be asked to provide educational programmes, develop online products, or work with a team to build its internal capability. This is only a sample of what might be asked of university consultants.

Invitations to be a consultant will generally link to a perceived need by the client. Consultants are expected to reflect that expectation. Their role is not to generate new opportunities for their research or teaching, but to guarantee successful achievement of the contracted outcome. This has particular implications for academics. In the role of consultant you will be devoting considerable effort to resolving a practical issue that may have little perceived value in your academic fraternity. Your recompense is likely to be in the form of intellectual, monetary or applied products, not academic publications. If there is potential for your engagement to support your teaching, extend your research or further the broader reputation of the university then you may consider the investment worthwhile. Funds from these types of activities may also supplement research grants or fund an assistant who can undertake particular roles to support your work. Many academics also use their consultancy funds to support their travel and related research costs. In some instances the contract may include a confidentiality agreement to limit your public conveyance of what has been learned. If this is the case, consider whether the role is an advisable use of your discretionary time, as it will have large implications for your visibility.

When approached to undertake a consultancy, establish a clear understanding about the scope and nature of the work. Some of the issues to discuss include:

- What is the background context for the project?
- What are the main deliverables to be accomplished? A report? A new product? A feasibility study?
- Are there support personnel in the organization or group who can offer assistance?
- What are the intended time frames?
- Has anything like this been tried before?
- Are there resources or historical material that can assist in scoping the project?
- Who holds the authority for the contract?
- What types of reports will they require, and how often?
- Will the funding be tied to particular milestones?

These questions will offer some guidance on the expectations and ultimate outcomes. At this stage, do not offer a cost estimate for the project. As with research proposals, first estimates are rarely accurate and could significantly underestimate time and associated costs. Instead, carefully undertake a review of the requirements and your capacity to deliver before providing an estimate.

Build familiarity with the university's expectations and protocols. It is likely that a formal contract will be developed to clarify the commitments of the various parties. In most cases this contract will be with the university, which will seek protection from litigation and preservation of your intellectual property rights. Your university may have particular policies relating to working as a consultant. Some will see it as an important part of their broader engagement strategy, while others may view it with suspicion, arguing that it is simply an opportunity to bring in more money. This is, of course, a very insular view of the benefits that will be achieved and demonstrates a limited understanding of the scholarship of engagement.

Cost your time very carefully. Academics often underestimate the amount of time and energy they will need to devote to the consultancy project. Face time with the client, which may be the basis for costing, will probably require threefold or more investment beyond that. Costing should therefore take account of these considerations. As a broad rule of thumb, consultancy fees would probably be three to four times the actual salary of the academic. Additional costs and overheads, including university infrastructure levies, may also need to be factored in.

Once the contract is signed, be vigilant in keeping to the agreed commitments. Academics can be poor in keeping to their contractual agreements as they regard time as fluid and renegotiable. From the client's perspective this is not the case. They will be expecting deliverables at agreed points in order to meet requirements for budget delivery and expenditure. There may be large numbers of stakeholders awaiting the outcomes, and subsequent expenditure and policies may also be pending on the project results. Thus, consultants have critical obligations in meeting contractual agreements and ensuring the expected outcomes are accomplished. The project management checklist relating to stakeholder management in Chapter 15 offers a particularly valuable overview of the processes that can enhance your relationship management with clients. It can also guide you in the process of managing your consultancy with respect to good time, cost, and risk management practices. Demonstrating a businesslike approach will ensure you reach a successful conclusion and encourage ongoing associations with these clients.

Creating and sustaining industry connections and research collaborations

Industry connections and collaborations operate in a similar vein. After building a profile that attracts potential collaborators, establish a clear understanding of what each party will bring to the partnership. Industry partners may offer know-how, connections, resources, access to data and information from their work setting, and/or applied knowledge that will assist your research. They will anticipate receiving regular communications, opportunities to influence the research, and benefits from the findings, products or outputs. Regular communication and ongoing meetings will also serve an important function in maintaining a two-way interchange. It will be necessary to clarify the role of each member, so that there is no misunderstanding around expectations and commitments. Your own professionalism, enthusiasm and commitment will be an important factor in keeping the relationship active and engaged.

Industry partners will expect their contributions to be acknowledged and valued. Any media features or publications from the collaboration will need to clearly state the role each group has played. Allow extra time when planning publications or other elements of the project so that approval can be obtained from the corporate group that oversees the project alliance. Contractual arrangements can also take much longer, given that they will involve the university and the partner's legal advisers.

Are you an effective, engaged academic?

Engagement and collaboration needs to be fed regularly. It is not something that you can expect to flourish if you are passive or absent. It will require regular cultivation and evidence that you are a valuable partner in the collaboration. Treating the partnership as a priority is the first step. Being prepared and well organized for any meetings is also critical.

You may need to acquire more extensive skills to contribute to critical collaborations. The engagement process will offer many different challenges and may require expertise in leading consultative processes, developing websites, preparing technical reports, facilitating workshops, designing events, negotiating, presenting to different audiences and through different mediums, or working with the media. These new skills will take time to acquire and may require additional development.

An occasional stocktake of your collaborative effectiveness can be a useful exercise. In speaking of networks, Cross and Thomas (2011) recommend a number of principles that could equally well apply to collaborations. They suggest four strategies that have been adapted to collaborations, and are outlined below.

1 *Analyse*: Review your collaborations and consider how well they are functioning. Are they offering good return for the effort being expended?
2 *De-layer*: Identify collaborations that need to stop. These may include relationships that deplete rather than excite you.
3 *Diversify*: Look for new collaborations that might enrich and extend your capacity. People who have complementary skills or high energy can be very productive targets.
4 *Capitalize*: Regularly review your strategies to make sure you are maximizing your opportunities.

Collaborations can be undermined by a number of factors: academic egos, lack of resources, an absence of leadership, hidden agendas, cynicism and many other barriers. Your role will be a critical one in contributing to a positive and effective collaborative community or partnership. It is worthwhile seeking feedback from fellow collaborators as to how well you are playing your part. The process of reflecting on your collaborative contribution can offer important guidance on the areas where you might improve. It may also make the difference between a collaboration that strengthens, and one that starts to languish. Given the amount of effort it takes to establish these partnerships, it is critically important not to have any wither on the vine.

Section 5

Strategic advancement in academic settings

18 Academic leadership

Many academics fail to develop a strong understanding of their leadership style and its impact on others. This can have immense consequences for how they operate and the well-being of any group they lead (Ramsden, 1998; Fullan and Scott, 2009). While it is unlikely that you will be assigned formal leadership duties in your first few years, you are likely to fulfil many leadership roles from the very first weeks that you work as an academic. The term *distributed leadership* recognizes that you will be asked to assume a range of responsibilities to guide others and ensure good outcomes – whether as a course coordinator, research supervisor, laboratory manager, project coordinator, or in many other capacities (Ramsden, 1998; Avolio et al., 2009; Bolden et al., 2009). In this chapter, then, we will explore some of the emerging principles of academic leadership and how you might construct a more conscious, reflective approach to your roles and responsibilities. The goal of this chapter is to highlight the critical importance of seeing leadership as another facet of academic work, that is also values-driven, not primarily outcome-focused.

Defining leadership (and management)

Table 18.1 offers a simple overview of how leadership and management are pictured in many textbooks. Using a travel analogy, leadership is the process of identifying the preferred direction, encouraging people to come with you, and keeping them motivated to stay with you once you begin. It relies strongly on communication and vision-setting to build a common understanding of the journey and its destination. Management, on the other hand, is the process of making that vision a reality. In terms of the trip, it involves good planning, resourcing, and establishing the processes that will be applied to make sure the group arrives safely at its destination. Leadership and management are complementary skills that need to work together (Yielder and Codling, 2004). A leader without good processes and structure will soon lose any followers. For the purposes of this chapter we will simply refer to leadership, but you will see that both components are integrated. (In more senior leadership roles you might have access to a professional manager. As a distributed leader, you will need to reflect both elements of the role.)

In your various positions you will be expected to enact different leadership roles. These might include: chairing committees, groups or projects; coordinating a research group; designing a new curriculum; serving as a deputy on a project; assisting with a change leadership strategy; sitting on an external board; working on an editorial

Table 18.1 Leadership and management

Leadership	Management
• Sets a clear vision that clarifies what needs doing and what the final goal will be. • Engages people in discussing and building the vision and associated goals. • Sets clear goals and targets. • Communicates regularly with followers. • Builds a constructive and supportive environment where all members can flourish.	• Establishes the systems, processes and protocols to facilitate achievement of the established goals. • Allocates resources equitably. • Offers clear feedback that assists in achieving high performance. • Monitors quality assurance and outcomes to ensure effective delivery of the desired outcomes.

committee; and many more. Each of these contexts will require careful consideration: how can you connect with and engage others and then ensure goals are well progressed?

As academic leaders we operate from a collegial focus (Yielder and Codling, 2004; Garrett and Davies, 2010). This means that the community being led expects to be effectively and respectfully engaged, included in decision-making and supported through the process. This is not always easy. Because academics are primarily rewarded for their individual performance, involvement in collective activities may be largely under-recognized. The individual's willingness to contribute to the collective good will influence their personal decision to be involved. You will see this in your work settings: some people will be generous contributors and others will be 'lone rangers', focused on their own priorities and largely ignoring their wider community.

In your leadership roles you will seek to influence others, and in turn will be influenced by them. You won't have all the answers, though you will hopefully have put time into planning and preparing for the exchange between group members. The interchange will be dynamic and reciprocal. The group requires a strong sense of shared purpose, supportive strategies to provide emotional and social assistance to each other and opportunities to share perspectives and give voice to issues.

Understanding your leadership style

Over many years there has been a gradual coalescing of understanding about leadership and how we express it. Lewin et al. (1939) identified three primary leadership styles: autocratic, laissez-faire and democratic. Since that early scoping there has been considerable development of more intensive theories and understanding as to how we interact with others. These three styles remain in currency, even so. (See, for example, http://psychology.about.com/library/quiz/bl-leadershipquiz.htm/ to test your leadership style.)

The three styles are very evident in academic settings. *Autocratic* or aggressive-defensive styles are leader-centric, aiming to direct the group's efforts towards a particular outcome and brooking little dissent. Autocratic leaders often use aggressive techniques to direct individuals, based on high competitiveness, power plays, perfectionism and opposing others' ideas. These bullying behaviours reduce the followers' confidence and can lead to very tentative, anxious members who lack confidence and operate at suboptimal levels. Many research leaders overuse this style as they operate from a task-driven approach, given their superior knowledge of the research domain. They can be regarded as bullies and may experience high turnover of the team. Autocratic approaches are not well suited to university workers, who draw on their knowledge to achieve work goals. These leaders may be viewed as argumentative, arrogant or volatile.

Laissez-faire or passive-defensive leaders may be people who feel insecure or uncertain about their context and authority. Some behaviours they may evidence include rigidly following the established rules, seeking approval from a higher authority or avoiding making decisions in case they are wrong. Groups led by these leaders tend to achieve little: they sit, paralyzed, waiting for someone else to make a decision. In these contexts, it is likely that a frustrated splinter group may emerge, taking action to get things moving. Leaders who operate in this manner will experience disrespect and factionalism, as they are offering little sense of direction or guidance.

Lewin's democratic leadership style is now described as *constructive leadership*. These leaders are positive in their focus: setting high goals and a vision that offers a clear sense of direction. They nurture their members, encouraging them to achieve their full potential, and ensure the group is inclusive and welcomes all members. There is a very strong association between constructive leaders and high performance – and it is particularly evident in academic communities. University members want to be engaged, included and respected. This style of leadership reflects a values-driven approach, based on accountability, morality, openness, ethics and transparency. It better matches the collegial setting in which your leadership best operates.

Learning to be a constructive leader

As with teaching, an important principle in being an effective leader is to be self-aware and reflective. What impact did my actions have on the group? Are we losing focus? How long is it since I caught up with everybody to see how they are progressing? If there is a problem, am I addressing it or avoiding the issue? Am I modelling positive, passionate engagement with the project? Are my communication practices effective, or do people's eyes glaze over when I talk to them? Am I building a consistent and effective approach to the decisions I take? Is everyone getting a chance to input into the process?

It is helpful to recognize that leadership will be a lifelong journey. Each time you take responsibility for a group or project you will have new opportunities to acquire greater understanding about how you operate and how your approaches impact on others (and outcomes). There is a vast array of literature that could be investigated, but one of the more effective ways to build your leadership capabilities is to participate in a leadership development programme that offers a chance to reflect deeply and clearly about your goals and processes. Programmes of this nature also offer a rewarding opportunity to build more diverse connections and identify powerful models.

Leading work groups

Group leadership is a role you will very likely assume quite early in your career. For the most part, the purpose of the group will be to achieve a particular task or goal. Members will be keen to get their commitments completed to a high quality and in the most efficient way possible. This is a very different focus from a longer-term group, which may seek to build more social engagement and time to learn about each other and 'play'.

Listed below are some principles that can assist in creating a positive experience for the group.

- Develop clear procedures and ensure decision-making and processes are systematic and clearly articulated.
- Ensure the group has a good understanding of issues and sufficient information on which to make decisions.
- Establish some clear protocols as to how interactions and discussions will be managed.
- Aim for a cooperative and respectful interchange between members.
- Ensure everyone is able to participate in discussions. Invite quieter members to share their views.
- Keep the group on task. If the conversation drifts, bring it back to the topic.
- If there are disagreements, provide an opportunity for each party to share their perspectives in an open, non-judgemental setting. Don't take sides. Your role will be to encourage each party to see different views and understand where the others are coming from.
- Keep the group processes flowing. Record outcomes from meetings and share them back as quickly as possible. Identify who has agreed to take responsibility for new tasks, and follow up on them promptly.
- Encourage openness and sharing. If a member is finding it hard to meet their commitments, the group will be better protected if members can share their difficulties.

Kellerman (2008) notes the critical importance of followers. She offers a typology of group members, ranging from 'isolates' and 'bystanders' to 'activists' and 'diehards'. Using an engagement continuum, she offers a range of ideas about how to bring people into groups and communities more fully. This is particularly important in work groups, where people may be included because of their functional skills rather than their desire to contribute.

As an engaged member or leader of the group you can personally enact a number of different roles that will support its development and the engagement of other members – particularly in meetings. Constructive roles include idea initiator, information or opinion giver, topic gatekeeper, consensus tester, encourager, energizer, progress monitor, celebrator, strategist, goal setter, information seeker, deadline setter and meeting convener. These are all important contributions to mobilize the group's resources and ensure it accomplishes its purpose. Unfortunately, you will potentially have to deal with a number of subversive behaviours that impede the group's efficacy. For example, you may encounter people who are avoiders, dominators, attention seekers, detractors, sarcastic responders, topic jumpers, personal anecdote raconteurs, nit-pickers, negative talkers, manipulators, and the list goes on... In these situations it is important to reaffirm the principles on which the group operates, bring the group back to the task, and open space for others to share their views. If a member is particularly destructive, take time outside the group sessions to discuss the impact. It may be necessary to *uninvite* them if they are particularly toxic and unwilling to change.

A useful model that can be applied to group dynamics is drawn from neural linguistic programming. Called *Perceptual Positions*, it encourages us to extend our reflection beyond our own responses to explore the other person's experience, and at a third level, the overall group dynamic (see: http://www.nlp-now.co.uk/perceptual.htm). This increased sensitivity to group dynamics can greatly enhance the group's functioning.

If you are working with a group of people for an extended period of time your role will focus more intensively on building the team. Teams are characterized by a common purpose and shared vision, concern for the well-being of each other, willingness to engage in robust discussion without taking offence, determination to work towards shared goals, and desire to create an environment that works for each individual. Honesty, trust and shared responsibility are core principles that need to be encouraged across the team.

When leading a group, you will find that the role you play will shift over time. In the first stage of development you will spend considerable time in shaping its understanding and sense of identity, and in designing suitable systems and processes. You will need to set clear expectations as to productivity and performance and encourage the development of group and individual capabilities and reflection. Over time, the balance between these tasks will recalibrate as processes become well established and group membership coheres. This opens up room for innovation and an increasing focus on strategy. Keeping the group fresh and engaged will be important goals for the long term.

In the next sections we will look at two particular leadership contexts that you may encounter in the early stage of your career: leading research or teaching teams.

Leading a research team

Your discipline will have a major influence on the type of research group you may lead. They can range from small investigative teams of two or three people to large laboratory groups where a programme of research is undertaken. There are some useful guides that can assist you in managing a laboratory-based team (Bushaway, 2003; Cohen and Cohen, 2005; Guberman et al., 2006). These guidelines emphasize the importance of understanding your research environment, being aware of your responsibilities as a scientific leader, building a vision as a leader, and maintaining your team. This can be a difficult role, given the need to maintain your own continuing trajectory as a leading researcher while also enacting research leadership. Using good management practices can reduce the time you lose in dealing with problems and crises. The project management checklist outlined in Chapter 15 provides many helpful hints as to how to manage a project-based research group. It emphasizes the need to operate from three perspectives: the project, the group's well-being and long-term strategy. These principles can be effectively applied to any research group.

Denney et al. (2011) offer a valuable overview of the different functions research leaders fill, identifying various leadership and management roles that are critical to successful research group outcomes. When leading a research group you will grapple with two conflicting priorities: getting the job done and encouraging the growth and development of each individual member. Recognize that each individual is seeking a career path that requires demonstration of growth and enhanced skill (Hobson et al., 2005). Your role as a research leader will be to seek opportunities for this development to occur and to encourage the individual to take advantage of them. If you are supervising research students you will need to ensure that they are prepared for future roles as well as the current requirements to graduate. Generosity in creating a strong publication culture and building the group's profile are important research leadership qualities.

It is very easy in research communities to focus primarily on executing the research project. But you will gain much by encouraging the group to take some time to be innovative and creative. These processes are not mutually exclusive to good research execution, but they are often seen as taking time away from the business of research. If you can create opportunities for your group to think about the future and identify possible paths that new projects might take, you can generate some exciting new possibilities that will keep your research alive and moving towards some more discursive futures. The secret is in balancing these particular strategies with the ongoing process of getting the agreed research completed.

Interestingly, the environment that best stimulates innovation also encourages high productivity. People function best under constructive leaders who encourage high performance, visualize clear goals and engage members as active and positive contributors. The opportunity to interact freely and openly with other people is a fertile ground for new ideas. The courage to acknowledge mistakes and to learn from them also offers the basis for both innovation and productive learning. Clearly, this requires a leader who is open to suggestions from others and keen to draw from the talents of all members of the group.

Leading a teaching team

Teaching teams face somewhat different challenges as they generally comprise individuals who are undertaking their roles in conjunction with many other responsibilities. This can lead to some personal tension around where energy and effort should be allocated. As a teaching leader you will play a large role in setting the tone, guiding the group directions, establishing standards and principles, and monitoring quality assurance. It is likely that you will be the main contact for students: a role that can be very demanding at peak times in a semester. This means that you will need to plan well ahead in preparing any guidelines or materials for your group. Teaching leadership cannot operate as a last minute strategy. That approach will result in chaos, disgruntled team members and many more students seeking individual advice from you.

While you may be the main driving force behind this group, it is important to recognize that each member of your team has particular skills and talents that they bring to their role. If you can harness this expertise your educational product will be vastly improved. Bring the group together regularly and encourage their input and guidance.

Quality assurance will be a big focus. Students anticipate receiving a consistent educational experience, regardless of who is teaching them. As a teaching coordinator you will need to monitor the effectiveness of the teaching being delivered and the quality of student outcomes that are evident. Regular review and evaluation of educational quality needs to be part of your management role. If you have members who are not performing effectively, particularly with respect to their teaching, it will be important to speak with them about the feedback you are receiving. This can be a very confronting experience the first time you encounter it. However, it is one of your core responsibilities as a coordinator. The issue needs to be handled with great sensitivity. Specific and targeted feedback on the problem area offers the greatest success in addressing the problem. You may also offer to provide some peer feedback, coach the individual or encourage them to observe others who are teaching in a similar area. Your teaching development staff and discipline head could assist you with this challenge.

Curriculum development is another form of teaching leadership that you may experience early in your career. In this context you are likely to take responsibility for investigating possible innovations or benchmarking against comparable curricula. Take time to fully investigate the options and strategies that might be adopted before identifying the most desirable solution. People often jump straight to the solution that they think is the most logical instead of canvassing a wider range of options. It is important to seek an optimal solution not just the most accessible. Convening a group that offers diversity of opinion and experience will be particularly helpful in reaching a good outcome. It also increases people's engagement with the change process and encourages them to become part of the solution, rather than resisting change in the future.

Effective academic leadership

This chapter has continued a thread that you may have detected throughout the whole book: the need to be a conscious leader who balances the complex demands of your work role with self-reflective practice that encourages growth and ongoing learning. Your leadership activities will comprise a number of different foci (Vilkinas et al., 2009). You will need to deliver good outcomes across the various responsibilities you are allocated; monitor the effectiveness of your initiatives and take action if they are not operating effectively; take care of others, and encourage them to reach their full potential; generate new opportunities, and increase your reach and profile within your school and beyond. These outcomes require a very conscious consideration of how you operate and the impact your behaviours have on others.

These skills are not learned overnight, and will require gradual development through workplace experience and other learning opportunities. Table 18.2 offers you

Table 18.2 Key leadership capabilities

Model good leadership	• What you model provides the most powerful demonstration of the values on which your leadership operates. Every action and attitude will be a cue to others.
Understand the political context	• Your mentors can guide you and explain how the context works. Be aware of who the key players are.
Shape strategic thinking	• Develop a clear understanding of your university strategy and consider how you can support those goals.
Encourage the involvement of others	• You will need to acquire a range of strategies to engage group members. These will range from building a common vision to drawing on the expertise of each individual.
Influence others	• Influence is a large part of leadership. It relies on good relationships and your credible enactment of your role.
Demonstrate reflective leadership practice	• Apply a reflective lens across your various activities to test your effectiveness, impact and credibility.
Learn new behaviours	• Regard leadership as an ongoing learning process, and regularly set new development goals.
Communicate effectively	• You will need many forms of effective communication. These will include written and verbal, small and large group, face to face and virtual. These skills will take time to develop.
Delegate effectively	• Delegation is a critical skill, but one that many people find hard to learn. People will accept responsibility for tasks if they have a clear sense of the scope of work and the role they are expected to play. Clear communication is therefore an important part of delegation.
Be sensitive to others	• Be empathetic to others' situations and issues. Provide support where you can and value their diverse perspectives.
Develop the team	• Focus on building your team so that it is high performing, confident and competent. Provide opportunities for members to develop further.
Encourage participative decision-making	• Encourage diverse opinions and perspectives when making decisions.

Table 18.2 (*Continued*)

Manage conflict	• Deal with conflict promptly. Avoiding the issue will only make things far worse. If the problem has already escalated, seek professional help from your Human Resources section.
Contribute to/conduct effective meetings	• Your meetings will range from formal structured meetings to less formal, collegial collaborations. You will need to acquire skills in handling these diverse settings. Observe the chairing of meetings that you attend. Identify useful models and read about meeting protocols.
Implement and monitor systems and processes	• Designing robust and efficient systems greatly facilitates team performance. This is particularly important when the team is not co-located or there is membership mobility.
Check for risks or pending problems	• Risk management is an important element of good leadership. Anticipating likely problems reduces the likelihood of them occurring, as precautions can be taken in advance.

a checklist of some of the key leadership skills that can assist you in this journey. It can be useful to target these as a matter of priority and to seek regular feedback on your effectiveness so that you can monitor your progressive success.

Recognize that leadership is a life journey: every one of us continues to reshape our persona and roles through the experiences we encounter. Feedback from others, monitoring of impact and reading about leadership can be important forms of learning that will guide your ongoing reflection and increasing effectiveness as an academic leader. Leaders are made, not born. We have the capacity to make a significant difference to the communities we serve, hopefully as constructive, reflective leaders.

19 Operating effectively in academic cultures

The word 'culture' is used to describe a complex mesh of attitudes and values that underpin the communities in which we operate. It comprises common philosophies, beliefs, ideologies, attitudes, values, expectations, assumptions and practices that we experience in our interactions with other colleagues. Culture has a very big impact on the way we operate and the degree to which we can achieve our best outcomes. It has a critical impact on academic well-being.

The dominant messages that university staff perceive and generate are significant cultural influences, sending particular cues about what is important and how things really work in that community. The cues can vary from the policies and reward systems that operate (e.g. research is most important), through to the stories that are shared around the water cooler or coffee machine. The real practices and values that are enacted provide a clear message as to what matters and how we will be judged in a particular community. The culture that is supported will be very evident to you as you watch the dynamics, observe the rules and regulations that are applied and hear the anecdotes about different things that have happened in the past. By understanding these various artefacts and patterns you will be more able to sieve out the principal cultural messages and start to reflect them – if you so choose. However, it is important to consider whether this culture is true to the values and principles by which you wish to operate. Thus, the cultural fit between yourself and your community will be an important aspect to monitor and assess.

Academic cultures are interesting phenomena: many academics experience minimal supervision or sponsorship, including little initial guidance or encouragement when they enter a new community. Others experience intensive cultures that are highly competitive, while some will experience highly managerialistic settings where they are rigidly controlled. In this chapter we will examine some of the cultural experiences you may encounter and how you can manage them – or at least better understand what is happening.

Flourishing in academe

In his aptly titled work *Flourish*, Martin Seligman (2011: 24) outlines a well researched model for living a full and rich life that ensures personal well-being. He identifies five key elements that contribute to well-being:

- positive emotion
- engagement
- relationships
- meaning
- achievement.

As knowledge workers who seek to be fulfilled and fully engaged in our roles, we operate best when we can experience all of these elements in our work setting. *Positive emotion* reflects our capacity to perceive life as pleasant and satisfying. It includes our capacity to feel safe and secure in the roles we undertake. *Engagement* relates to the capacity to be immersed in an activity. As academics we enter into this state through our research, writing and possibly our broader interactions with the public. *Relationships* encourage social connectedness, and affirm your relevance to others. *Meaning* relates to feeling that your life has purpose and value: that it makes a difference. And, finally, *achievement* reflects the desire to accomplish something – whether to meet personal goals or more altruistic outcomes. This framing of well-being has been widely adopted and recognized as offering an important insight into how people flourish. It helps to explain why some work settings are places where you can thrive and others may impede your health and progress. If you are in a setting that allows you to work in a conducive environment, where you can find meaning, work on tasks that keep you engaged, accomplish your goals, and build enjoyable relationships, your overall well-being will be greatly encouraged. The culture that you work in will have a large impact on these different elements.

The ideal work environment

What do we seek in an ideal work environment? As intelligent, self-managing individuals we enjoy high levels of autonomy and appreciate a constructive and supportive setting that offers sufficient sponsorship to allow us to pursue our dreams. We generally appreciate being recognized for our achievements and hope to be given opportunities to stretch and grow. A collegial atmosphere that encourages and supports each other provides a rich dynamic from which we feed. Leaders who model constructive behaviours and operate with an inclusive management style bring out the best in their communities. In these situations it is likely that there will be high engagement by most members, providing regular opportunities to excel. Unsuccessful risk-taking or innovation will be seen as learning points, not punished.

The leadership of a community has a high impact on the type of culture that is generated. Constructive leaders strive to encourage full engagement of their members. They place considerable importance on modelling good leadership, recognizing its considerable benefits for the academic community. In reviews of effective academic leadership the word *generosity* is often noted, reflecting recognition that these leaders operate for the good of others, and sometimes sacrifice some of their career potential to create an ideal environment for others to flourish. These are the settings that we all try to find when we are looking for new workplaces. Unfortunately, it is not always possible to find utopia. Instead, we generally settle for something a little less salubrious, where many of those characteristics may be somewhat evident, but not fully.

Academics are high-end knowledge workers (Debowski, 2006). Their primary activities focus on knowledge critique, generation, exchange and dissemination. This requires access to suitable resources and sufficient space to undertake the different knowledge activities. To be fully effective we need to operate across the broad domain of knowledge work: investigating the *what, how, why, where* and *when* of our particular specialism and work context. We rely on a reasonable degree of discretionary time and the capacity to deploy our energy in a way that allows us to be as productive as possible. In recent years we have seen increasing difficulty in finding that discretionary time as higher workloads and more complex roles have required attention. For example, those with teaching responsibilities have experienced a growth in administrative functions that must also be supported. Researchers have also found that there are increasing ethical and governance requirements that must be reflected in their roles. Some academics have claimed that universities are moving towards managerialistic cultures that do not value the academic role. However, the situation is much more complex, reflecting the evolving context in which the sector sits.

Heads of schools and deans face an unenviable task as they balance the university requirements to be financially and resource responsible with academic staff desires to be well resourced and sponsored in their quest towards excellence. The role of head is even more vulnerable given that many will return into the collegial setting after a period of working in the head role. This can be a factor that leads to laissez-faire leadership where decisions are avoided because of concerns that there may be repercussions in the future. Heads often spend considerable energy in trying to support the myriad demands that come their way. As one of many needy people, you may find that the level of support is not as much as you would hope. If this is the case, it is important to understand why your head is unable to offer the full sponsorship that you thought was reasonable. What they may provide, however, is encouragement to find other resource avenues and to connect with sources that might provide that level of support. Fortunately, as individuals with high motivation and the capacity to mobilize our own resources, we can work within more constrained settings. (Interestingly, resource constraints may also stimulate increased collaboration and innovation.)

Academics are fortunate in that they do have some degree of choice as to where they deploy their energies and who they choose to interact with. There are always some people who are going to be more challenging. Hopefully you won't need to work too closely with them. To optimize your work setting, identify people who are constructive collaborators and colleagues and those who ideally should be avoided.

Difficult work communities

Sometimes academic communities can be difficult work settings, particularly with the increasing push towards higher achievement and tightening resources. As finances tighten, leaders may corral resources and deploy their power base to focus activities on key priorities. While this is recognized as a powerful leadership strategy (Pfeffer, 2010), it can be overused. Autocratic processes designed to promote a particular outcome can reduce individual autonomy, particularly if people are regulated as to how discretionary time is deployed or required to account for their activities in minute detail. This leadership practice, called micromanagement, can be very distressing if you are seeking a more creative environment in which to work. This leadership approach generates high uncertainty, risk aversion and, potentially, ill health. Certainly, it is not conducive to well-being or to optimizing academic outcomes.

If you have entered a difficult work community you may find your approach to work does alter. You'll be likely to minimize your contact with other individuals and to focus on the work that you can control. You may move into a more defensive style of operation where you protect your reputation and outputs as best you can. The energy you expend on protectionism will be considerable. You may find yourself interpreting people's motives in a less trusting way and looking for the catch, even when you are treated generously. A risk in this situation is that you may become part of the problem rather than part of the solution. Finding individuals who demonstrate a positive outlook and support their colleagues will be an important survival mechanism. If they are not readily apparent in your immediate environment, look further afield and find colleagues within or beyond the university who might offer you the sustenance you cannot obtain locally. This would be a good time to look for university committees and external engagement that allows you to develop your career in a more congenial setting.

In some cases, people may not be aware that their practices are causing distress. Many universities select leaders because of their research track record. They may be much more in tune with tasks to be done rather than people and their responses. The rapid transition into complex academic leadership roles can offer limited opportunity to learn about leadership. In some instances the first time leaders realize they are seen as bullies may occur when a complaint is lodged in the university system. This can be an immense shock. These individuals may also avoid participating in leadership development programmes because they lack self-awareness as to their leadership effectiveness or needs. It is helpful to understand this background, as it makes it easier to see why these situations occur. When a leader is ineffective, the whole community will feel under siege. However, collegiality through adversity can be a strong bonding influence and it may encourage some deep friendships through supporting each other.

When bad things happen

A more challenging scenario occurs if you are singled out for bullying. It has been estimated that one in five people will experience bullying at some time in their life (Field, 2010). Recognizing that you are being bullied is in itself a traumatic journey for any individual – no matter how old or experienced. Fortunately, bullying and its practices are now much better understood and more overtly addressed in universities and other workplaces.

Bullies target individuals for a variety of reasons. They may feel threatened, wish to undermine that individual so that they are not competition, desire their resources, or fear their limited skills or capabilities may be exposed. In some instances the bullied individual may just be different. In other cases the bully may be a sociopath who has risen through the ranks by removing anybody who could possibly expose them (Babiak and Hare, 2006). (In fact, many academics find it hard to differentiate between robust academic interchange and bullying. They interpret the concept of academic freedom of speech as meaning they can say anything to anybody.)

In the academic world it is very easy to undermine a person's reputation. Commentary around their performance, innuendo about the quality of their research, questions around their teaching effectiveness… It becomes very easy to imply that someone is ineffective. The challenge is that you may not know this is being done until it is too late. Because we operate primarily on soft measures that draw on interpretation or qualitative assessments it can be easier to judge someone harshly. To protect yourself against this form of bullying, make sure you regularly document your successes and develop your evidence of achievements. More importantly, share these with sponsors and mentors on a regular basis and meet with your head of school or other significant disciplinary colleagues to discuss your progress. Make sure you are not invisible, as that will make you an ideal target.

When people are bullied they often accept responsibility for causing the bullying, internalizing the blame. This can cause great distress, considerably reducing coping skills and productivity. If you are being bullied you may spend hours at night agonizing over emails, mulling over what you said and feeling anxious about what the next day will bring. You will have several choices: tolerate the bullying, leave, or address the issue. The first option is only a short-term possibility as you will eventually find your health and well-being considerably affected. The second option is traumatic but will at least give you respite. It may mean that you have to abandon particular career opportunities that were important to you.

The third option has a number of benefits. First, it allows you to take control of the situation and reduces your disempowerment. Second, it is likely to stop the bullying as you will no longer be demonstrating the behaviours that allowed you to be targeted in the first place. Third, by standing up to your bully you are also demonstrating the values and courage that will help to turn the culture around. You will need to be very courageous. While universities have policies on bullying, their handling of these matters can still be clumsy. This is one of the reasons many people delay making a complaint. The following set of steps offers you some guidance on how to address the issue. You will note that obtaining some additional support is a very important part of this strategy.

1   ***Recognize you have a problem but are not the problem***. It can take some time to move past the point of feeling responsible for the problem. It is worthwhile reading some of the key works to get a better understanding of what is happening and why you have been targeted (Babiak and Hare, 2006; J. Clarke, 2007; Field, 2010). It is highly possible that you are seen as the

most talented, and therefore challenging, colleague. Regaining your sense of worth and value is an important step in combating this difficult experience.

2 ***Speak to the perpetrator***. Sometimes bullies do not realize they are operating in a way that is perceived to be abusive. Sharing your perceptions and the way their behaviours are making you feel may arrest the problem at an early stage. To start, review your university policy so that you understand how those behaviours are seen in the university policy. This can offer you some words and guidelines on what is acceptable or not. Rehearse what you are going to say and pick a time that will give you sufficient opportunity to explore the situation with the bully. (You may decide to bring a third party along as a support.) Be very clear about the particular behaviours that are causing you consternation, including some specific incidents that you can outline.

3 ***Seek help***. Your university is likely to have some form of assistance programme that is conducted by an external agency. Don't be afraid to seek help. It will be very important to you to explore the issue with an objective listener. Your counsellor can offer assistance and advice on some of the strategies that might work for you. Another source of assistance might be a coach. These individuals will work more intensively with you and offer you strong support through the tough times. You may also know of people who have been through a similar experience. Make contact with them and ask to meet. All of these people will offer important emotional support.

4 ***Use your mentors and sponsors***. You will need to use your mentors and sponsors in a fairly strategic way. If they are associated with the bully tread carefully. Sociopaths, for example, are very expert at manipulating people who they see as influential or more senior. Your account of being bullied may seem bizarre if that individual's experience of the bully is at odds with your story. Instead, maintain a strong relationship with your mentors and/or sponsors: reviewing your career, current progress, avenues for development and career goals. Your mentors or sponsors will be important voices in challenging any malicious messages that are being circulated.

5 ***Don't play the game***. A major part of a bully's strategy is to whittle away your confidence piece by piece. Email messages will be used to increase your vulnerability. Ignore them. The bully will lose interest if they cannot get a response from you. If you are being undermined in meetings the first response is often to go quiet or to get angry. If you feel strong enough, you might challenge your bully in a way that shows you have control. For example, a smile and shake of the head in disbelief can show that you recognize the unpleasantness of that individual. They will look foolish and you will have alerted others to the toxic approach that is being employed. These strategies are best discussed with your counsellor or an expert so that you feel confident in managing any likely interchanges.

6 ***Show courage and resilience***. The way you deal with your bully will partially determine how they approach you. If you are forthright and maintain a stoic and courageous approach to your interchanges, you may find that the

pressure reduces. People who stand up to bullies and are not cowed by their actions become less desirable targets.

7   *Wait it out?* If you think the individual is likely to move on to another victim or a new work setting, you may choose to wait it out. You will need strong resilience and considerable tenacity to hold yourself together. Make sure you keep your evidence of good performance in case you need it, as waiting passively may result in some difficulties. If you are located on the margins and find you are limited in your opportunities within the university don't be afraid to look for more adventurous creative spaces outside. You may discover some very new and exciting opportunities await you (Debowski, 2009).

8   *Lodge a complaint*. This is a serious decision that may be necessary if you feel your actions have led to very little improvement. To make your complaint stick, you will need to have good evidence of the bullying. A dossier that maps the interchanges, captures the emails and documents various incidents will need to be retained. Whenever you experience a difficult encounter, keep an accurate log, date and sign the record. This may be necessary if you have to take the problem through to more formal proceedings. This will be a difficult experience but a necessary one to hopefully stop the behaviours. If there are several people who might make a complaint it can be useful to take action collectively. You may find that your complaint will encourage the person to think more carefully about their actions. While some might be sociopathic, many more are just lacking self-awareness and emotional intelligence.

One of the key qualities academics need to develop is resilience. Bullying is an extreme form of academic behaviour and hopefully you won't experience it in your career. But chances are, you will. Don't be afraid to deal with it. And recognize that it does not relate to your self-worth, but instead reflects poorly on the bully and their inappropriate responses and actions.

Change and renewal: supporting university reforms

Your university may be undertaking some significant reforms in its efforts to remain competitive. In times of change, academics can be part of the solution or part of the problem. In some institutions they resist new ideas, undermine strategies and obstruct leadership efforts to create a new work environment. In others, they are active agents in leading the change and reform processes. In this section we will explore some of the reasons for these differences and discuss how you might become a force for innovation and change.

Change is a necessary part of university life and likely to escalate in the forthcoming years. There are various levels of change, ranging from simple process enhancement to major structural reform that affects people's work identities, roles and functions.

Academics' identities are strongly linked to the teaching and research that they undertake. When academic work or structures are targeted for review, there can be strong emotions generated. The destabilization of traditional practices and patterns may lead to some very agitated and negative responses as people work through transitionary processes.

Universities do not always handle these change processes very effectively. They often focus on redesigning processes and systems instead of engaging the community that will be affected. People respond better if they can see that the changes will benefit their students, their work context or other elements that are important to their particular values. They need time to come to terms with the change, to let go of the old history, test the new concepts and then transition to a new beginning. Because people make those transitions at different rates, the process of change can be lumpy and unpredictable. As an individual with less historical attachment to the past, you are likely to be more open to moving on early in the process. This provides you with an opportunity to think about the future and how it might be used to create some new and engaging options.

Leaders are very appreciative of positively engaged staff. This is a good time to establish your identity as an enthusiastic emergent leader who demonstrates the qualities that will support new innovations. You may see opportunities to contribute to working groups, consultations, reviews of options or other strategies that are being put in place. You can make a big difference by accepting the need for change and helping to move the community forward.

This chapter has highlighted some of the ways that culture can impact on your academic role and work context. Although it explored some of the more difficult situations that you may encounter, it is important to recognize that these will be exceptions, not the rule. Most academic communities offer space for you to grow and maximize your opportunities. However, the chapter does highlight the value of viewing your work setting with an analytical focus to guard against potentially toxic situations. If you work in a poorly led community, you will hopefully feel more confident about your ability to cope and progress your career path. Most importantly, understanding the leadership context can also encourage you to contribute to your community's development in times of change. This provides you with yet another opportunity to make a difference and to establish yourself as a key leader in the community.

20 Effective career and priority management

One of the last traditions to be reshaped in higher education is the academic recognition and reward system. We have seen massive changes in teaching and research; increasing casualization of the workforce to accommodate shifts in demand; aggressive attraction and recruitment of students; shifts in student expectations as to the quality learning experience they require and need; more focused concern for academic engagement; expanding requirements of academics; university marketing and branding and the financial and management strategies underpinning university work; ... and yet, very little shift in how academics are recruited, appointed, managed and recognized for the roles they play. Part of the reason for this inertia may relate to the preservation of long-held traditions by those who have come through the system. Partly, it may relate to the international pressure to be research-focused to demonstrate success.

No matter the reason, it will need to change as the diversity of academic work continues to grow and the existing generation of baby boomers finally surrenders to retirement, leaving way for a new generation of academics who have entered a very different world to that experienced by their older colleagues. New academics will straddle two worlds: the established, predictable and buttoned down world of a traditional enterprise, and an embryonic, somewhat unpredictable sector that will need to review and modify its practices to better support a precious and limited supply of future academics as those sitting in senior roles gradually fade away.

Universities are experiencing an increasingly dynamic work setting, where the types of academic work are expanding and employment conditions are becoming less predictable. In this work setting, effective career management can be more challenging but also more creative and opportunistic. This chapter explores some of the new theories relating to career management, offering some useful perspectives in which to position your planning for the future. It will show that careers are likely to take many turns and that your preparation for serendipitous chance events, multiple career paths and maximizing your talents will be critical factors in preparing you for whatever lies ahead (Raabe et al., 2007). The final section of the chapter will explore priorities and their management to achieve a balanced and healthy life.

Mapping a career in higher education

Academic career paths have taken some interesting twists in the last few years (Gappa et al. 2007). An increasingly competitive and resource-constrained higher education setting has resulted in more diversity of career options. Academics may, for example, move into research-intensive, teaching-intensive, teaching-research, support or adjunct roles. They may stay in academe or move between industry and academic settings. The globalized context encourages work across national boundaries, particularly when pursuing promotional roles. Tenured roles are diminishing and contract-based employment is more common – at both junior and senior levels. A particular challenge relates to the variability of conditions and functions of key roles, particularly for postdoctoral researchers, where career tracks and roles are highly diverse (Akerlind, 2005). Industry–university research work has also changed markedly over the last decade (Dany and Mangematin, 2004; Dietz and Bozeman, 2005), challenging traditional assumptions about research roles and careers.

These shifts are part of a bigger global context: the world of work has notably changed, particularly with respect to the roles and expectations of employer and employee (Wilson, 2010). The concept of a psychological contract that guaranteed employer and employee loyalty based on mutual benefit (high-quality work and loyalty in exchange for long-term security) has moved to a more pragmatic realization that each party seeks quite different outcomes from the partnership (high-quality work in exchange for career enhancement and enriching work contexts). The expectation that the employer will monitor and manage career advancement no longer holds currency: it has been clear for some time that career management is the responsibility of the employee, and the predictable, hierarchical progression up a career ladder is less assured (Baruch, 2004).

A challenge for higher education institutions is the dogged adherence to traditional structures that were established for a very different time and academic context. Promotional paths generally emphasize a single career channel that supports traditional teaching/research profiles, despite the growth of more diverse roles and contexts. There has been some softening of performance expectations to accommodate diversity or those who have had limited career opportunities due to child rearing or part-time roles. However, the gender differential at more senior levels remains significant (Mason and Goulden, 2002; Earle Reybold and Alamia, 2008). The preponderance of women filling transient roles and casual appointments (Earle Reybold and Alamia, 2008) is a phenomenon that remains concerning. This pattern highlights the need for university employers to be more conscious of the growing diversity of employment structures that must be more effectively managed.

It is likely that academe will change markedly in its work structures and arrangements over the coming years (Marginson, 2000). People may shift across different role compositions and employers as opportunities arise. Certainly, they will need to consciously prepare for their future options – particularly through clear understanding of current and future expectations, well planned career management, strategic use of mentors, regular professional development and monitoring of opportunities (Adcroft and Taylor, 2009). We can either see this era of transformation as depressing, or as an era where the inertia of many years will finally be challenged, encouraging changes to internal university practices and assumptions about work.

Career management in a changing context

Each of us will experience a unique career path that is influenced by our personal choices, interpretation of the organizational structures and culture in which we operate, opportunities that occur at suitable moments, and the particular capabilities and expertise that we bring to our roles.

There has been considerable development of theories around career management, reflecting the changing environment in which professional work occurs. Careers are now regarded as dynamic, fluid constructions that will generate multiple employment opportunities (Baruch, 2004). They encourage a sense of identity, facilitate relationships and associations, offer meaningful work and provide paid employment. The focus of traditional career management on working towards a single aspirational target (such as promotion) has moved towards a more discursive emphasis on developing a career that offers multidirectional paths to achieve enrichment, life balance, autonomy and meaningfulness. As academics we are at the forefront of this shift towards 'intelligent careers' that adapt to evolving conditions (Arthur et al., 1995).

Many emerging career theories and models are very pertinent when considering academic career management. Table 20.1 offers an overview of some of the dominant theories that now guide our understanding of career management. They highlight the various considerations that you may bring to your analysis of your context and possible options.

This brief glimpse into the new view of career management theory highlights several key principles that relate to your academic career context.

- Think carefully about the main reasons and goals that you seek to achieve through working in academe: they may relate more to values than traditional career recognition.
- Prepare for a range of career possibilities that might support your personal aspirations and targets.
- Take responsibility for your career and monitor its evolution.
- Recognize that there will be different channels you might pursue, and that these will potentially change the future you achieve.
- Integrate career planning into your regular strategies relating to teaching, research and engagement: they all help to build an intelligent career that assists your goals.

Planning your intelligent career strategy

In Table 20.1 the key elements of an intelligent career were outlined. In this section, we will apply those principles to guide you in planning your own strategy. To succeed

Table 20.1 Career management theories applicable to academic work

Theory	Components
Intelligent careers (Arthur et al., 1995; Jones and DeFillippi, 1996)	• *Know why*: developing an understanding of your motivations and reasons for pursuing a particular career • *Know how*: acquiring the professional and academic capabilities that are necessary to do the required work • *Know who*: building networks, relationships and sponsors; identifying helpful people • *Know what*: monitoring opportunities, threats and risks, requirements for the role • *Know where*: sourcing opportunities to enter the field, develop your capabilities and progress your career • *Know when*: judging the best timing for decisions and actions
Career resilience (Waterman et al., 1994)	• The capacity to bounce back from upsets or disappointments
Protean careers (Hall, 1996; Briscoe et al., 2006)	• The career is driven by the individual • A values-driven career orientation guides career planning • The primary goal is psychological success, not vertical success (salary, promotion) • Employability is more critical than job security • The career goals change and adapt to match the individual's growth and evolving context
Multidirectional career paths (Baruch, 2004)	• Careers can take many forms and move horizontally, vertically or downwards • Upward mobility is more limited due to flatter structures or ceilings on opportunity • Career planning emphasizes professional challenge, merit and past achievements

in your chosen career, you will need to be proactive in building a strong understanding of what you seek from your career and how you will invest in that perceived strategy. Career planning is a very critical element of a successful career. It best operates as a conscious cycle of reflection and evaluation, setting goals, mobilizing resources, identifying opportunities and reviewing your overall effectiveness and profile. Knowledge of your motivations and yourself, the career context and your likely sources of support all underpin a successful strategy. The following sections offer some useful points of reflection to assist you in this process.

What is academic success?

This book has explored the concept of academic success, as it is currently measured and evaluated in most institutions. You may have a different view of what you seek to achieve from your role and engagement with the sector. The list below may assist you in thinking about your main motivations for working in higher education.

- Contribute to the nation's productivity agenda.
- Leave a legacy in your discipline.
- Establish a name as a leading commentator in your field.
- Build a high-level profile as a researcher.
- Win a Nobel Prize.
- Gain patents and other forms of intellectual excellence.
- Promote better practice in your discipline/the sector/your specialist role.
- Obtain stable employment.
- Access a reasonable income.
- Be recognized as a leading figure.
- Enjoy opportunities to learn and grow.
- Undertake rich and meaningful work.
- Work in an innovative and engaging employment context.
- Encourage students.
- Make a difference to society.
- Work flexibly.
- Operate in a research-rich setting.
- Acquire new skills and capabilities.

There may be other factors that you might add. Consider which would be your top five motivations for wishing to be associated with the sector. As reflected in the Protean Career Model, these motivations may be very different to the sector's espoused reasons for working in academe. Keep these in mind and think about their implications for the types of roles you might seek. Are you targeting the right opportunities?

Know yourself

An important part of career planning is to be very clear about your strengths and talents, acquired skills and capabilities, and future potential. Take the time to think about what you bring to your role – not just in traditional academic track record terms but in your personal approach to work and your own unique personality. There are various ways you might undertake this self-assessment. Some of these are listed below, offering interesting perspectives on how you work and your overall suite of capabilities.

- ***Are you a 'high potential' employee?*** If you are a significant performer who ranks in the top 3–5 per cent of your cohort, you may fit this category

(Ready et al., 2010). Features of high potentials include a capacity to deliver credible results; master new skills and expertise; operate as a role model and exemplar; and support the organizational culture and values. Your drive, quest for excellence and capacity to innovate can be both a strength and a risk. Your employer will have high expectations, and you will need to keep the momentum up while maintaining a suitable balance to ensure you last the distance.

- **What are your signature strengths?** (See: http://www.authentic happiness.sas.upenn.edu/Default.aspx) This website offers you an insight into the five factors identified by Seligman as critical to a life that enables you to flourish. (You may also enjoy working through the other tests to more fully explore characteristics that will support your well-being.)
- **What is your preferred work context?** Free online versions of the Myers Brigg Type Inventory (MBTI) offer you a quick insight into your dominant work preferences and the type of work setting you may prefer. (For example, see: http://www.developandgrow.com/lifecoach/blog/free-on-line-myers-briggs-personality-tests/).
- **What are you key talents?** Identify the top five talents that you believe you bring to your role/activities. Now ask your colleagues to note the top five talents that they see in you. Do they identify something different to what you have noted? Why? Are they having trouble identifying five? Perhaps this offers a cue to think about the degree to which you are connecting and engaging with your colleagues?
- **Review your CV and academic portfolio**. What are the main messages they offer as to your skills and capabilities? Have they really captured the richness of your talents, strengths, achievements and expertise? If not, redevelop them to better showcase what you bring to your career. (Buller (2010) offers a useful overview of building an effective CV.)

Appraise your career strategy and impact

Regular appraisal of your career strategy enables you to review and sculpt your profile so that you are attractive to a prospective employer and better positioned to move towards identified goals. When thinking about your competitiveness, it is useful to think about how employers view candidates. While there will be some predictable assessment areas (such as your research and teaching track record), you will find that they are also looking for points of difference: the things that distinguish you from others. It is here that your engagement strategy may stand out. While engagement may be less acknowledged in traditional promotional systems, it is highly valued by employers looking for new members who demonstrate good citizenship. A track record that shows a capacity to work across different communities and to successfully undertake different roles will be an added asset when you are seeking new avenues of employment.

A useful exercise is to map your career according to its depth and breadth. On a large sheet of paper, draw a large 'T', with a thick trunk and head. Figure 20.1 offers

⬅ **Breadth** ➡

Committees (workplace, university, national, international); working groups, leadership roles, project responsibilities; achievements; consultancies; collaborations; position papers; community roles; editorial committees; reviewing; boards etc…

Depth
⬇

Specialist expertise
Skills
Knowledge
Research methods
Broader capabilities
Talents
Strengths

Demonstrated by:
Grants
Publications
Invitations
Collaborative partnerships
Citations
Impact factor of journals
H-index
Translation
Patents
Keynotes, workshops, seminars
Roles
Teaching
Engagement activities

Figure 20.1   The Career T

a list of some of the elements that you might integrate into your figure. These are described below.

In the trunk of the T, summarize your track record in terms of your competencies, knowledge and skills – that is, your *depth* of expertise in your specialist area. As a starter, list the areas of expertise that you have developed. (Consider process and methodological skills as well as content knowledge.) Now review your evidence of success across your different areas of specialist work. For example, if you are building a research track record, you might identify the number and types of publications, grants, citations, student projects or any other elements that contribute to your emerging profile. If you are teaching, you might focus on the areas in which you have taught, the types of students and methodologies that you have applied. If engagement has been part of your focus, identify the skills and expertise that you have developed through that work. These might include chairing committees, undertaking community consultations, overseeing complex projects, and many other areas. Thus, the trunk captures the many areas of expertise and the depth of knowledge and skills that you have developed to date.

If you feel your depth is thin, you may need to focus on accessing more development and learning opportunities.

The head of the T maps the *breadth* of activities and roles you have undertaken in your work, professional activities and beyond. Employers look for candidates who show a range of personal qualities that can be translated into their work setting. These include the capacity to work in teams, contribute to the diversity of activities that occur, take on leadership roles, manage projects or groups, support the discipline or university, and many more. In the top bar of the T, then, list all of the experiences you have engaged in to date. If they are sparse, think about how you might supplement them. (Chapters 16 and 17 would be worth rereading if this is the case.)

This exercise highlights the importance of building a strategy that ensures progressive development of both depth and breadth. Recognize that this complex strategy won't be developed overnight. Regular mapping in this way will offer useful guidance on how you might best position your efforts and focus.

Take the time to think about your career strategy on a regular basis. The goal is to build a repertoire that offers a number of interesting angles as to your capabilities. Depth and breadth will both be important in consolidating your expertise and competitiveness.

Scan the horizon and options

A fascinating element of higher education is that as you work towards a particular career path, others may be operating in parallel, offering different but equally enriching options. It is important to regularly scan the horizon to keep abreast of emergent opportunities. If you see a different but interesting role, review the advertised criteria and consider how you might present your capabilities. Be open to taking a fork in your career journey. Some of the most worthwhile careers can emerge from unplanned opportunities.

Bright and his colleagues investigated the impact of chance events on career strategies (Bright et al., 2005; Bright et al., 2009). In some instances, these events may be a series of compounding factors that are outside your control, but force you to take stock and consider your options. Not all chance experiences are positive, unfortunately. While distressing and potentially debilitating, negative experiences may unleash considerable creativity and energy as you work towards alternative options. Understanding your strengths, talents and motivations will assist in scoping a more constructive path forward.

When considering various employment options, carefully evaluate the employer as well as the role. Universities have very diverse approaches to developing their organizational setting. Their mission, values, strategic orientation, principles, particular emphases on teaching, research and/or engagement, funding base, likely workloads, role expectations and the level of support they provide once you are employed will all influence an academic's work context.

To remain competitive and attractive, look for useful developmental programmes, mentorship, enrichment roles, and possibly more substantive leadership opportunities (Ready et al., 2010; Fernandez-Araoz et al., 2011). Some questions to consider include: What support will your prospective employer be able to offer? Will you be expected to be at your desk in working hours (face time) or will you be judged on your overall performance and effectiveness (Sullivan and Mainiero, 2008)? (This could be an important issue if you are managing a young family.) If you are considering working overseas to advance your career, how much support will the employer provide as you acculturate?

As noted in Table 20.1 above, *knowing when* is an important consideration. Opportunities may come along but, for personal or professional reasons, be poorly timed for you. While it can be reasonable to not put yourself forward in that case, consider carefully before letting a highly desirable opportunity go. If it is right for you, those other issues will resolve themselves, particularly if you have support. The opportune moment may never happen. On the other hand, personal priorities such as family can be much more critical concerns at times, despite their potential career-limiting impact.

Marshall your resources

The intelligent careerist ensures a strong career base is established and that other sources of support are employed to assist. Drawing on your networks, sponsors, development opportunities (both formal and informal) and other avenues, keep building your profile and visibility to set yourself up for success. If you are dutiful and biddable, operating as a much relied on 'hidden treasure' you will be unlikely to flourish in this tough world, unfair as it seems. You will need to move yourself into a more visible space and to build your sponsors to take your career forward. Being aware of the situation is the first, important step.

Evaluate your progress

Regular review of your career strategy will be critical to your success. Each year should see you building more breadth and depth, a stronger profile and a wider network of supporters. Setting clear career goals and moving towards those goals in a considered but energetic way will ensure you are seen as a star performer. Key supports in evaluating your progress will be your mentors.

An important part of your evaluation will be seeking feedback from your supervisor. There are two forms of feedback that you might solicit. The first might operate as formative feedback relating to particular tasks or activities you have undertaken. Feedback of this nature often occurs near the event and can assist in refining your approach. Summative feedback will be more formally scheduled and may reflect your university's aim of providing regular reviews for all staff. The discussion will explore your holistic performance over a period of time, and will offer an invaluable opportunity to evaluate how well you are developing. Treat these reviews as important opportunities to monitor your successes, and to discuss your emerging goals and further support your university and supervisor might offer. You will gain a more complete understanding as to how you are performing compared with other colleagues and may receive guidance on areas that now require further enhancement. The exchange with your supervisor can also alert them to your evolving development needs and desire for increased sponsorship. Maximize the opportunity! Be well prepared and offer a strong and confident vision of your goals and directions.

Career phases and transitions

Your career management strategy will need to change as you progress. In the early stages of your career, you will need to focus on building your capabilities, profile, relationships and capacity to operate efficiently and effectively. Mentors and sponsors are critical strategies to help you navigate through this time, particularly if you are also finding it difficult to secure predictable employment.

After the first seven years you will be deemed to be an experienced academic who should be moving into leading groups, teams and projects. The skills you require to undertake these roles draw on leadership and management capabilities. The complexity and range of responsibilities that you assume over those ensuing years will depend on your particular focus. Some individuals will move into laboratory-based leadership, while others may emphasize university or teaching leadership. At this point, one of your challenges will be to maintain your academic track record and profile while leading others. This is a stage where some individuals reach a point of 'middlescence' – that is, their research has become stale and they lack the resources or initiative to reignite their focus. This can be avoided by maintaining a close watch over your track record, goals and priorities, recognizing that the early goals will not be suited to the long term. We all need to change and evolve to match the shifting contexts in which we operate, and to build on our established expertise.

By the time you move towards a senior role, you will be thinking carefully about the legacy you leave behind. This may be in research, or teaching, or engagement, or all three. The profile you have developed will be very much a product of years of planning, dedicated focus and determination. While some chance events may have played a role in bringing you to this point, the majority of the credit will be attributable to your own careful nurturing of a stellar career.

Diversity issues

There is considerable discussion as to the ways in which gender and race may influence career opportunity. Academic diversity remains challenging. If you are from a diverse background you may find that you are not being offered the same experiences and opportunities as your mainstream colleagues. This oversight is not necessarily intentional, but it does mean you need to be more active in monitoring your career landscape. Mentors and sponsors will be a very critical part of your strategy and profile building will be even more essential, as you may not be noticed as readily as you should be.

We do make choices that can significantly influence our options. Babies *will* impact on an academic career (Mason and Goulden, 2002) – your focus and priorities will shift and you may choose to compromise your choices in order to accommodate your family or personal needs. These are personal decisions that support our broader values and life goals. Universities are striving to better acknowledge these complexities by judging academic performance in terms of 'achievement relative to opportunity'. However, this remains a troubling accommodation and still requires more debate, testing and consideration.

Women sometimes wait longer to seek promotion or recognition – they like to be sure they will be successful. If this fits you, be adventurous. Don't wait to be 100 per cent sure – test the waters much earlier. You may be successful, much to your surprise! At the least, you will find the experience educative and may be offered valuable feedback in readiness for a second round.

It's not for me. . .

Academic work is challenging. There is very little room for taking a few years out and then returning to the fray. The constant need to maintain profile, effectiveness and impact may be more than you wish to invest. In some instances, the opportunities relating to your specialism may be limited in your particular region. If this is the case, there are many other roles that will productively use your skills and expertise (Denholm and Evans, 2009). Don't be afraid to move laterally or externally to explore life outside academe. You may return with many new skills and capabilities. On the other hand, you may also find that your academic grounding has offered you a perfect basis for a new, alternative role. This interchange between academe and general work settings can be a productive and engaging option. In weighing up the choices, think about what you want from your intelligent career. Don't be afraid to move away if you do feel this competitive world is not for you.

Putting it all together

Career planning must ally with effective execution of your plan. Time and priority management ensure your key intentions are translated into actions. Although we have already covered many principles of working effectively and efficiently in the teaching and research contexts, this final element will explore the bigger picture: of building a composite strategy so that you flourish across your complex world – professional, personal and other.

Before exploring specific strategies, there is an essential preliminary step: be clear about your critical priorities for the coming five years. What do you wish to pursue in your personal and professional spheres? Building an academic profile? Being a great parent and partner? Keeping physically fit and healthy? Establishing your publication profile? Gaining that prestigious fellowship or grant? Achieving recognition as an excellent teacher? Clear priorities will help to set your direction and focus. You then need to devote sufficient strategic attention to achieve those goals. The following tips may assist you.

- Prioritize your work so that you make time for your major goals. We spend considerable time on less urgent, unimportant tasks. Make space for your priorities. Prepare a list of your top achievement targets for the coming week and integrate time for them. Be firm about your availability, putting a sign on your door to indicate you are involved in a complex task and would appreciate not being disturbed.
- Set high performance goals. Don't go for low fruit. Think like an athlete and be ambitious, aiming for a personal best that is well above your norm. You may not reach your target, but you will achieve more than you would otherwise have accomplished.
- Structure your time to spend your high-performance period each day on your key priorities.
- Keep lists of anything you need to do. This will prevent you getting distracted by things you have missed. Then prioritize your lists, identifying the key actions that need to be taken. You may find it helpful to group particular activities (such as phone calls) together.
- Take breaks. We are not machines. We need space to regenerate. Aim for high-intensity periods that are then rewarded with some space for thinking and relaxing. In fact, if you need it, keep a pillow in the office for a power nap!
- Learn to say no. It is important to keep a manageable portfolio. Remember to focus on win-win-win so that your activities support your professional, career and personal needs.
- When you are considering a task, critically review its worth. Is it a good use of your time? Will it help you achieve your long-term goals? You will need to be very focused. There will be many opportunities. Select those that help build breadth, depth or profile, while also supporting the university and its mission.
- Set time limits on tasks. Don't seek perfection: 'satisficing' is fine.
- Don't procrastinate. Use your available time to maximum effect. Learn to focus and switch into your work rapidly.
- Use your technology; don't let it abuse you. If you are ruled by your email, it is time to stop letting it control your life. Turn off the sound and check your email several times a day, not by the minute. You will find that you have much more intensive opportunities to do work.
- Stay fit and healthy. Your body needs to be here for the long haul.
- Make time for your loved ones. Treat them as a priority and give them focused attention. If you need to work on weekends, block out other spaces that will be 'theirs' – without compromise. You will find that the partitioning of your discretionary time will make you more efficient when you switch back to your work roles, and your family will appreciate the dedicated time.

- Don't aim for perfection. It will be one of your largest stressors and will impact on your health. Recognize you are human and accept that you can't control every element of your world. If you don't reach your targets, so be it. Forgive yourself and move to the next goal. Your academic journey has many years ahead.

This chapter has offered some different perspectives on career and priority management. In thinking about your career, recognize that there is not a single path in academe. You have many potential journeys. The choices you make will determine which paths become the most readily travelled. Once you have determined your priorities, keep them in focus and give them sufficient time to be enacted. Regular checks will be important to monitor your degree of success. Above all, aim for balance to ensure you are not just a brilliant academic, but also a person who others enjoy being around.

21 Enacting your strategy

The concept of academic identity has been a strong motif throughout this work, positioning you as an active participant in shaping your destiny and building your capacity to operate as an effective, reflective, consciously engaged scholar and professional academic. You have been offered a range of perspectives to assist your optimization of your talents and opportunities. This final chapter provides a holistic perspective that will further assist you in being strategic in managing your career. It emphasizes the need to review and manage your actions and growth with care and deliberation, deploying all of the avenues for support that are available.

There are three key areas of activity that are necessary to activate your career and build a range of viable futures as an academic, as depicted in Figure 21.1. The model illustrates three levels of activity that will assist in your career management: building your academic toolkit, mobilizing the support and other resources within your local university setting, and then acting in a strategic and focused manner. Each of these areas will be reviewed, highlighting the importance of being self-aware and reflective, pursuing challenging goals and priorities, and creating a setting where you can flourish (Seligman, 2011).

The academic toolkit

The academic toolkit encompasses the key capabilities, knowledge, skills and attributes you bring to your role(s). Over time it will deepen and broaden (reflecting the Career T concept discussed in Chapter 20), as you extend your experience and expertise into new contexts and expand your repertoire. The toolkit draws on your specialist disciplinary knowledge base and the professional skills that you employ in your various academic activities and functions.

Experience

Experience is an important educative process that helps us to build new insights about ourselves, extend our repertoire and expand our deep knowledge of different academic contexts. This experiential base is enriched by all activities that you undertake: teaching, research, engagement and leadership. As you interact with new roles, different work contexts, students, colleagues and members of the community you will build a stronger understanding of academic work.

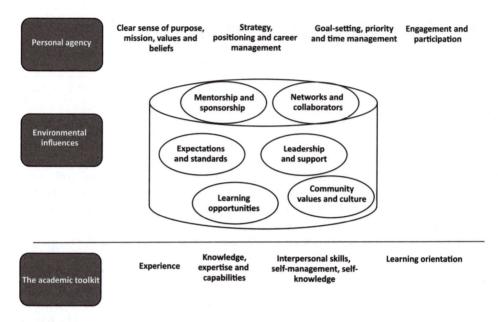

Figure 21.1 Academic identity

In building your track record, think carefully about the breadth of roles you are integrating and how they build a coherent but expansive story around your potential and proven capacity to operate across the broad domain of academic activity. Seek opportunities to work across disciplines to see the commonalities and differences. Consider how you have enacted scholarship and reflective practice in these different roles – particularly in critically assessing your effectiveness, impact and learning from the experiences.

Knowledge, expertise and capabilities

You are embarking on a long journey where your toolkit will need ongoing supplementation. As you develop your foundational skills, you will see new learning paths opening up, particularly as you build expertise in an area. Keep track of your overall knowledge base to monitor how your skills are evolving. Your teaching role will need ongoing enhancement, adding to your repertoire of strategies and skills. Your research will continue to challenge and extend you, particularly when supervising research students or through collaboration. Monitor your repertoire so that you can articulate your depth of expertise and capabilities. This will be a major differentiator when you are seeking employment, recognition or advancement. The Career T exercise can help map your progress.

Interpersonal and relationship management skills

Academic work is strongly allied to the capacity to interact effectively with others. Your career will necessitate the development of alliances and effective relationships with a huge range of people and groups. Students, colleagues and community members anticipate respectful and effective communication. When interacting with different individuals, practise the principles relating to *Perceptual Positions* to think about how others perceive a particular situation. Developing high levels of interpersonal skills will be an important asset. You need to be someone who people *like* to work with, who is respected and valued. As you develop these skills, you will find that people are seeking you out, rather than having to orchestrate opportunities.

The development of these important skills will take time and practise. You may feel tentative initially. That is quite normal. The presence of a sponsor when moving into more challenging opportunities can be a helpful support. A particularly useful strategy may be to rehearse scripts ahead of time so that you feel prepared for possible eventualities. If the thought of working with others fills you with trepidation, consider investing in a coach who can lead you through small challenges to build your confidence.

Learning orientation, reflective practitioner and scholar

Academic work is predicated on learning. The whole profession operates in an evolving, unpredictable and dynamic context. To thrive, you will need to be agile: seek opportunities to develop new capabilities, expand your experiential base and challenge your existing assumptions. A strong learning orientation will be an important asset in your career: it will ensure you remain current and, potentially, at the top of your field in your skills and knowledge. At no point should you feel that you have reached your goal of being 'the expert'. In fact, it is the quest to *be* expert that helps to focus your continual improvement. Set new learning goals on a regular basis, and evaluate your progress. At the least, an annual review of your achievements and evidence of growth will help you to assess your effectiveness in building new capabilities.

In tandem, building a reflective view of your work and impact is an essential professional practice. As the individual most closely associated with the roles you play, you must build a strong critical lens as to how you are performing. Take the time to review your effectiveness and your impact on others. This may require support from experts to build a deeper understanding of the indicators of excellence to guide your assessment. Reviewing your performance to identify new areas of learning and personal challenge informs your development plan. Remember, though, that you will not benefit from trying to be perfect or overly self-critical. Negative thoughts and talking yourself down will be detrimental to your well-being. The focus of reflective practice is to seek continual improvement to achieve a high standard of performance and enhancement of your depth of expertise. Your academic portfolio is a particularly helpful tool in reflecting on your learning and insights.

A scholarly approach to your activities will support your ongoing learning and reflective practice. Monitor the work of others to keep abreast of new developments and contribute to that body of knowledge through your own research and scholarship. These activities will enrich and inform your growing learning and insights.

Environmental influences

Regularly scanning your academic environment will be an important element of your strategic practice. There are many sources of support and influence that you can access in building your intelligent, strategic career, as outlined below. Note, however, that each context will be likely to comprise a different mix of opportunities that require review and assessment. Keep informed of new developments and work on building your political and personal 'radar' as to both opportunities and threats.

Institutional context

Your institutional context is a composite of the university and its mission, purpose and priorities; your work group and its strategic focus, and your particular role and how it operates in this organization. Maintain a watching brief over your institutional trends and the institution's responses to broader sectoral change. It is important to keep informed of likely developments and to assess the potential impacts these may have on your role and opportunities. Become familiar with your university leaders and look for chances to contribute to your institution's development. Focus on building connections and watch for new initiatives that might complement your existing repertoire. This broader view will also help you to adjust your learning or career strategy during future shifts in organizational practice.

Leadership and support

Leaders can greatly support your career strategy by providing advice, offering targeted feedback, explaining the political landscape and its implications, and linking you to key groups, projects or individuals. Build solid connections with them and share your career and development goals. This embedded support will be very important as your strategy to build more profile, share your knowledge or explore more lateral opportunities emerges.

You may also look for ways in which you can support the leadership group in your school or department. Accepting responsibility for small projects and contributing to any organizational change initiatives are some ways you can establish your presence and credibility as a good addition to the community. In the process, you will continue to develop your own leadership capabilities and confidence in your capacity to lead groups.

Community values and culture

As noted in Chapter 19, you will be situated in a particular academic culture that can strongly impact on your strategy. If the culture is inclusive and constructive, you can access many avenues for growth and development. Mentors and sponsors may be readily sourced within your own work area. If the environment is less supportive, recognize that it may offer limited support, and focus instead on accessing other sources.

Identify people with whom you enjoy interacting and focus on building mutually respectful and valued relationships. Close allegiances of this nature are important sources of social sustenance, increasing your capacity to be socially connected. When reviewing your own work culture, consider how closely your values ally with that community. If you sense a strong disconnection, you will need to consider new career avenues in the long term. Your well-being is an important priority.

Learning opportunities

The key to being strategic is to act on learning opportunities. You will be surrounded by supportive sources – both within your institution and beyond. Start by participating in foundational programmes or workshops that guide your core professional practices. You need to demonstrate proficiency in teaching, research and supervision as a matter of urgency. Once these are consolidated, devise an annual development plan to continually extend your repertoire and enrich your academic toolkit. You might access university support, work with a mentor or draw on your professional and disciplinary networks. Review your participation at the end of each year to make sure you have maximized the benefits from these sources. Just doing your job is insufficient if you wish to be a strategic, well positioned academic.

Expectations and standards

In planning your academic career, monitor the institutional (and sectoral) expectations and standards of performance. These will help you to assess your effectiveness and to consider your overall strategic focus. If, for example, you are seen as less competitive in your research, you will need to build a development strategy to escalate your outcomes in that area. Seek regular feedback from your supervisor to establish a clear sense of performance expectations. Find exemplars who might act as models. Aim for a high standard that prepares you for your next career jump. You will achieve more if you set aspirational targets.

Regularly review your performance with comparators: integrate checks of your h-index, citations and impact factors and evaluate your teaching results against institutional benchmarks. Prepare submissions for external recognition of excellence to obtain feedback and assessments of your competitiveness. All of these sources of information will help you to calibrate how you compare.

Mentorship and sponsorship

The most critical sources of support you need to mobilize are mentors and sponsors. Aim for at least one mentor a year to strategically build your support crew. Ensure your relationships are positive, highly achievement-focused and reflective. Invest the necessary time to make these opportunities work. You will need to treat them as the highest priority to ensure the mentor or sponsor feels their support is valued. Don't forget that the most productive way to engage your mentors is to do some preparatory work in reviewing your strategy to date and your perceived goals for development. This preparedness sets the tone for productive partnerships.

In the first instance, aim for a single or very limited range of mentoring relationships. Learn to manage these interchanges before expanding your connections. Your initial efforts to act on your mentor's advice may take longer in the initial learning phase. Devote the necessary time to act on the agreed priorities. Remember, too, that sponsors are best deployed when you reach a certain level of capability that is ready to be leveraged. Work on building your profile and toolkit to the point where you are credible and sufficiently developed to launch from your sponsor's connections and knowledge.

Networks and collaboration

Aim to increase your profile and connections with networks and collaborators. This will be particularly critical as you start to build a credible research base or particular niches where you are an identified source of knowledge. These partnerships are two-way: you will learn much from your contacts, while also finding opportunities to share your knowledge and expertise. Taking the time to build and maintain these relationships will be particularly important. Allocate sufficient space to manage your interactions so that you maintain a regular presence and interaction.

Collaborations will be particularly critical in increasing the quality and quantity of your outcomes. Keep a watchful eye out for potential collaborators and be ready to act on suitable opportunities. Recognize that you may need to take a more active role in building associations initially. However, once you have proven your calibre as a research, teaching or engagement colleague, you will find the relationships are much easier to develop and sustain.

Personal agency

In conjunction with a good professional toolkit and effective harnessing of institutional and external support, the capacity to optimize your performance and impact will contribute to your intelligent career. You will need to be targeted in your priorities and goals, aiming for good synergy with the factors that will also contribute to your overall well-being. Four key factors can be identified.

Clear sense of purpose, mission, values and beliefs

Hopefully, your exploration of this book has prompted you to think about your underlying values and beliefs. These underpin your sense of identity, informing your long-term and short-term goals. Take time to think about what you hope to achieve in your role, and the type of contributions or priorities that should be accentuated. Strong self-awareness will provide more support when you face complex choices and decisions.

Strategy, positioning and career management

Essential to your career management is the development and implementation of a clear strategy. Think carefully about the type of academic you wish to be, and your career goals. Build a strong vision of your aspirations and think carefully about the options you might follow. In some cases, you may have several choices. Explore your options with mentors and other valued colleagues to build a strong understanding of the implications of any decisions. Consider then how you will build your intelligent career and the key strategies that will help you achieve those goals.

Recognize that your academic profile will partly relate to your talented efforts and partly to the ways in which others note those outcomes. Don't work in isolation. Consider how you can increase your profile and reach so that people are aware of your work and seek your input.

Goal-setting and priority management

At the next level, develop clear goals and ensure you have a strong understanding of the priorities that will achieve those targets. Keep the goals in clear sight and treat them as a very high priority. If you become distracted with busy but less essential tasks, you will find that your progress is becoming less notable. It will be important to review your priorities and goals on a regular basis.

At a basic level, maintain your CV as a current working tool. Enter any new accomplishment as soon as it is confirmed. Take the time to review your profile regularly to see how it appears and check that you are balancing your various commitments so that you have a balanced portfolio. If you are finding your time management is poor, attend a relevant course to assist you.

Engagement and participation

How committed and engaged are you? Waiting for someone to notice you or to recognize your talent will be largely disappointing. This is your career. Take ownership of it and treat it as an important project. Think about the various steps that you need to take and prepare a clear plan that will ensure you have benefited from any opportunities. For example, pre-prepare for a conference to ensure you have identified key people who you should meet. Volunteer for strategic roles, and actively look for new opportunities. Stay engaged. Passive academics do not thrive.

Final comments

This work has offered a clear road map on how to deploy your talents and energies in an academic role. It has explored many complex facets of academic work, particularly with respect to the social context in which your role will operate. It recognizes that career strategies need to be realistically allied to your own capabilities and the environment in which you operate. Most particularly, it challenges you to take stronger ownership: to build a strategic perspective on both working and thinking as an academic. Hopefully you have found yourself thinking deeply about your assumptions and current context. That is a healthy first step in building an effective and dynamic role that truly supports your full potential.

Don't be afraid to look laterally and creatively at different opportunities that might emerge. The world of academe can be a very vibrant, evolving setting if you take ownership of your role. The key will be linking to your own embedded values and needs, thinking about the intelligent career you wish to establish and weighing up the pros and cons of various options. A keen knowledge of your own talents, motivations and signature strengths is a critical component of strategic career management.

Do more than simply survive in academe. This strategic handbook provides you with many ideas to build your strategy and to strengthen it over time. It will help you to thrive and flourish... You are the next generation academic. Move positively forward to your strategic, intelligent future!

References

Adcroft, A. and Taylor, D. (2009) Developing a conceptual model for career support for new academics, *International Journal of Teaching and Learning in Higher Education*, 22(3): 287–98.

Adkins, B. (2009) PhD pedagogy and the changing knowledge landscapes of universities, *Higher Education Research & Development*, 28(2): 165–78.

Adler-Kassner, L. and O'Neill, P. (2010) *Reframing Writing Assessment to Improve Teaching and Learning*. Logan, Utah: Utah State University Press.

Aitchison, C. (2010) *Publishing Pedagogies for the Doctorate and Beyond*. New York: Routledge.

Akerlind, G. (2009) Making your doctorate work in an academic career, in C. Denholm and T. Evans (eds) *Beyond Doctorates Downunder*. Camberwell Vic.: ACER Press, pp. 138–45.

Akerlind, G.S. (2005) Postdoctoral researchers: roles, functions and career prospects, *Higher Education Research & Development*, 24(1): 21–40.

Alexander, P.A. (2004) A model of domain learning: reinterpreting expertise as a multidimensional, multistage process, in D.Y. Dai and R.J. Sternberg (eds) *Motivation, Emotion and Cognition*. Mahwah, NJ: Erlbaum, pp. 273–98.

Allen, T. (2003) Relationship effectiveness for mentors: factors associated with learning and quality, *Journal of Management*, 29(4): 469–86.

Amundsen, C. and McAlpine, L. (2009) 'Learning supervision': trial by fire, *Innovations in Education and Teaching International*, 46(3): 331–42.

Arthur, M.B., Claman, P.H. and DeFillippi, R.J. (1995) Intelligent enterprise, intelligent careers, *Academy of Management Executive*, 9(4): 7–22.

Arum, R. and Roksa, J. (2011) *Academically Adrift: Limited Learning on College Campuses*. Chicago, IL: University of Chicago Press.

Avolio, B.J., Walumbwa, F.O. and Weber, T.J. (2009) Leadership: current theories, research, and future directions, *Annual Review of Psychology*, 60(1): 421–49.

Babiak, P. and Hare, R.D. (2006) *Snakes in Suits: When Psychopaths go to Work*. New York: Regan Books.

Barnard, A. et al. (2011) Peer partnership to enhance scholarship of teaching: a case study, *Higher Education Research & Development*, 30(4): 435–48.

Barnett, R. (1997) *Higher Education: A Critical Business*. Buckingham: Open University Press.

Barnett, R. and Coate, K. (2005) *Engaging the Curriculum in Higher Education*. Maidenhead, England; New York: Society for Research into Higher Education and Open University Press.

Barrie, S.C. (2007) A conceptual framework for the teaching and learning of generic graduate attributes, *Studies in Higher Education*, 32(4): 439–58.

Baruch, Y. (2004) Transforming careers: from linear to multidirectional career paths: organizational and individual perspectives, *Career Development International*, 9(1): 58–73.

Becher, T. and Trowler, P.R. (2001) *Academic Tribes and Territories: Intellectual Enquiry and the Culture of Disciplines*. Buckingham: Society for Research into Higher Education and Open University Press.

Bell, M. (2012) *Peer Observation Partnerships in Higher Education*. 2nd ed. Milperra, NSW: Higher Education Research and Development Society of Australasia (HERDSA).

Benzie, H.J. (2010) Graduating as a 'native speaker': international students and English language proficiency in higher education, *Higher Education Research & Development*, 29(4): 447–59.

Biggs, J. (2012) What the student does: teaching for enhanced learning, *Higher Education Research & Development*, 31(1): 39–55.

Biggs, J.B. and Tang, C.S. (2011) *Teaching for Quality Learning at University: What the Student Does*, 4th edn. Maidenhead, England; New York: Society for Research into Higher Education and Open University Press.

Billot, J. (2010) The imagined and the real: identifying the tensions for academic identity, *Higher Education Research & Development*, 29(6): 709–21.

Bista, K.K. (2011) Academic dishonesty among international students in higher education, in J.E. Miller and J.E. Groccia (eds) *To Improve the Academy: Resources for Faculty, Instructional, and Organizational Development*. San Francisco, CA: Jossey-Bass, pp. 159–72.

Bland, C.J. et al. (2005) *The Research-Productive Department: Strategies from Departments that Excel*. Bolton, MA: Anker Publishing.

Blaxter, L., Hughes, C. and Tight, M. (1998) *The Academic Career Handbook*. Buckingham: Open University Press.

Boettcher, J.V. and Conrad, R.-M. (2010) *The Online Teaching Survival Guide: Simple and Practical Pedagogical Tips*. San Francisco, CA: Jossey-Bass. Available at: http://site. ebrary.com/id/10388345 [accessed 30 January 2012].

Bolden, R. et al. (2010) *Strategies for Effective Employer–HE engagement: Defining, Sustaining and Supporting Higher Skills Provision*. Exeter: University of Exeter.

Bolden, R. and Petrov, G. (2008) *Employer Engagement with Higher Education: A Literature Review*. Exeter: University of Exeter.

Bolden, R., Petrov, G. and Gosling, J. (2009) Distributed leadership in higher education: rhetoric and reality, *Educational Management Administration & Leadership*, 37(2): 257–77.

Borrell-Damian, L. et al. (2010) Collaborative doctoral education: university–industry partnerships for enhancing knowledge exchange, *Higher Education Policy*, 23(4): 493–514.

Boud, D. and Tennant, M. (2006) Putting doctoral education to work: challenges to academic practice, *Higher Education Research & Development*, 25(1): 293–306.

Bourn, D. (2011) From internationalisation to global perspectives, *Higher Education Research & Development*, 30(5): 559–71.

Bovill, C., Cook-Sather, A. and Felten, P. (2011) Students as co-creators of teaching approaches, course design, and curricula: implications for academic developers, *International Journal for Academic Development*, 16(2): 133–45.

Boye, A. and Meixner, M. (2011) Growing a new generation: promoting self-reflection through peer observation, in J.E. Miller and J.E. Groccia (eds) *To Improve the Academy: Resources for Faculty, Instructional, and Organizational Development*. San Francisco, CA: Jossey-Bass, pp. 18–31.

Boye, A.P. and Tapp, S. (2010) MacGyvers, Medeas, and bionic women: patterns of instructor response to negative feedback, in J.E. Miller and L.B. Nilson (eds) *To Improve the Academy: Resources for Faculty, Instructional, and Organizational Development*. San Francisco, CA: Jossey-Bass, pp. 139–57.

Boyer, E.L. (1990) *Scholarship reconsidered: Priorities of the professoriate*. New York: Carnegie Foundation for the Advancement of Teaching.

Bozionelos, N. (2004) Mentoring provided: Relation to mentor's career success, personality, and mentoring received, *Journal of Vocational Behavior*, 64(1): 24–46.

Bradmore, D.J. and Smyrnios, K.X. (2009) The writing on the wall: responses of Australian public universities to competition in global higher education, *Higher Education Research & Development*, 28(5): 495–508.

Brew, A. (2010a) Imperatives and challenges in integrating teaching and research, *Higher Education Research & Development*, 29(2): 139–50.

Brew, A. (2010b) Transforming academic practice through scholarship, *International Journal for Academic Development*, 15(2): 105–16.

Brew, A. and Sachs, J. (2007) *Transforming a University: The Scholarship of Teaching and Learning in Practice*. Sydney: Sydney University Press.

Bright, J.E.H. et al. (2009) Chance events in career development: influence, control and multiplicity, *Journal of Vocational Behavior*, 75(1): 14–25.

Bright, J.E.H., Pryor, R.G.L. and Harpham, L. (2005) The role of chance events in career decision making, *Journal of Vocational Behavior*, 66(3): 561–76.

Bringle, R.G. and Hatcher, J.A. (2002) Campus-community partnerships: the terms of engagement, *Journal of Social Issues*, 58(3): 503–16.

Briscoe, J.P. and Hall, D.T. (2006) The interplay of boundaryless and protean careers: combinations and implications, *Journal of Vocational Behavior*, 69(1): 4–18.

Brockbank, A. and McGill, I. (1998) *Facilitating Reflective Learning in Higher Education*. Buckingham; Philadelphia, PA: Society for Research into Higher Education and Open University Press.

Brookfield, S. (1995) *Becoming a Critically Reflective Teacher*. San Francisco, CA: Jossey-Bass.

Brown, G.T. (2010) Assessment: principles and practices, in R. Cantwell and J.J. Scevak (eds) *An Academic Life: A Handbook for New Academics*. Camberwell, Vic.: ACER Press, pp. 35–44.

Brown, R.T., Daly, B.P. and Leong, F.T.L. (2009) Mentoring in research: a developmental approach, *Professional Psychology: Research and Practice*, 40(3): 306–13.

Buller, J.L. (2010) *The Essential College Professor: A Practical Guide to an Academic Career*. San Francisco, CA: Jossey-Bass.

Bushaway, R. (2003) *Managing Research*. Philadelphia, PA: Open University.

Cannon, R. and Knapper, C. (2011) *Lecturing for Better Learning*. Milperra, NSW: Higher Education Research and Development Society of Australasia (HERDSA).

Cantwell, R. (2010) *An Academic Life: A Handbook for New Academics*. Camberwell Vic.: ACER Press.

Cantwell, R., Scevak, J.J. and Parkes, R.J. (2010) Aligning intellectual development with curriculum instruction and assessment, in R. Cantwell and J.J. Scevak (eds) *An Academic Life: A Handbook for New Academics*. Camberwell Vic.: ACER Press, pp. 16–24.

Cargill, M. (2009) *Writing Scientific Research Articles: Strategies and Steps*. Hoboken, NJ: Wiley-Blackwell.

Chalmers, D. (2011) Progress and challenges to the recognition and reward of the scholarship of teaching in higher education, *Higher Education Research & Development*, 30(1): 25–38.

Cipolle, S.B. (2010) *Service-Learning and Social Justice: Engaging Students in Social Change*. Lanham, MD: Rowman & Littlefield Publishers.

Clarke, B.R. (2004) *Sustaining Change in Universities: Continuities in Case Studies*. Bletchley, Buckinghamshire: Open University Press.

Clarke, J. (2007) *Pocket Psycho*. Milsons Point, NSW: Random House.

Clarke, M. (2007) The impact of higher education rankings on student access, choice and opportunity, *Higher Education in Europe*, 32(1): 59–70.

Coates, H. and Goedegebuure, L. (2010) *The Real Academic Revolution: Why we need to Reconceptualise Australia's Academic Workforce, and Eight Possible Strategies for how to go about This*. Melbourne: LH Martin Institute.

Cohen, C.M. and Cohen, S.L. (2005) *Lab Dynamics: Management Skills for Scientists*. Cold Spring Harbor, NY: Cold Spring Harbor Laboratory Press.

Cranton, P. (2011) A transformative perspective on the scholarship of teaching and learning, *Higher Education Research & Development*, 30(1): 75–86.

Crisp, G. (2009) *Designing and Using e-assessments*. Milperra, NSW: Higher Education Research and Development Society of Australasia.

Crosling, G. and Heagney, M. (2009) Improving student retention in higher education, *Australian Universities Review*, 51(2): 9–18.

Cross, B. and Thomas, R. (2011) A smarter way to network, *Harvard Business Review*, July–August: 149–53.

Crozier, G. and Reay, D. (2011) Capital accumulation: working-class students learning how to learn in HE, *Teaching in Higher Education*, 16(2): 145–55.

Cryer, P. (1996) *The Research Student's Guide to Success*. Milton Keynes: Open University Press.

Cuthbert, D., Spark, C. and Burke, E. (2009) Disciplining writing: The case for multidisciplinary writing groups to support writing for publication by research candidates in the humanities, arts and social sciences, *Higher Education Research & Development*, 28(2): 137–50.

Dany, F. and Mangematin, V. (2004) Beyond the dualism between lifelong employment and job insecurity: some new career promises for young scientists, *Higher Education Policy*, 17(2): 201–19.

Darwin, A. and Palmer, E. (2009) Mentoring circles in higher education, *Higher Education Research & Development*, 28(2): 125–36.

Davies, M. (2011) Introduction to the special issue on critical thinking in higher education, *Higher Education Research & Development*, 30(3): 255–60.

Debowski, S. (2005) Across the divide: teaching a transnational MBA in a second language, *Higher Education Research & Development*, 24(3): 265–80.

Debowski, S. (2006) *Knowledge Management*. Milton, Qld: Wiley Press.

Debowski, S. (2007) Finding the right track: Enabling early career academic management of career, teaching and research, in *Enhancing Higher Education, Theory and Scholarship, Proceedings of the 30th HERDSA Annual Conference*, Adelaide, 8–11 July 2007, pp. 138–149.

Debowski, S. (2009) Pencilled at the margins: dealing with bullies at work, in K. Naidoo and F. Patel (eds) *Working Women: Stories of Strife, Struggles and Survival*. San Francisco, CA: Sage Publications, pp. 65–78.

Debowski, S. (2012) Leading higher education teaching, learning, and innovation, in J.E. Groccia, M.A.T. Alsudairi and W.H. Bergquist (eds) *Handbook of University and College Teaching: A Global Perspective*. San Francisco, CA: Sage Publications, pp. 251–67.

Deem, R., Mok, K.H. and Lucas, L. (2008) Transforming higher education in whose image? Exploring the concept of the 'World-Class' university in Europe and Asia, *Higher Education Policy*, 21: 83–97.

Delamont, S. (1997) *Supervising the PhD: A Guide to Success*. Buckingham; Bristol: Society for Research into Higher Education and Open University Press.

Delamont, S. and Atkinson, P. (2004) *Successful Research Careers: A Practical Guide.* Maidenhead, Berkshire: Society for Research into Higher Education and Open University Press.

Denholm, C. (2006) *Doctorates Downunder: Keys to Successful Doctoral Study in Australia and New Zealand.* Camberwell, Vic.: ACER Press.

Denholm, C.J. and Evans, T.D. (2009) *Beyond Doctorates Downunder: Maximising the Impact of your Doctorate from Australia and New Zealand.* Camberwell, Vic.: ACER Press.

Denney, F., Mead, J. and Toombs, P. (2011) *The Leading Researcher: Explore and Develop your Potential.* Cambridge, UK: Vitae.

Denson, N., Loveday, T. and Dalton, H. (2010) Student evaluation of courses: what predicts satisfaction?, *Higher Education Research & Development*, 29(4): 339–56.

Department of Innovation, Industry, Science and Research (2010) *Meeting Australia's research workforce needs.* Canberra: Department of Innovation, Industry, Science and Research, Australian Govt. Available at: http://www.innovation.gov.au/Research/ResearchWorkforceIssue/Documents/ResearchWorkforceStrategyConsultationPaper.pdf [accessed 18 July 2012].

Deuchar, R. (2008) Facilitator, director or critical friend?: contradiction and congruence in doctoral supervision styles, *Teaching in Higher Education*, 13(4): 489–500.

Devlin, M. and Samarawickrema, G. (2010) The criteria of effective teaching in a changing higher education context, *Higher Education Research & Development*, 29(2): 111–24.

Dietz, J.S. and Bozeman, B. (2005) Academic careers, patents, and productivity: industry experience as scientific and technical human capital, *Research Policy*, 34(3): 349–67.

DiPietro, M. (2010) Theoretical frameworks for academic dishonesty: a comparative review, in J.E. Miller and L.B. Nilson (eds) *To Improve the Academy: Resources for Faculty, Instructional, and Organizational Development.* San Francisco, CA: Jossey-Bass, pp. 250–62.

Driscoll, A. and Lynton, E. (1999) *Making Outreach Visible: A Guide to Documenting Professional Service and Outreach.* Washington, DC: American Association for Higher Education.

Duda, R. (2004a) Mentorship in academic medicine: a critical component for all faculty and academic advancement, *Current Surgery*, 61(3): 325–7.

Duda, R. (2004b) Physician and scientist leadership in academic medicine: strategic planning for a successful academic leadership career, *Current Surgery*, 61(2): 175–7.

Duncan, S. and Spicer, S. (2010) *The Engaging Researcher.* Cambridge, UK: Careers Research and Advisory Centre. Available at: http://www.vitae.ac.uk/researcherbooklets [accessed 21 May 2012].

Dunham-Taylor, J. et al. (2008) What goes around comes around: improving faculty retention through more effective mentoring, *Journal of Professional Nursing*, 24(6): 337–46.

Dunne, C. (2011) Developing an intercultural curriculum within the context of the internationalisation of higher education: terminology, typologies and power, *Higher Education Research & Development*, 30(5): 609–22.

Earle Reybold, L. and Alamia, J.J. (2008) Academic transitions in education: a developmental perspective of women faculty experiences, *Journal of Career Development*, 35(2): 107–28.

Edwards, D. and Coates, H. (2011) Monitoring the pathways and outcomes of people from disadvantaged backgrounds and graduate groups, *Higher Education Research & Development*, 30(2): 151–63.

El Hassan, K. (2009) Investigating substantive and consequential validity of student ratings of instruction, *Higher Education Research & Development*, 28(3): 319–33.

Ellis, R.A., Ginns, P. and Piggott, L. (2009) E-learning in higher education: some key aspects and their relationship to approaches to study, *Higher Education Research & Development*, 28(3): 303–18.

Fairlie, P. (2011) Meaningful work, employee engagement, and other key employee outcomes: implications for human resource development, *Advances in Developing Human Resources*, 13(4): 508–25.

Feldman, D.C. and Turnley, W.H. (2004) Contingent employment in academic careers: relative deprivation among adjunct faculty, *Journal of Vocational Behavior*, 64(2): 284–307.

Fernandez-Araoz, C., Groysberg, B. and Nohria, N. (2011) How to hang onto your high potentials, *Harvard Business Review*, October: 76–83.

Field, E. (2010) *Bully Blocking at Work: A Self-Help Guide for Employees and Managers*. Bowen Hills, Qld.: Australian Academic Press.

Fielden, J. and Leadership Foundation for Higher Education (Great Britain) (2011) *Leadership And Management Of International Partnerships: Final Report*. London: Leadership Foundation for Higher Education.

Fitzgerald, H.E., Burack, C. and Seifer, S.D. (2010) *Handbook of Engaged Scholarship: Contemporary Landscapes, Future Directions*. East Lansing, MI: Michigan State University Press.

FitzPatrick, M.A. and Spiller, D. (2010) The teaching portfolio: institutional imperative or teacher's personal journey?, *Higher Education Research & Development*, 29(2): 167–78.

Foote, K.E. and Solem, M.N. (2009) Toward better mentoring for early career faculty: results of a study of US geographers, *International Journal for Academic Development*, 14(1): 47–58.

Foreman-Peck, L. and Winch, C. (2010) *Using Educational Research To Inform Practice: A Practical Guide To Practitioner Research In Universities And Colleges*. London; New York: Routledge.

France, K. (2004) Problem-based service-learning: rewards and challenges with undergraduates, in C.M. Wehlberg and S. Chadwick-Blossey (eds) *To Improve the Academy: Resources for Faculty, Instructional, and Organizational Development*. San Francisco, CA: Jossey-Bass, pp. 239–50.

Freudenberg, B., Brimble, M. and Cameron, C. (2010) Where there is a WIL there is a way, *Higher Education Research & Development*, 29(5): 575–88.

Fullan, M. and Scott, G. (2009) *Turnaround Leadership for Higher Education*. San Francisco, CA: Jossey-Bass.

Gale, H. (2011) The reluctant academic: early-career academics in a teaching-orientated university, *International Journal for Academic Development*, 16(3): 215–27.

Gappa, J.M., Austin, A. and Trice, A.G. (2007) *Rethinking Academic Work: Higher Education's Strategic Imperative*. San Francisco, CA: Jossey-Bass.

Gardiner, M. and Kearns, H. (2010) *Turbocharge your Writing: How to Become a Prolific Academic Writer*. Adelaide, SA: Flinders University.

Garrett, G. and Davies, G. (2010) *Herding Cats: Being Advice to Aspiring Leaders and Research Leaders*. Axminster, Devon, UK: Triarchy Press.

Garrison, D.R. and Vaughan, N.D. (2008) *Blended Learning in Higher Education: Framework, Principles, and Guidelines*. San Francisco, CA: Jossey-Bass.

Gatfield, T. (2005) An investigation into PhD supervisory management styles: development of a dynamic conceptual model and its managerial implications, *Journal of Higher Education Policy and Management*, 27(3): 311–25.

George-Walker, L.D. and Keeffe, M. (2010) Self-determined blended learning: a case study of blended learning design, *Higher Education Research & Development*, 29(1): 1–13.

Gibson, S.K. (2005) Whose best interests are served? The distinction between mentoring and support, *Advances in Developing Human Resources*, 7(4): 470–88.

Gikandi, J.W., Morrow, D. and Davis, N.E. (2011) Online formative assessment in higher education: a review of the literature, *Computers & Education*, 57(4): 2,333–51.

Giles, D.E. (2008) Understanding an emerging field of scholarship: toward a research agenda for engaged, public scholarship, *Journal of Higher Education Outreach and Engagement*, 12(9): 97–106.

Ginsberg, S.M. (2011) Support needs of university adjunct lecturers, in J.E. Miller and J.E. Groccia (eds) *To Improve the Academy: Resources for Faculty, Instructional, And Organizational Development*. San Francisco, CA: Jossey-Bass, pp. 32–45.

Golding, C. (2011) Educating for critical thinking: thought-encouraging questions in a community of inquiry, *Higher Education Research & Development*, 30(3): 357–70.

Gratton, L. (2007) *Hot Spots: Why Some Teams, Workplaces, and Organizations Buzz with Energy – And Others Don't*. San Francisco, CA: Berrett-Koehler Publishers.

Guberman, J. et al. (2006) *Making The Right Moves: A Practical Guide to Scientific Management for Postdocs and New Faculty*, 2nd edn. Chevy Chase, Maryland: Burroughs Wellcome Fund/Howard Hughes Institute. Available at: http://www.hhmi.org/resources/labmanagement/moves.html [accessed 21 May 2012].

Haigh, N. (2011) Sustaining and spreading the positive outcomes of SoTL projects: issues, insights and strategies, *International Journal for Academic Development*, 1–13.

Hall, D.T. (1996) Protean careers of the 21st century, *The Academy of Management Executive* 10(4): 8–16.

Halse, C. and Malfroy, J. (2010) Retheorizing doctoral supervision as professional work, *Studies in Higher Education*, 35(1): 79–92.

Hammer, S.J. and Green, W. (2011) Critical thinking in a first year management unit: the relationship between disciplinary learning, academic literacy and learning progression, *Higher Education Research & Development*, 30(3): 303–15.

Hanover Research (2010) *Strategies for Teaching Large Undergraduate Classes*. Washington, DC: Hanover Research. Available at: http://www.businessandeconomics.mq.edu.au/intranet/learning_and_teaching/leading_discussions_projects/Strategies_for_Teaching_Large_Undergraduate_Classes.pdf [accessed 21 May 2012.

Harris, L., Jones, M. and Coutts, S. (2010) Partnerships and learning communities in work-integrated learning: designing a community services student placement program, *Higher Education Research & Development*, 29(5): 547–59.

Hattie, J. (2008) *Visible Learning: A Synthesis of Meta-Analyses Relating to Achievement*. London; New York: Routledge.

Hay, I. (2011) *Inspiring Academics: Learning with the World's Great University Teachers*. Maidenhead, England: Open University Press. Available at: http://site.ebrary.com/id/10476270 [accessed 4 February 2012].

Healey, M. (2000) Developing the scholarship of teaching in higher education: a discipline-based approach. *Higher Education Research & Development*, 19(2): 169–89.

Healey, M. and Jenkins, A. (2009) *Development undergraduate research and enquiry*. York: The Higher Education Academy. Available at: http://www.heacademy.ac.uk/assets/York/documents/resources/publications/DevelopingUndergraduate_Final.pdf [accessed 18 July 2012].

Hegstad, C.D. and Wentling, R.M. (2004) The development and maintenance of exemplary formal mentoring programs in Fortune 500 companies, *Human Resource Development Quarterly*, 15(4): 421–48.

Hénard, F. (2010) *Learning our Lesson: Review of Quality Teaching in Higher Education*. Paris: OECD (Organisation for Economic Co-operation and Development).

Heppner, F. (2007) *Teaching the Large College Class: A Guidebook for Instructors with Multitudes*. San Francisco, CA: Jossey-Bass.

Hermanowicz, J.C. (2003) Scientists and satisfaction, *Social Studies of Science*, 33(1): 45–73.

Higgins, M.C. (2000) The more, the merrier? Multiple developmental relationships and work satisfaction, *Journal of Management Development*, 19(4): 277–96.

Hirsch, J.E. (2005) An index to quantify an individual's scientific research output, *Proceedings of the National Academy of Sciences of the United States of America (PNAS)*, 102(46): 16: 569–72.

Hobson, J., Jones, G. and Deane, E. (2005) The research assistant: silenced partner in Australia's knowledge production?, *Journal of Higher Education Policy and Management*, 27(3): 357–66.

Holland, B. (1999) Factors and strategies that influence faculty involvement in public service, *Journal of Public Service and Outreach*, 4(1): 37–44.

Hubball, H., Clarke, A. and Poole, G. (2010) Ten-year reflections on mentoring SoTL research in a research-intensive university, *International Journal for Academic Development*, 15(2): 117–29.

Hughes, M. (2005) The mythology of research and teaching relationships in universities, in R. Barnett (ed.) *Reshaping the University: New Relationships between Research, Scholarship and Teaching*. New York: SHRE and Open University Press, pp. 14–26.

Jackson, D. (2009) Mentored residential writing retreats: a leadership strategy to develop skills and generate outcomes in writing for publication, *Nurse Education Today*, 29(1): 9–15.

Jackson, N.J. (2010) From a curriculum that integrates work to a curriculum that integrates life: changing a university's conceptions of curriculum, *Higher Education Research & Development*, 29(5): 491–505.

James, R. et al. (2002) *Assessing Learning In Australian Universities: Ideas, Strategies and Resources for Quality in Student Assessment*. Melbourne; Canberra: Centre for the Study of Higher Education; Australian Universities Teaching Committee.

de Janasz, S.C. and Sullivan, S.E. (2004) Multiple mentoring in academe: developing the professorial network, *Journal of Vocational Behavior*, 64(2): 263–83.

Johnson, R. and Kumar, M. (2010) The Monsoon wedding phenomenon: understanding Indian students studying in Australian universities, *Higher Education Research & Development*, 29(3): 215–27.

Johnston, B. (2010) *The First Year at University: Teaching Students in Transition*. Maidenhead: Open University Press.

Jones, C. and DeFillippi, R.J. (1996) Back to the future in film: combining industry and self-knowledge to meet career challenges of the 21st century, *The Academy of Management Executive*, 10(4): 89–104.

Kamler, B. and Thomson, P. (2006) *Helping Doctoral Students Write: Pedagogies For Supervision*. London; New York: Routledge.

Kearns, H. (2006) *Time for Research: Time Management for PhD Students*. Adelaide, SA: Flinders University, Staff Development and Training Unit.

Kellerman, B. (2008) *Followership: How Followers are Creating Change and Changing Leaders*. Boston, MA: Harvard Business Press.

Kiley, M. and Wisker, G. (2009) Threshold concepts in research education and evidence of threshold crossing, *Higher Education Research & Development*, 28(4): 431–41.

King, M.F., Denecke, D.D. and Council of Graduate Schools in the United States (2003) *On the Right Track: A Manual for Research Mentors*. Washington, DC: Council of Graduate Schools.

Kligyte, G. (2011) Transformation narratives in academic practice, *International Journal for Academic Development*, 16(3): 201–13.

Kochan, F.K. (2002) Examining the organizational and human dimensions of mentoring: a textual data analysis, in F.K. Kochan (ed.) *Perspectives in Mentoring: The Organizational and Human Dimensions of Successful Mentoring Programs and Relationships*. Greenwich, CT: Information Age Publishing, pp. 269–84.

Kubler, M. and Western, M. (2007) *PhD Graduates 5 to 7 Years Out: Employment Outcomes, Job Attributes and the Quality of Research Training: Summary Results for The Australian National University*. Brisbane, Qld: University of Queensland.

Kuh, G.D. (2003) What we're learning about student engagement from NSSE: benchmarks for effective educational practices, *Change: The Magazine of Higher Learning*, 35(2): 24–32.

Kuh, G. (2008) *High-Impact Educational Practices: What They Are, Who Has Access to Them, and Why They Matter*. Washington DC: Association of American Colleges and Universities. Available at: http://www.aacu.org/leap/hip.cfm [accessed 21 May 2012].

Laird, T.F.N. and Ribera, T. (2011) Institutional encouragement of and faculty engagement in the scholarship of learning and teaching, in J.E. Miller and J.E. Groccia (eds) *To Improve the Academy: Resources for Faculty, Instructional, and Organizational Development*. San Francisco, CA: Jossey-Bass, pp. 112–25.

Land, R. (2011) There could be trouble ahead: using threshold concepts as a tool of analysis, *International Journal for Academic Development*, 16(2): 175–8.

Layton, C. and Brown, C. (2011) Striking a balance: supporting teaching excellence award applications, *International Journal for Academic Development*, 16(2): 163–74.

Leach, L. and Zepke, N. (2011) Engaging students in learning: a review of a conceptual organiser, *Higher Education Research & Development*, 30(2): 193–204.

Lee, A. (2008) How are doctoral students supervised? Concepts of doctoral research supervision, *Studies in Higher Education*, 33(3): 267–81.

Lee, A., Dennis, C. and Campbell, P. (2007) Nature's guide for mentors, *Nature*, 447: 791–7.

Levy, D.C. (2006) Market university?, *Comparative Education Review*, 50(1): 113–24.

Lewin, K., Llippit, R. and White, R.K. (1939) Patterns of aggressive behavior in experimentally created social climates, *Journal of Social Psychology*, 10: 271–301.

Light, R.J. (2004) *Making The Most of College: Students Speak Their Minds*. Cambridge, MA; London: Harvard University Press.

Litchfield, A., Frawley, J. and Nettleton, S. (2010) Contextualising and integrating into the curriculum the learning and teaching of work-ready professional graduate attributes, *Higher Education Research & Development*, 29(5): 519–34.

Lublin, J. and Sutherland, K.A. (2009) *Conducting Tutorials*. Milperra, NSW: Higher Education Research and Development Society of Australasia.

McAlpine, L. (2010) Fixed-term researchers in the social sciences: passionate investment, yet marginalizing experiences, *International Journal for Academic Development*, 15(3): 229–40.

McArthur, J. (2011) Reconsidering the social and economic purposes of higher education, *Higher Education Research & Development*, 30(6): 737–49.

McBeath, C. (2010) Professional activities and community service, in R. Cantwell and J.J. Scevak (eds) *An Academic Life: A Handbook for New Academics*. Camberwell, Vic.: ACER Press, pp. 150–8.

McDowall-Long, K. (2004) Mentoring relationships: implications for practitioners and suggestions for future research, *Human Resource Development International*, 7(4): 519–34.

McGrail, M.R., Rickard, C.M. and Jones, R. (2006) Publish or perish: a systematic review of interventions to increase academic publication rates, *Higher Education Research & Development*, 25(1): 19–35.

McKinney, K. (2007) *Enhancing Learning Through the Scholarship of Teaching and Learning: The Challenges and Joys of Juggling.* Bolton, MA: Anker Pub. Co. Available at: http://public.eblib.com/EBLPublic/PublicView.do?ptiID=484887 [accessed 30 January 2012].

Marginson, S. (2000) Rethinking academic work in the global era, *Journal of Higher Education Policy and Management*, 22(1): 23–35.

Marginson, S. (2010) Higher education in East Asia and Singapore: rise of the Confucian Model, *Higher Education*, 61(5): 587–611.

Marginson, S. and Considine, M. (2000) *The Enterprise University: Power, Governance and Reinvention in Australia.* Cambridge: Cambridge University Press.

Marginson, S. and van der Wende, M. (2007) To rank or to be ranked: the impact of global rankings in higher education, *Journal of Studies in International Education*, 11(3–4): 306–29.

Markwell, D. (2007) *'A Large and Liberal Education': Higher Education for the 21st Century.* North Melbourne, Vic.: Australian Scholarly Publishing and Trinity College, The University of Melbourne.

Marsh, H.W. and Hattie, J. (2002) The relationship between research productivity and teaching effectiveness: complementary, antagonistic or independent constructs?, *The Journal of Higher Education*, 73(5): 603–41.

Martin, E. (1999) *Changing Academic Work.* Buckingham, England; Philadelphia, PA: Society for Research into Higher Education and Open University Press.

Martinsuo, M. and Turkulainen, M. (2011) Personal commitment, support and progress in doctoral studies, *Studies in Higher Education*, 36(1): 103–20.

Marton, F. and Säljö, R. (1976) On qualitative differences in learning: outcome and process, *British Journal of Educational Psychology*, 46(1): 4–11.

Mason, M.A. and Goulden, M. (2002) Do babies matter? The effect of family formation on the lifelong careers of academic men and women, *Academe Online*. Available at: http://www.aaup.org/AAUP/pubsres/academe/2002/ND/Feat/Maso.htm [accessed 27 February 2012].

Matthews, K.E., Andrews, V. and Adams, P. (2011) Social learning spaces and student engagement, *Higher Education Research & Development*, 30(2): 105–20.

Maxwell, T.W. and Smyth, R. (2010) Research supervision: the research management matrix, *Higher Education*, 59(4): 407–22.

Moore, T.J. (2011) Critical thinking and disciplinary thinking: a continuing debate, *Higher Education Research & Development*, 30(3): 261–74.

Morosanu, L., Handley, K. and O'Donovan, B. (2010) Seeking support: researching first-year students' experiences of coping with academic life, *Higher Education Research & Development*, 29(6): 665–78.

Mullins, G. and Kiley, M. (2002) 'It's a PhD, not a Nobel Prize': how experienced examiners assess research theses, *Studies in Higher Education*, 27(4): 369–86.

Murray, R. and Newton, M. (2009) Writing retreat as structured intervention: margin or mainstream?, *Higher Education Research & Development*, 28(5): 541–53.

Nakamura, J. and Shernoff, D.J. (2009) *Good Mentoring: Fostering Excellent Practice In Higher Education.* San Francisco, CA: Jossey-Bass/John Wiley.

National Academy of Sciences (US), National Academy of Engineering and Institute of Medicine (US) (1997) *Adviser, Teacher, Role Model, Friend: On Being a Mentor to Students in Science and Engineering.* Washington, DC: National Academy Press. Available at: http://search.ebscohost.com/login.aspx?direct=true&scope=site&db=nlebk&db=nlabk &AN=1019 [accessed 29 January 2012].

Nicoll, C. (2009) Dispelling myths about doctorates in the Australian public service, in C. Denholm and T. Evans (eds) *Beyond Doctorates Downunder*. Camberwell, Vic.: Australian Council for Educational Research, pp. 47–56.

Ning, H.K. and Downing, K. (2011) The interrelationship between student learning experience and study behaviour, *Higher Education Research & Development*, 30(6): 765–78.

Nsibande, R. and Garraway, J. (2011) Professional development through formative evaluation, *International Journal for Academic Development*, 16(2): 97–107.

O'Meara, K. (2003) Reframing incentives and rewards for community service-learning and academic outreach, *Journal of Higher Education Outreach and Engagement*, 8(2): 201–20.

O'Meara, K. (2008) Motivation for public scholarship and engagement: listening to exemplars, *Journal of Higher Education Outreach and Engagement*, 12(1): 7–30.

OECD (2010) *Education at a Glance 2010: OECD Indicators*. Paris, France: OECD.

OECD (2011) *A Tuning-AHELO Conceptual Framework of Expected Desired/Learning Outcomes in Engineering*. Paris, France: OECD. Available at: http://www.oecd-ilibrary.org/education/a-tuning-ahelo-conceptual-framework-of-expected-desired-learning-outcomes-in-engineering_5kghtchn8mbn-en [accessed 21 May 2012].

Omary, B. (2008) Mentoring the mentor: another tool to enhance mentorship, *Gastroenterology*, 135: 13–16.

Overall, N., Deane, K.L. and Peterson, E.R. (2011) Promoting doctoral students' research self-efficacy: combining academic guidance with autonomy support, *Higher Education Research & Development*, 30(6): 791–805.

Paivitynjala, J.V. and Sarja, A. (2003) Pedagogical perspectives on the relationships between higher education and working life, *Higher Education*, 46: 147–66.

Palmer, P.J., Zajonc, A. and Scribner, M. (2010) *The Heart of Higher Education: A Call to Renewal: Transforming the Academy through Collegial Conversations*. San Francisco, CA: Jossey-Bass. Available at: http://site.ebrary.com/id/10399075 [accessed 30 January 2012].

Parker, R. (2009) A learning community approach to doctoral education in the social sciences, *Teaching in Higher Education*, 14(1): 43–54.

Parkes, R.J. and Muldoon, N. (2010) The tutorial as cognitive apprenticeship: developing discipline-based thinking, in R. Cantwell and J.J. Scevak (eds) *An Academic Life: A Handbook for New Academics*. Camberwell, Vic.: ACER Press, pp. 55–64.

Peelo, M.T. and Wareham, T. (2002) *Failing Students in Higher Education*. Buckingham, England; Philadelphia, PA: Society for Research into Higher Education and Open University Press.

Pepper, C. (2010) 'There's a lot of learning going on but NOT much teaching!': student perceptions of problem-based learning in science, *Higher Education Research & Development*, 29(6): 693–707.

Percy, A. et al. (2008) *The RED Report, Recognition - Enhancement - Development: The Contribution of Sessional Teachers to Higher Education*. Sydney: Australian Learning and Teaching Council.

Pfeffer, J. (2010) Power play, *Harvard Business Review*, July–August: 85–92.

Phillips, E.M. and Pugh, D.S. (2010) *How to Get a PhD: A Handbook for Students and their Supervisors*. Berkshire, England: McGraw-Hill/Open University Press.

Plate, C. (2006) Publish and flourish, *Campus Review*, 13.09–19.09: 10–11.

Project Management Institute (2008) *A Guide to the Project Management Body of Knowledge*. Pennsylvania, PA: Project Management Institute.

Quiddington, P. (2010) The new politics of Australian higher education: why universities get rumbled in the budget, *Higher Education Research & Development*, 29(4): 475–87.

Raabe, B., Frese, M. and Beehr, T.A. (2007) Action regulation theory and career self-management, *Journal of Vocational Behavior*, 70(2): 297–311.

Ramsden, P. (1998) *Learning to Lead in Higher Education*. London; New York: Routledge.

Ransome, P. (2011) Qualitative pedagogy versus instrumentalism: the antinomies of higher education learning and teaching in the United Kingdom, *Higher Education Quarterly*, 65(2): 206–23.

Räsänen, K. (2009) Understanding academic work as practical activity – and preparing (business-school) academics for praxis?, *International Journal for Academic Development*, 14(3): 185–95.

Ready, D.A., Conger, J.A. and Hill, L.A. (2010) Are you a high potential?, *Harvard Business Review*, June: 79–84.

Reio, T. (2011) Toward expert publishing practice, *Human Resource Development Review*, 10(2): 119–22.

Richard, O.C. et al. (2009) Mentoring in supervisor–subordinate dyads: antecedents, consequences, and test of a mediation model of mentorship, *Journal of Business Research*, 62(11): 1,110–8.

Rochon, P.A. et al. (2002) Comparison of review articles published in peer-reviewed and throwaway journals, *Journal of the American Medical Association*, 287(21): 2,853–6.

Ruiz-Gallardo, J.-R. et al. (2011) Assessing student workload in problem based learning: relationships among teaching method, student workload and achievement. A case study in natural sciences, *Teaching and Teacher Education*, 27(3): 619–27.

Ruohoniemi, M. and Lindblom-Ylänne, S. (2009) Students' experiences concerning course workload and factors enhancing and impeding their learning – a useful resource for quality enhancement in teaching and curriculum planning, *International Journal for Academic Development*, 14(1): 69–81.

Ryan, J. (2011) Teaching and learning for international students: towards a transcultural approach, *Teachers and Teaching: theory and practice*, 17(6): 631–48.

Sadler, D. (2009) *Up the Publication Road: A Guide to Publishing in Scholarly Journals for Academics, Researchers and Graduate Students*, 3rd edn. Milperra NSW: Higher Education Research and Development Society of Australasia.

St George, E. (2006) Positioning higher education for the knowledge based economy, *Higher Education*, 52: 589–610.

Sambrook, S., Stewart, J. and Roberts, C. (2008) Doctoral supervision... a view from above, below and the middle!, *Journal of Further and Higher Education*, 32(1): 71–84.

Sampson, K.A. and Comer, K. (2010) When the governmental tail wags the disciplinary dog: some consequences of national funding policy on doctoral reserach in New Zealand, *Higher Education Research & Development*, 29(3): 275–89.

Sanderson, G. (2011) Internationalisation and teaching in higher education, *Higher Education Research & Development*, 30(5): 661–76.

Sandmann, L.R. (2008) Conceptualization of the scholarship of engagement in higher education: a strategic review, 1996–2006, *Journal of Higher Education Outreach and Engagement*, 12(1): 91–104.

Sandmann, L.R., Saltmarsh, J. and O'Meara, K. (2008) An integrated model for advancing the scholarship of engagement: creating academic homes for the engaged scholar, *Journal of Higher Education Outreach and Engagement*, 12(1): 47–63.

Sandmann, L.R., Thornton, C.H. and Jaeger, A.J. (2011) *Institutionalizing Community Engagement in Higher Education: New Directions for Higher Education*. Hoboken, NJ: John Wiley & Sons.

Sawatzky, J.-A.V. and Enns, C.L. (2009) A mentoring needs assessment: validating mentorship in nursing education, *Journal of Professional Nursing*, 25(3): 145–50.

Scandura, T.A. and Williams, E.A. (2004) Mentoring and transformational leadership: the role of supervisory career mentoring, *Journal of Vocational Behavior*, 65(3): 448–68.

Scevak, J.J. (2010) Lectures, in R. Cantwell and J.J. Scevak (eds) *An Academic Life: A Handbook For New Academics*. Camberwell, Vic.: ACER Press, pp. 45–54.

Schapper, J. and Mayson, S.E. (2010) Research-led teaching: moving from a fractured engagement to a marriage of convenience, *Higher Education Research & Development*, 29(6): 641–51.

Seldin, P. and Miller, J.E. (2009) *The Academic Portfolio: A Practical Guide to Documenting Teaching, Research, and Service*. San Francisco, CA: Jossey-Bass.

Seligman, M.E.P. (2011) *Flourish*. North Sydney, NSW: Random House Australia.

Shaker, G.G., Palmer, M.M. and Chism, N.V.N. (2011) Understanding and supporting full-time non-tenure track faculty: a needed change, in J.E. Miller and J.E. Groccia (eds) *To Improve the Academy: Resources of Faculty, Instructional, and Organizational Development*. San Francisco, CA: Jossey-Bass, pp. 46–59.

Shattock, M. (2003) *Managing Successful Universities*. Maidenhead, Berkshire: Society for Research into Higher Education and Open University Press.

Smith, L. (2009) Sinking in the sand? Academic work in an offshore campus of an Australian university, *Higher Education Research & Development*, 28(5): 467–79.

Souza, T.J. et al. (2010) Communication Climate, Comfort, and Cold Calling: an Analysis of discussion-based courses at multiple universities, in J.E. Miller and L.B. Nilson (eds) *To Improve the Academy: Resources for Faculty, Instructional, and Organizational Development*. San Francisco, CA: Jossey-Bass, pp. 227–49.

Stassen, M.L.A., Herrington, A. and Henderson, L. (2011) Defining critical thinking in higher education: determining assessment fit, in J.E. Miller and J.E. Groccia (eds) *To Improve the Academy: Resources for Faculty, Instructional, and Organizational Development*, Vol. 30. San Francisco, CA: Jossey-Bass, pp. 126–41.

Stevens, M.L., Armstrong, E.A. and Arum, R. (2008) Sieve, incubator, temple, hub: empirical and theoretical advances in the sociology of higher education, *Annual Review of Sociology*, 34: 127–51.

Sullivan, S.E. and Mainiero, L. (2008) Using the kaleidoscope career model to understand the changing patterns of women's careers: designing HRD programs that attract and retain women, *Advances in Developing Human Resources*, 10(1): 32–49.

Sullivan-Brown, K. (2002) The Missouri teachers' academy: mentoring for organizational and personal transformation, in F.K. Kochan (ed.) *Perspectives in Mentoring: The Organizational and Human Dimensions of Successful Mentoring Programs and Relationships*. Greenwich, CI: Information Age Publishing, pp. 141–52.

Svinicki, M.D., McKeachie, W.J. and Nicol, D. (2011) *Mckeachie's Teaching Tips: Strategies, Research, and Theory for College and University Teachers*. Belmont, CA: Wadsworth, Cengage Learning.

Sword, H. (2009) Writing for higher education differently: a manifesto on style, *Studies in Higher Education*, 34(3): 319–36.

Sword, H. (2011) *Stylish Academic Writing*. Cambridge, MA: Harvard University Press.

Szumacher, E. et al. (2006) The development of an interprofessional mentorship program for faculty at the Department of Radiation Oncology, University of Toronto – a new beginning, *CARO*, September: S64.

Taylor, J. and Machado, M. (2006) Higher education leadership and management: from conflict to interdependence through strategic planning, *Tertiary Education and Management*, 12: 137–60.

Taylor, O.L. and Carter, T.P. (2005) High attrition in doctoral education: is it inevitable?, in J.E. Groccia and J.E. Miller (eds) *On Becoming a Productive University: Strategies for Reducing Costs and Increasing Quality in Higher Education*. Bolton, MA: Anker Publishing Company, pp. 206–15.

Tennant, M., McMullen, C. and Kaczynski, D. (2009) *Teaching, Learning and Research in Higher Education: A Critical Approach*. London: Routledge.

Thoma, M. (2011) New forms of communication and the public mission of economics: overcoming the great disconnect, *Transformations of the Public Sphere*, 11 November. Available at: http://publicsphere.ssrc.org/thoma-new-forms-of-communication-and-the-public-mission-of-economics/ [accessed 25 February 2012].

Toohey, S. (1999) *Designing Courses for Higher Education*. Buckingham, England; Philadelphia, PA: Society for Research into Higher Education and Open University Press.

Trahar, S. and Hyland, F. (2011) Experiences and perceptions of internationalisation in higher education in the UK, *Higher Education Research & Development*, 30(5): 623–33.

Trevitt, C., Stocks, C. and Quinlan, K.M. (2011) Advancing assessment practice in continuing professional learning: toward a richer understanding of teaching portfolios for learning and assessment, *International Journal for Academic Development*, 1–13.

Trigwell, K. et al. (2000) Scholarship of teaching: a model, *Higher Education Research & Development*, 19(2): 155–68.

Vardi, I. (2011) The changing relationship between the scholarship of teaching (and learning) and universities, *Higher Education Research & Development*, 30(1): 1–7.

Vilkinas, T. et al. (2009) *Academic Leadership: Fundamental Building Blocks*. Strawberry Hills, NSW: Australian Learning and Teaching Council.

Visser-Wijnveen, G.J. et al. (2010) The ideal research–teaching nexus in the eyes of academics: building profiles, *Higher Education Research & Development*, 29(2): 195–210.

Waitere, H.J. et al. (2011) Choosing whether to resist or reinforce the new managerialism: the impact of performance-based research funding on academic identity, *Higher Education Research & Development*, 30(2): 205–17.

Wang, T. (2011) 'Tell me what to do' vs 'guide me through it': feedback experiences of international doctoral students, *Active Learning in Higher Education*, 12(2): 101–12.

Waterman Jr., R.H., Waterman, J.A. and Collard, B.A. (1994) Toward a career-resilient workforce, *Harvard Business Review*, 72(4): 87–95.

Waters, L. (2004) Protégé–mentor agreement about the provision of psychosocial support: the mentoring relationship, personality, and workload, *Journal of Vocational Behavior*, 65(3): 519–32.

Watts, J.H. (2009) From professional to PhD student: challenges of status transition, *Teaching in Higher Education*, 14(6): 687–91.

Weimer, M. (2002) *Learner-Centered Teaching: Five Key Changes to Practice*. San Francisco, CA: Jossey-Bass.

White, B. (2011) *Mapping Your Thesis: The Comprehensive Manual of Theory and Techniques for Masters and Doctoral Research*. Camberwell, Vic.: ACER Press.

Willcoxson, L. (2010) Factors affecting intention to leave in the first, second and third year of university studies: a semester-by-semester investigation, *Higher Education Research & Development*, 29(6): 623–39.

Willcoxson, L., Kavanagh, M. and Cheung, L. (2011) Leading, managing and participating in inter-university teaching grant collaborations, *Higher Education Research & Development*, 30(4): 533–48.

Williams, D. et al. (2004) Effective peer evaluation in learning teams, in C.M. Wehlberg and S. Chadwick-Blossey (eds) *To Improve the Academy: Resources for Faculty, Instructional, and Organizational Development*. San Francisco, CA: Jossey-Bass, pp. 251–67.

Willis, D. and Millis, B.J. (2004) An international perspective on assessing group projects, in C.M. Wehlberg and S. Chadwick-Blossey (eds) *To Improve the Academy: Resources for Faculty, Instructional, and Organizational Development*. San Francisco, CA: Jossey-Bass, pp. 268–83.

Wilson, K.L., Lizzio, A. and Ramsden, P. (1997) The development, validation and application of the Course Experience Questionnaire, *Studies in Higher Education*, 22(1): 33–53.

Wilson, P. (2010) *People@Work/2020: The Future of Work and the Changing Workplace: Challenges and Issues for Australian HR Practitioners*. Melbourne: Australian Human Resources Institute.

VanWynsberghe, R. and Andruske, C. (2007) Research in the service of co-learning: sustainability and community engagement, *Canadian Journal of Education*, 30(1): 349–76.

Yielder, J. and Codling, A. (2004) Management and leadership in the contemporary university, *Journal of Higher Education Policy and Management*, 26(3): 315–28.

Yorke, M. and Longden, B. (2004) *Retention and Student Success in Higher Education*. Maidenhead, England: Society for Research into Higher Education and Open University Press.

Young, A. and Perrewe, P.L. (2000) What did you expect? An examination of career-related support and social support among mentors and protégés, *Journal of Management*, 26(4): 611–32.

Index

TEACHING FOR QUALITY LEARNING AT UNIVERSITY
Fourth Edition

John Biggs and Catherine Tang

9780335242757 (Paperback)
September 2011

eBook also available

Teaching for Quality Learning at University, now in its fourth edition, is a bestselling book for higher education teachers and administrators interested in assuring effective teaching. The authors outline the constructive alignment of outcomes based teaching, including how to implement it and why it is a good idea to do so. Clearly organized and written, with practical examples, the new edition is thoroughly updated.

Key features:

- Clearly organized and written, with practical examples
- Aids staff developers in providing support for teachers
- Provides a framework for administrators interested in quality assurance and enhancement of teaching across the whole university

www.openup.co.uk

GIVING STUDENTS EFFECTIVE WRITTEN FEEDBACK

Deirdre Burke and Jackie Pieterick

9780335237456 (Paperback)
2010

eBook also available

This book focuses on one of the key issues in student assessment - delivering student feedback. It considers feedback from both the perspective of tutor provider and student receiver to offer new insights into the impact feedback has on student performance

Key features:

- Provides an opportunity to explore research and contemporary concerns about the function and impact of written feedback
- Offers practical guidance on how to give more appropriate and effective feedback
- Explores strategies for tutors to use with students to ensure that they make full use of tutor feedback

www.openup.co.uk

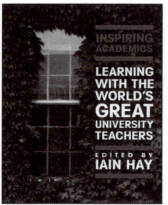

INSPIRING ACADEMICS
Learning with the World's Great University Teachers

Iain Hay (Ed)

9780335237425 (Paperback)
2011

eBook also available

Inspiring Academics draws on the experience and expertise of award-winning university teachers to illuminate exemplary teaching practice. It is structured around five core themes: inspiring learning, command of the field, assessment for independent learning, student development and scholarship.

Key features:

- Brings together the work of top academics from around the world
- Highlights practical ways to improve university teaching
- Openly discusses what does not work, as well as what does

www.openup.co.uk

OPEN UNIVERSITY PRESS
McGraw - Hill Education

WRITING FOR ACADEMIC JOURNALS
Second Edition

Rowena Murray

9780335234585 (Paperback)
2009

eBook also available

"Academics are expected to write but seldom consider and discuss the nature of academic writing. As a result, the practice is shrouded in mystery. Writing for Academic Journals *makes explicit much of what is normally opaque and it should be among the first ports of call for any academic who is contemplating getting published. This new edition achieves the near-impossible: improving on what was already acknowledged as a first-rate compendium".*
Professor Ronald Barnett, Institute of Education, University of London, UK

Key features:

- Comprehensively updated to include the most recent research and theory
- Offers practical and tested strategies for good academic writing
- Unravels the process of writing academic papers

www.openup.co.uk

OPEN UNIVERSITY PRESS
McGraw - Hill Education